Second Timothy

Preaching Verse by Verse

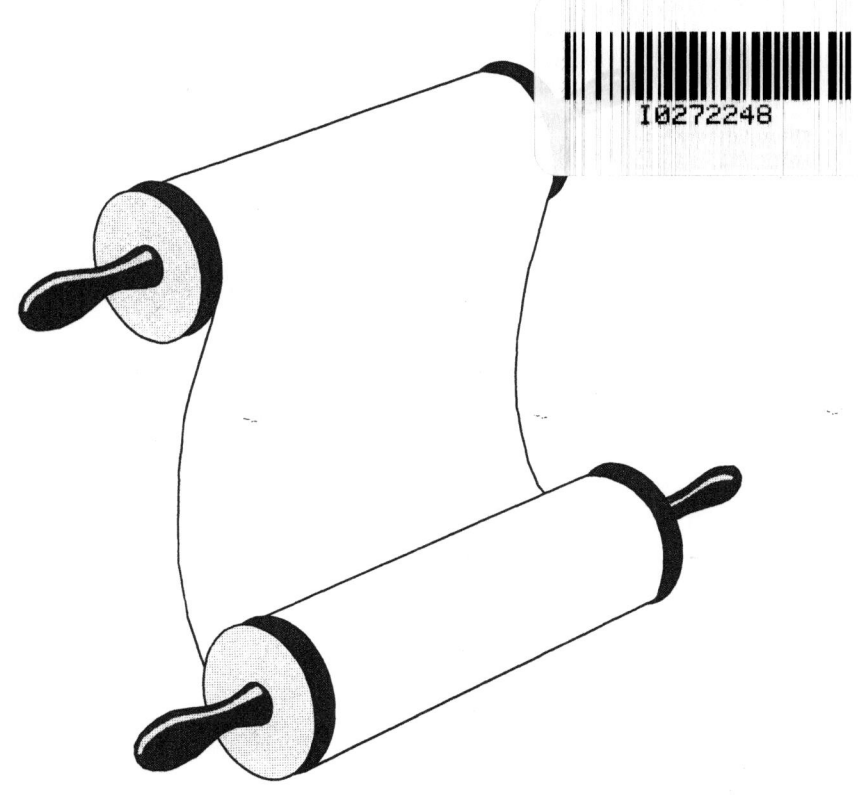

Pastor D. A. Waite, Th.D., Ph.D.

Published by

THE BIBLE FOR TODAY PRESS
900 Park Avenue
Collingswood, New Jersey 08108
U.S.A.

Church Phone: 856-854-4747
BFT Phone: 856-854-4452
Orders: 1-800-John 10:9
e-mail: BFT@BibleForToday.org
Website: www.BibleForToday.org
fax: 856-854-2464

**We Use and Defend
the King James Bible**

**September, 2008
BFT 3105 BK**

Copyright, 2008
All Rights Reserved

ISBN #1-56848-060-1

Acknowledgments

I wish to thank and to acknowledge the assistance of the following people:

The Congregation of the **Bible For Today Baptist Church**, for whom these messages were prepared, to whom they were delivered, and by whom they were published. They listened attentively and encouraged their pastor as he preached;

Dianne W. Cosby, for typing these messages from the original cassette tapes and putting them in computer format;

Yvonne Sanborn Waite, my wife, who encouraged the publication of these sermons, read the manuscript several times, suggested the various boxes, and gave other helpful suggestions and comments;

Barbara Egan, our Bible For Today secretary who proofread the manuscript and, as usual, offered valuable suggestions and comments.

Julia Monaghan, a faithful supporter of our Bible For Today ministry and an attender via the Internet of our **Bible For Today Baptist Church** services, who read the manuscript and gave helpful comments for correction.

Daniel S. Waite, the Assistant to the Bible For Today Director, who kept my computer working, guided the book through the printing process, and made important suggestions.

Dr. H. D. Williams, a friend in the Bible For Today and the Dean Burgon Society ministries. His expertise in "print on demand" (POD) technology has made it possible for us to print this book in this manner, thus saving us thousands of dollars.

Foreword

- **The Beginning.** This book is the **eighth** in a planned series of books based on expository preaching from various books of the Bible. It is an attempt to bring to the minds of the readers two things: (1) the **meaning** of the words in the verses and (2) the practical **application** of those words to the hearts and lives of Bible-believing Christians.
- **Preached Sermons.** These are messages that have been preached to our **Bible For Today Baptist Church** in Collingswood, New Jersey, broadcast over radio, over the Internet by streaming, and placed on our Website as follows: **(http://www.BibleForToday.org/audio_sermons.htm)** This site is for people all over the world to listen to, should they wish. As the messages were originally preached, I took half a chapter during our Sunday morning services, spending about forty-five minutes on each message.
- **Other Verses.** In connection with both the meaning and application of the verses in this book, there are many verses from other places in the Bible that have been quoted for further elaboration of Paul's discussion. One of the unique features of this study is that all the various verses of Scripture that are used to illustrate further truth are written out in full for easy reference.
- **A Transcription.** It should be noted that this book is made up largely from the transcription of the tape recordings of the messages as they were preached. These recordings are available in both audio and video formats **(Audio is BFT #3105/1-4; or Video is BFT #3105VC1-2, or DVD #3105DV1-2).** Though there has been some editing, the words are basically the same as the ones I used as I preached the sermons. Though different in emphasis, this was also the method Dr. H. A. Ironside used in his Bible exposition books.
- **The Audience.** The audience intended is the same as the audience that listened to the messages in the first place. These studies are not meant to be overly scholarly, though there is some reference to various Greek words used by Paul. My aim and burden is to try to help believers to understand the Words of God. It is my hope that I can get as many as possible of my expositions in print so that my children, grandchildren, great grand-children, and many others might profit thereby.

        Yours For God's Words,
        Pastor D. A. Waite, Th.D., Ph.D.
        Bible For Today Baptist Church

Table of Contents

Publisher's Data i

Acknowledgments ii

Foreword iii

Table of Contents iv

2 Timothy Chapter One 1

2 Timothy Chapter Two 51

2 Timothy Chapter Three 99

2 Timothy Chapter Four 159

Index of Words and Phrases 215

About the Author 235

Order Blank Pages 236

Defined King James Bible Orders 241

Second Timothy
Chapter One

Introductory Remarks

Though there is a dispute as to whether Paul was in the prison in Rome once or twice, I believe the evidence points to two imprisonments. This letter to Pastor Timothy was written at the end of these two confinements. It was his last letter that Paul wrote before being martyred.

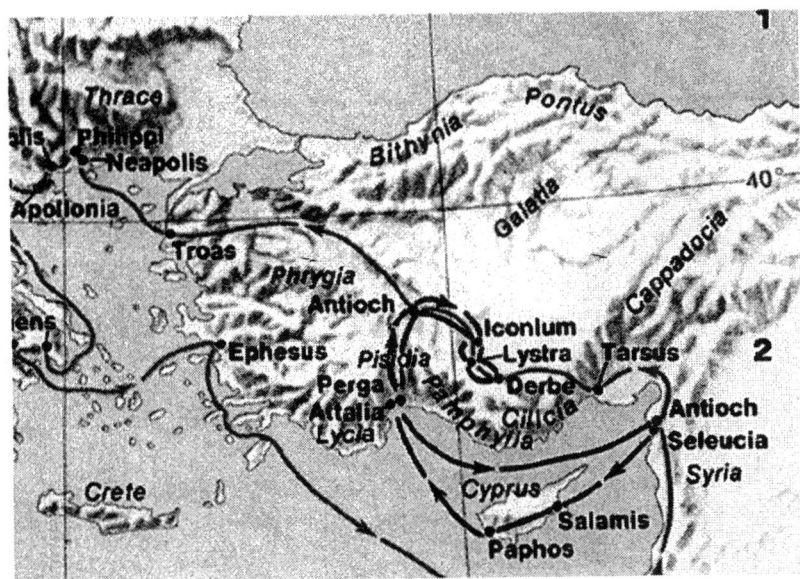

Along with 1 Timothy and Titus, 2 Timothy is a part of what are called the Pastoral Epistles because they were written to two pastors in the early church, Timothy and Titus.

According to tradition, Timothy was the pastor of the church at Ephesus. From the map above, you can see that Ephesus was located in Asia Minor which is now called Turkey. It was a major seaport in the Mediterranean Sea in its day. Timothy evidently had been led to the Lord Jesus Christ by Paul and is referred to as *"my own son in the faith"* (1 Timothy 1:2).

Timothy joined Paul when Paul visited the areas of Lystra and Derbe (Acts 16:1). Timothy's mother was a Jewess and his father was a Gentile. Timothy accompanied Paul in the events from Acts 16:1 through at least 20:4 where his name is mentioned.

Writing His Last Letter From Prison

In this book, Paul tells his dear friend, and fellow minister, Timothy, some of the most important things he can impart before he goes home to be with the Lord Jesus Christ in Heaven. From the last chapter of this book, Paul, writing from his cold prison cell in Rome, knew very well that his life was drawing to a close. He did not whine or cry to Pastor Timothy even though he knew the end was near. Instead, he summoned up all the courage and wisdom that the Lord Jesus Christ could give him and discussed some of the most important topics upon which any Pastor should be grounded.

Paul makes specific mention that he is in prison in the following verses.

- 2 Timothy 1:8
Be not thou therefore ashamed of the testimony of our Lord, **nor of me his prisoner**: but be thou partaker of the afflictions of the gospel according to the power of God;

During the first Roman imprisonment Paul wrote Ephesians, Philippians, Colossians and Philemon. Now, he has been recommitted to prison because he kept on preaching.

- 2 Timothy 1:16
The Lord give mercy unto the house of Onesiphorus; for he oft refreshed me, and **was not ashamed of my chain**: But, when he was in Rome, he sought me out very diligently, and found me.

2 Timothy 1:1

"Paul, an apostle of Jesus Christ by the will of God according to the promise of life which is in Christ Jesus."

Paul was called to be an "*apostle*" by the "*will of God.*" His call is referred to in various places.

2 Timothy 1:1

- **Acts 9:1-6a**
And Saul, yet breathing out threatenings and slaughter against the disciples of the Lord, went unto the high priest, And desired of him letters to Damascus to the synagogues, that if he found any of this way, whether they were men or women, he might bring them bound unto Jerusalem. And as he journeyed, he came near Damascus: and **suddenly there shined round about him a light from Heaven: And he fell to the earth, and heard a voice saying unto him, Saul, Saul, why persecutest thou me?** And he said, Who art thou, Lord? And the Lord said, I am Jesus whom thou persecutest: *it is* hard for thee to kick against the pricks. And he trembling and astonished said, **Lord, what wilt thou have me to do?** And the Lord *said* unto him, Arise, and go into the city, and it shall be told thee what thou must do.

- **Acts 22:4**
And **I persecuted this way unto the death**, binding and **delivering into prisons** both men and women.

.Paul imprisoned and even killed Christians before the Lord changed him.

- **Acts 22:14**
And he said, **The God of our fathers hath chosen thee**, that thou shouldest know his will, and see that Just One, and shouldest hear the voice of his mouth.

He was "*chosen*" of God to be an apostle.

- **Acts 26:10**
Which thing I also did in Jerusalem: and **many of the saints did I shut up in prison, having received authority from the chief priests; and when they were put to death**, I gave my voice against *them*.

Paul was killing Christians and all of a sudden he repented of his sins, trusted in the Lord Jesus Christ as his Saviour, and began to serve Him. Paul is called an "*apostle*" in many of the epistles and letters that he wrote. He mentions it over and over. Here are a few examples.

- **1 Corinthians 1:1**
Paul, called *to be* **an apostle** of Jesus Christ through the will of God, and Sosthenes *our* brother,

- **2 Corinthians 1:1**
Paul, **an apostle** of Jesus Christ by the will of God, and Timothy *our* brother, unto the church of God which is at Corinth, with all the saints which are in all Achaia:

Paul did not make himself an "*apostle*," it was by the will of God.

- Galatians 1:1
  Paul, **an apostle**, (not of men, neither by man, but **by Jesus Christ, and God the Father**, who raised him from the dead;)
Paul was called of God like it says in this first verse of 2 Timothy.
- 2 Timothy 1:1
  Paul, **an apostle** of Jesus Christ **by the will of God**, according to the promise of life which is in Christ Jesus,
- Ephesians 1:1
  Paul, **an apostle** of Jesus Christ **by the will of God**, to the saints which are at Ephesus, and to the faithful in Christ Jesus:
- Colossians 1:1
  Paul, **an apostle** of Jesus Christ **by the will of God**, and Timotheus *our* brother,
- 1 Timothy 1:1
  Paul, **an apostle** of Jesus Christ by the commandment of God our Saviour, and Lord Jesus Christ, *which is* our hope;

Paul was called an "*apostle*." He introduces himself as an "*apostle*" when he was in a prison in Rome. His first letter to Timothy (1 Timothy) was written when he was out of prison.

2 Timothy 1:2

"To Timothy, my dearly beloved son: Grace, mercy, and peace, from God the Father and Christ Jesus our Lord."

Paul calls Timothy his "*dearly beloved son.*" Timothy was not Paul's physical son, but he was his son in the faith. Paul evidently led Timothy to Christ. Timothy was half Jew and half Gentile.
- Acts 16:1
  Then came he to Derbe and Lystra: and, behold, a certain disciple was there, named **Timotheus, the son of a certain woman, which was a Jewess, and believed; but his father *was* a Greek:**
- 1 Corinthians 4:17
  For this cause have I sent unto you **Timotheus, who is my beloved son**, and faithful in the Lord, who shall bring you into remembrance of my ways which be in Christ, as I teach every where in every church.

When you lead someone to Christ, if he is a man, he is your son in the faith, if she is a woman, she is your daughter in Christ.

- 1 Timothy 1:2
  Unto **Timothy,** *my* **own son in the faith**: Grace, mercy, *and* peace, from God our Father and Jesus Christ our Lord.
- 1 Timothy 1:18
  This charge **I commit unto thee, son Timothy**, according to the prophecies which went before on thee, that thou by them mightest war a good warfare;

Grace, Mercy And Peace

Notice the greetings, *"grace, mercy, and peace."* *"Grace"* is the greeting of the Greeks. *"Mercy"* is also one of the terms that God has used many times. *"Peace"* is the Jewish greeting which, in Hebrew, is *"Shalom."* *"Grace"* has been defined as something positive: *"Getting something we don't deserve."* *"Mercy"* has been defined as something negative: *"Not getting something we do deserve."* Every living person deserves Hell. God's *"grace"* was manifested by sending His Son into this world to die for sins so those who trust Him might be saved.

Peace has been defined as:
"the tranquil state of a soul, assured of its salvation through Christ, and so fearing nothing from God and content with it's earthly lot of whatsoever sort it is."
That's what real *"peace"* is. *"Peace"* can be pictured as the state of a mother bird and her babies under Niagara Falls who is happily singing despite the roar of those powerful falls nearby. That is *"peace."*

I remember, in 1961, I preached on *"peace"* in my church after I came out of the chaplaincy. That sermon was the last sermon I preached in that church. I called it, *"The Gift of Peace."* I gave that illustration about those birds under the falls. After the sermon, there was the biggest riot any church had ever seen. Some of the church leaders stormed the platform, turned off the power to the organ, and made the pianist stop playing the closing hymn. After that, it didn't take too long for many of us to leave that particular church and start a new church.

Notice that *"peace"* is *"from God the Father **and** Christ Jesus the Lord."* God the Son is equal to God the Father. The Roman Catholic teachings hold that the Lord Jesus Christ can be found in a little wafer. That is not the Christ of the Bible. The modernists and liberals do not believe that God the Son (the Lord Jesus Christ) is equal with God the Father. They believe that Jesus was just a man and not God, rather than perfect Man and perfect God. This verse shows the equality of the Father and the Son. We see that *"peace, grace, and mercy"* are all from both the Father and the Son. They are equal in all of their Divine attributes.

2 Timothy 1:3

"I thank God, whom I serve from my forefathers with pure conscience that without ceasing I have remembrance of thee in my prayers night and day."

Paul thanks God continuously. The word for *"thank"* is in the present tense which implies continuous action. Paul not only *"thanks"* the Lord, he also *"serves"* him *"with pure conscience."* *"Service"* is part of the Christian faith. When God saves us He wants us to *"serve"* Him.

- Romans 1:9
  For God is my witness, **whom I serve** with my spirit in the gospel of his Son, that without ceasing I make mention of you always in my prayers;
- Galatians 5:13
  For, brethren, ye have been called unto liberty; only *use* not liberty for an occasion to the flesh, but **by love serve one another**.

God wants us to *"serve"* one another as believers.

- Colossians 3:24
  Knowing that of the Lord ye shall receive the reward of the inheritance: for **ye serve the Lord Christ**.

That is the duty of every Christian.

- 1 Thessalonians 1:9
  For they themselves shew of us what manner of entering in we had unto you, and how ye turned to God from idols **to serve the living and true God;**
- Hebrews 9:14
  How much more shall the blood of Christ, who through the eternal Spirit offered himself without spot to God, purge your conscience from dead works **to serve the living God?**
- Revelation 7:15
  Therefore are they before the throne of God, and **serve him day and night in his temple**: and he that sitteth on the throne shall dwell among them.

We who are saved are going to serve the Lord in Heaven.

2 Timothy 1:3

- **Revelation 22:3**
  And there shall be no more curse: but the throne of God and of the Lamb shall be in it; and **his servants shall serve him**:

  There is not going to be anymore curse in Heaven. Paul says to Timothy that he has *"served"* God *"from his forefathers with pure conscience."* Our *"conscience"* must be pure.

- **Acts 24:16**
  And herein do I exercise myself, **to have always a conscience void of offence toward God, and *toward* men**.

  Paul reminded Timothy that *"without ceasing"* he had *"remembrance"* of him *"in his prayers night and day."* Timothy especially needed prayer, because he was an active pastor. Prayer is needed by Christians everywhere and for everything.

- **Acts 12:5**
  Peter therefore was kept in prison: but **prayer was made without ceasing of the church unto God for him**.

  God answered *"prayer"* for Peter's release from prison. It was amazing and miraculous.

- **Romans 1:9**
  For God is my witness, whom I serve with my spirit in the gospel of his Son, that **without ceasing I make mention of you always in my prayers;**

- **1 Thessalonians 1:2**
  We give thanks to God always for you all, **making mention of you in our prayers;**

- **1 Thessalonians 5:17**
  Pray without ceasing.

  We are to always have an attitude of prayer. When we walk, when we talk, when we go to bed, when we get up, when we are in church, we should have an attitude of prayer.

- **1 Corinthians 11:24**
  And **when he had given thanks**, he brake *it*, and said, Take, eat: this is my body, which is broken for you: this do in remembrance of me.

  The Lord Jesus Christ prayed before instituting the Lord's supper. Paul followed his Saviour in the practice of prayer.

ABOVE THE DIN

Above the din and noise and strife,
Above the cares of my own life;
Oh Lord, I come to Thee and pray;
Now teach me, Lord, just what to say.

For self I cry, I need Thy touch,
For I do murmur ever much;
For others dear I yearn and plead
That Thou wilt grant their every need.

My Lord, I long to come to Thee
So free and oft that I may be
In reverent attitude all day
To lift my heart and learn to pray.
(By Gertrude Grace Sanborn, August 1961)

2 Timothy 1:4

"Greatly desiring to see thee, being mindful of thy tears, that I may be filled with joy;"

The reason for Timothy's *"tears"* is not mentioned. There are many kinds of *"tears."*

- Psalm 116:8
  For **thou hast delivered** my soul from death, **mine eyes from tears**, *and* my feet from falling.

It is a thing that is not seen too much today, *"tears"* of joy.

- Mark 9:24
  And straightway **the father of the child cried out, and said with tears, Lord, I believe**; help thou mine unbelief.

- Acts 20:19
  Serving the Lord with all humility of mind, and with many tears, and temptations, which befell me by the lying in wait of the Jews:

- Acts 20:31
  Therefore watch, and remember, that by the space of three years **I ceased not to warn every one night and day with tears**.
  Paul was warning "*with tears*." In our warnings today, we should not forget Paul's experience here.
- 2 Corinthians 2:4
  For out of much affliction and anguish of heart **I wrote unto you with many tears**; not that ye should be grieved, but that ye might know the love which I have more abundantly unto you. Paul had a tearful remembrance of those who had done evil.
- Revelation 7:17
  For the Lamb which is in the midst of the throne shall feed them, and shall lead them unto living fountains of waters: and **God shall wipe away all tears from their eyes**.

TEARS

O, Father, thank you for them,
For the depths of deeds
Which drew them to our eyes;
For the balm of soul their dampness brought us
For that anguish sore they materialized.

For by those tears
We knew our hearts were human,
Not made of stone, insensitive to pain,
Not pumping ice in veins just mortal;
But instruments revealing our domain
of care, regret, of love, of longing,
of loneliness and grief, of soul, of mind,
of loss, of indispensable need for relief.

> For, in those tears, O Lord, we found Thee
> Closer than a human hand,
> Closer than a friend unfaithful,
> Closer than an insincere command
> To care for us--
>
> Who could do it?
> To comfort and caress with grace,
> To touch with tenderness our feelings,
> To transform that hopeless empty space?
>
> Only Thee, a faithful Father,
> Only Thee the God of years unknown,
> Only Thee holding tomorrow's promise,
> Only Thee, eternal on the throne.
>
> I thank Thee, Father, for them--
> Those tears of grief and deep despair,
> I thank Thee for Thy hand that wipes them
> And the peace left by Thy perfect care.
> (By Yvonne S. Waite)

Paul wanted Timothy to take the trip from Ephesus to Rome and see him in prison so that he would be *"filled with joy."* When somebody comes to see you, do they bring you *"joy"*? I guess it depends on who comes to see you. When you go to see someone, do you bring him or her *"joy"*? I guess it depends on how you act to them. Timothy brought Paul the apostle *"joy."* They were fellowsoldiers.

2 Timothy 1:5

"When I call to remembrance the unfeigned faith that is in thee which dwelt first in thy grandmother Lois, and thy mother Eunice, and I am persuaded that in thee also."

The Biblical *"faith"* in Pastor Timothy was because of both his *"grandmother Lois"* and his *"mother Eunice."* Remember Timothy's mother is described in Acts as being a *"Jewess"* who *"believed"* (Acts 16:1) in the Lord Jesus Christ. His grandmother Lois was also a believer. Timothy's faith was *"unfeigned"* [ANUPOKRITOS]. There are a number of things, which should be *"unfeigned."*

- 1 Timothy 1:5
Now the end of the commandment is charity out of a pure heart, and *of* a good conscience, and *of* <u>faith unfeigned</u>:
- 1 Peter 1:22
Seeing ye have purified your souls in obeying the truth through the Spirit <u>unto unfeigned love of the brethren</u>, *see that ye love one another with a pure heart fervently:*

Timothy's Spiritual Heritage

Unfeigned" [ANUPOKRITOS] means *"without any hypocrisy, true, genuine, sincere, and honest."* Timothy had a spiritual heritage. Do you have a heritage? Some of us do. Some of us have had Christian parents. Some of us have had unsaved parents. It depends upon how we have been brought up. If you are saved and you have children, you should *"bring them up in the nurture and admonition of the Lord"* (Ephesians 6:4) as Eunice, and Lois, brought up Timothy.

2 Timothy 1:6

"Wherefore I put thee in remembrance that thou stir up the gift of God, which is in thee by the putting on of my hands."

Paul refers to stirring up Timothy's *"gift of God"* that he received by Paul's special apostolic action. That word for *"stir up"* [ANAZOPUREO] means *"to kindle a flame and to make zealous."* We do not know what *"gift"* it was that Timothy received by the apostle's hands. There are many *"gifts"* in Scripture.

- Romans 1:11
  For **I long to see you, that I may impart unto you some spiritual gift,** to the end ye may be established;
- Romans 11:29
  For **the gifts and calling of God** *are* **without repentance.**
- Romans 12:6-8
  Having then gifts differing according to the grace that is given to us, whether prophecy, *let us prophesy* according to the proportion of faith; Or ministry, *let us wait* on *our* ministering: or he that teacheth, on teaching; Or he that exhorteth, on exhortation: he that giveth, *let him do it* with simplicity; he that ruleth, with diligence; he that sheweth mercy, with cheerfulness.
  These are some gifts that are still with us.

Some Gifts Are Temporary

Some of the gifts mentioned in Scripture are no longer with us. We believe they are gone with the completion of the Scripture.

- 1 Corinthians 1:7
  So that **ye come behind in no gift**; waiting for the coming of our Lord Jesus Christ:
- 1 Corinthians 7:7
  For I would that all men were even as I myself. **But every man hath his proper gift of God, one after this manner, and another after that.**
  I believe Paul was a widower, that is, he had been married, but his wife had died. One of the proofs for this is that he was a member of the Jewish Sanhedrin which required that its members be married.
- 1 Corinthians 12:4
  Now **there are diversities of gifts**, but the same Spirit.

Differing Gifts

Everyone does not have the same gift.

2 Timothy 1:6

- **1 Corinthians 12:8-10**
  For **to one is given by the Spirit the word of wisdom**; to another the word of knowledge by the same Spirit; To another faith by the same Spirit; to another the gifts of healing by the same Spirit; To another the working of miracles; to another prophecy; to another discerning of spirits; to another *divers* kinds of tongues; to another the interpretation of tongues:

  There are nine spiritual gifts that we believe have passed away after the Bible was completed in 90 or 100 A.D. These are the charismatic gifts, which the Pentecostals still practice.

- **Ephesians 4:7-8**
  But **unto every one of us is given grace according to the measure of the gift of Christ**. Wherefore he saith, When he ascended up on high, he led captivity captive, and gave gifts unto men.

  There are some spiritual gifts that are permanent and some that have passed away. Here are the gifts that are mentioned.

  "Apostles" – I do not believe there are any more *"apostles."* The Mormons have *"apostles"* in the Mormon Church. I do not believe that is Scriptural.

  "Prophets" – I believe the gift of *"prophets"* is gone.

  The next three gifts are still with us.

  "Evangelists" – The Lord Jesus gave the gift of *"evangelists."*

Missionaries Are "Evangelists"

Our friend, Missionary David Bennett, taught our church that *"evangelists"* were *"missionaries."*

"Pastors" – they are still with us.

"Teachers" – These are still with us also.

What is the purpose of these gifts that the Lord Jesus Christ gave to the church? It was to the *"apostles"* and the *'prophets'* that He gave the Words of God.

Three Purposes For Christ's Gifts

There are three reasons for God's giving us His Words:
1. for the perfecting of the saints,
2. for the work of the ministry, and
3. for the edifying of the body of Christ.

How long are these gifts for? *"Till we all come in the unity of the faith."*

- Ephesians 4:13
 Till we all come in the unity of the faith, and of the knowledge of the Son of God, unto a perfect man, unto the measure of the stature of the fulness of Christ:

The spiritual gifts of the church are so that Christians do not act like children. This is what we must do until the Lord Jesus Christ returns and all the saved ones are unified. We must teach the Words of God so that Christians will grow up. We must be strong, and mature. I think about one of the members of the second church where I was the pastor. He recently sent us a Christmas card and told us he appreciated the teaching he received in our church years ago. The purpose of a pastor's teaching the Words of God is to ground the people of the church. So when hard times come, they will not move away from the Words of God. Later, the pastor who came after me in that church wanted to merge that church into a church that was not the right kind of church. This member stood up for what was right. Soon after that, that pastor left that church. This same pastor who followed me in that church came to see me in my home. I told him that the church asked him what he believed and he told them. We have his answers on tape. He said he did believe certain things and yet he did not believe these things. I asked him why he contradicted himself. I scolded him for his lying. Soon, that man resigned as pastor of that church.

- 2 Timothy 4:14
 Alexander the coppersmith did me much evil: the Lord reward him according to his works:

- Hebrews 2:3-4
 How shall we escape, if we neglect so great salvation; which at the first began to be spoken by the Lord, and was confirmed unto us by them that heard *him*; **God also bearing *them* witness, both with signs and wonders, and with divers miracles, and gifts of the Holy Ghost**, according to his own will?

In the apostolic days, there were these spiritual gifts, but now that the Bible is

completed, many of those gifts are no longer with us.
- **1 Peter 4:10**
  As every man hath received the gift, *even so* **minister the same one to another,** as good stewards of the manifold grace of God.
  If you have a gift, minister it as a good steward.

2 Timothy 1:7

"For God hath not given us the spirit of fear, but of power, and of love, and of a sound mind."

We are not to have the *"spirit of fear."*
- **Psalm 23:4**
  Yea, though I walk through the valley of the shadow of death, **I will fear no evil:** for thou *art* with me; thy rod and thy staff they comfort me.
- **Psalm 27:1**
  The LORD *is* my light and my salvation; **whom shall I fear? the LORD** *is* **the strength of my life; of whom shall I be afraid**?

If we are saved, God has *"not given us the spirit of fear."* We should not have that *"fear."*
- **Psalm 27:3**
  Though an host should encamp against me, **my heart shall not fear:** though war should rise against me, in this *will* I *be* confident.
- **Acts 5:5**
  And Ananias hearing these words fell down, and gave up the ghost: and **great fear came on all them that heard these things.**

The cause of this *"fear"* is because they lied to the Holy Spirit.
- **1 Timothy 5:20**
  Them that sin rebuke before all, **that others also may fear.**

There is to be *"fear"* on the part of pastors and others who have sinned and done wrong.
- **Hebrews 2:14-15**
  Forasmuch then as the children are partakers of flesh and blood, he also himself likewise took part of the same; that through death he might destroy him that had the power of death, that is, the devil; **And deliver them who through fear of death were all their lifetime subject to bondage**.

Do You Have "Fear Of Death"?

If you are unsaved you should be in *"fear of death."* You must trust the Lord Jesus Christ sincerely and personally; otherwise, eternal Hell and judgment is waiting.

- Hebrews 11:7
  By faith Noah, being warned of God of things not seen as yet, **moved with fear, prepared an ark** to the saving of his house; by the which he condemned the world, and became heir of the righteousness which is by faith.

  Noah was a man of faith, but he was also a man of *"fear."* He feared that if he didn't do something, there would be no one left alive on the earth through which the Saviour would come.

- 1 John 4:18
  There is no fear in love; but perfect love casteth out fear: because fear hath torment. He that feareth is not made perfect in love.

  I remember as a student at the University of Michigan in Ann Arbor. I was preparing to be a medical doctor. The Lord put *"fear"* in my heart and life so that I would change from medicine to the work of the Lord. Every time an ambulance went by, I was afraid. Every time I went to an accident, I was afraid. I told you about the woman I saw who was in front of her car trying to fix it. Her car went into gear and ran right over her. There was blood all over the street. I was watching in *"fear."*

  The Lord used this *"fear"* to change the direction of my life. The Lord took that *"fear"* away from me once I yielded to His will. I have not been afraid of an accident since. As a Navy chaplain I saw death and all sorts of accidents. God wanted me into a different area of life, so He used that *"fear"* to put me where He wanted me.

"but of power"
- Psalm 147:5
  Great *is* our Lord, and of great power: his understanding *is* infinite.

  God has given us *"power"* through the Spirit of God.

- Acts 1:8
  But ye shall receive power, after that the Holy Ghost is come upon you: and ye shall be witnesses unto me both in Jerusalem, and in all Judaea, and in Samaria, and unto the uttermost part of the earth.
- Romans 1:16
  For I am not ashamed of the gospel of Christ: for it is the power of God unto salvation to every one that believeth; to the Jew first, and also to the Greek.

Gnostic Texts Remove "Christ" Here

In the Gnostic Westcott and Hort Greek Text and other Gnostic Critical Texts, the word *"Christ"* is taken out of this verse. The modern versions that follow this Critical Text just say *"gospel."* It is the *"gospel of Christ."*

- 1 Corinthians 1:18
  For the preaching of the cross is to them that perish foolishness; but **unto us which are saved it is the power of God.**
- 1 Corinthians 1:24
  But unto them which are called, both Jews and Greeks, **Christ the power of God**, and the wisdom of God.
- 1 Corinthians 2:5
  That your faith should not stand in the wisdom of men, **but in the power of God.**
  God has given the saved ones this *"power."*
- Ephesians 6:10
  Finally, my brethren, be strong in the Lord, **and in the power of his might.**
  It is not the might or the strength of the Christian, but the *"power"* of God that is important.
- 1 Peter 1:5
  Who are kept by the power of God through faith unto salvation ready to be revealed in the last time.

We who are saved should have no fear. We are connected to the power of God.

"and of love"

- **John 13:34-35**
  A new commandment I give unto you, **That ye love one another; as I have loved you, that ye also love one another.** By this shall all *men* know that ye are my disciples, **if ye have love one to another.**
  God wants us to love one another. That is part of our Christian faith.
- **Romans 5:5**
  And hope maketh not ashamed; because **the love of God is shed abroad in our hearts by the Holy Ghost** which is given unto us.
- **Romans 8:35-39**
  Who shall separate us from the love of Christ? *shall* tribulation, or distress, or persecution, or famine, or nakedness, or peril, or sword? As it is written, For thy sake we are killed all the day long; we are accounted as sheep for the slaughter. Nay, in all these things we are more than conquerors through him that loved us. For I am persuaded, that neither death, nor life, nor angels, nor principalities, nor powers, nor things present, nor things to come , **Nor height, nor depth, nor any other creature, shall be able to separate us from the love of God,** which is in Christ Jesus our Lord.
- **Galatians 5:22**
  But **the fruit of the Spirit is love**, joy, peace, longsuffering, gentleness, goodness, faith,
  The Holy Spirit of God who enables Christians to be filled gives us that love.
- **1 John 2:15**
  Love not the world, neither the things *that are* in the world. **If any man love the world, the love of the Father is not in him.**
  We who are saved must be careful whom we love and what we love. We ought to love the Lord.

"and a sound mind."

- **Isaiah 26:3**
  Thou wilt keep *him* in perfect peace, **whose mind *is* stayed on thee**: because he trusteth in thee.
- **Matthew 22:37**
  Jesus said unto him, Thou shalt love the Lord thy God with all thy heart, and with all thy soul, and **with all thy mind.**

- **Mark 5:15**
  And they come to Jesus, and see him that was possessed with the devil, and had the legion, **sitting, and clothed, and in his right mind:** and they were afraid.
  The Lord Jesus Christ gave this man a *"sound mind."*
- **1 Corinthians 1:10**
  Now I beseech you, brethren, by the name of our Lord Jesus Christ, that ye all speak the same thing, and *that* there be no divisions among you; but *that* **ye be perfectly joined together in the same mind** and in the same judgment.
- **2 Corinthians 7:7**
  And not by his coming only, but by the consolation wherewith he was comforted in you, when he told us your earnest desire, your mourning, **your fervent mind toward me**; so that I rejoiced the more.
- **2 Corinthians 8:12**
  For **if there be first a willing mind**, *it is* accepted according to that a man hath, *and* not according to that he hath not.
- **2 Corinthians 8:19**
  And not *that* only, but who was also chosen of the churches to travel with us with this grace, which is administered by us to the glory of the same Lord, and **declaration of your ready mind**:
- **2 Corinthians 9:2**
  For I know **the forwardness of your mind**, for which I boast of you to them of Macedonia, that Achaia was ready a year ago; and your zeal hath provoked very many.
- **Philippians 2:3**
  Let nothing *be done* through strife or vainglory; but **in lowliness of mind** let each esteem other better than themselves.
- **Romans 8:7**
  Because **the carnal mind *is* enmity against God**: for it is not subject to the law of God, neither indeed can be.
- **Colossians 2:18**
  Let no man beguile you of your reward in a voluntary humility and worshipping of angels, intruding into those things which he hath not seen, **vainly puffed up by his fleshly mind**,

- **Colossians 3:12**
  Put on therefore, as the elect of God, holy and beloved, bowels of mercies, kindness, **humbleness of mind**, meekness, longsuffering;

God has given us *"minds."* Some people don't have much of a *"mind."* This is sometimes due to birth injuries and sometimes for other causes. God wants us to be in control of our *"mind"* and to have a *"sound mind."* The *"mind"* is not a place for wickedness or evil thoughts. That's the trouble with so many people whose *"minds"* have been trained by the world. Their *"mind"* is trained not to believe in the Lord. That's a terrible thing. Our *"minds"* must be sound and able to think. I realize that we can't choose the kind of *"mind"* that we have from birth, but whatever *"mind"* the Lord has given us should be given over to His control land leadership.

It might be that some might develop Alzheimer's disease. That's a condition of the *"mind."* We can't control that. One of our relatives has dementia. He used to be a strong football player in high school and in college. He was a very successful businessman, and now he has dementia. He can't drive anymore. His wife has to take care of him.

Sometimes our *"minds"* go bad, no matter how great the mind was to start with. My dad had a tremendous *"mind."* He was a chemical engineer. He held various patents in his field. He was a director of research at a chemical company in Cleveland, Ohio. In the last two or three years of his life his *"mind"* went almost completely. Sometimes minds go bad and they can't be stopped. Until the *"minds"* of us who are Christians go bad, God has promised to give us *"sound minds."* As we read the Words of God, and apply them to our lives, our *"minds"* can get even more sound.

2 Timothy 1:8

"Be not thou therefore ashamed of the testimony of our Lord, nor of me, his prisoner, but be thou partaker of the afflictions of the gospel according to the power of God."

Two Kinds Of Negative Commands

You will remember that I have told you on many occasions that there are two kinds of negative commands or prohibitions. If the Greek aorist tense is used, it means that the action is not even to be begun. If the present tense is used, it means to stop an action that had already begun.

In this verse, the aorist tense is used. This means that Paul told Pastor Timothy not even to begin to be *"ashamed"* of him or the testimony of the Lord. Timothy was not *"ashamed"* of the Lord or of Paul, but Paul did not want him to start being *"ashamed."* Sometimes you might not be *"ashamed"* of people up to a certain point, but all of the sudden, for some reason, you begin to be :*ashamed"* of them.

Paul also told Pastor Timothy, *"be thou partaker of the afflictions of the gospel according to the power of God."* Did Paul mean there are sometimes *"afflictions"* as the gospel is preached? You better believe that there are *"afflictions."* There are all kinds of *"afflictions."* If you don't believe it, just start telling somebody about the gospel of Christ and see how many *"afflictions"* come upon you. Part of the *"gospel"* is that all people are sinners who will go to the lake of fire in Hell unless they genuinely receive the Lord Jesus Christ as their Saviour. Pastors especially must be prepared for *"afflictions"* as they faithfully proclaim the true gospel of the Saviour.

Don't Be Ashamed Of The Lord

Despite the presence of any *"afflictions,"* the born-again Christian should never be *"ashamed"* of *"the testimony of our Lord."*

- Psalm 25:2
 O my God, I trust in thee: **let me not be ashamed**, let not mine enemies triumph over me.
- Psalm 25:20
 O keep my soul, and deliver me: **let me not be ashamed**; for I put my trust in thee.
- Mark 8:38
 Whosoever therefore shall be ashamed of me and of my words in this adulterous and sinful generation; of him also shall the Son of man be ashamed, when he cometh in the glory of his Father with the holy angels.
- Romans 1:16
 For **I am not ashamed of the gospel of Christ:** for it is the power of God unto salvation to every one that believeth; to the Jew first, and also to the Greek.

- Romans 5:5
And **hope maketh not ashamed**; because the love of God is shed abroad in our hearts by the Holy Ghost which is given unto us.
- Romans 9:33
As it is written, Behold, I lay in Sion a stumblingstone and rock of offence: and **whosoever believeth on him shall not be ashamed.**
- 2 Timothy 1:12
For the which cause I also suffer these things: nevertheless **I am not ashamed**: for I know whom I have believed, and am persuaded that he is able to keep that which I have committed unto him against that day.
- 2 Timothy 1:16
The Lord give mercy unto the house of **Onesiphorus; for he oft refreshed me, and was not ashamed of my chain** :
- 2 Timothy 2:15
Study to shew thyself approved unto God, **a workman that needeth not to be ashamed,** rightly dividing the word of truth.
- Hebrews 2:11
For both he that sanctifieth and they who are sanctified *are* all of one: for which cause **he is not ashamed to call them brethren,**
- 1 Peter 4:16
Yet if *any man suffer* as a Christian, **let him not be ashamed**; but let him glorify God on this behalf.
- 1 John 2:28
And now, little children, abide in him; that, when he shall appear, we may have confidence, **and not be ashamed before him at his coming.**

Are you going to be *"ashamed"* when the Lord Jesus returns? You have to live for Christ every day and not be *"ashamed."* There is a hymn called, *"Ashamed of Jesus."* Here are the words:

ASHAMED OF JESUS

Jesus, and shall it ever be A mortal man ashamed of Thee?
Ashamed of Thee Whom angels praise,
Whose glories shine thru' endless days.
Ashamed of Jesus! that dear Friend
On Whom my hopes of heav'n depend!
No! when I blush, be this my shame,
That I no more revere His Name.
(Words by Joseph Griggs)

Paul told Pastor Timothy that he should be a *"partaker of the afflictions of the gospel."* "Afflictions" are spoken about in many places in the Bible.

- Psalm 34:19
  Many are the afflictions of the righteous: but the LORD delivereth him out of them all.
- Acts 7:9-10
  And the patriarchs, moved with envy, sold Joseph into Egypt: but God was with him, **And delivered him out of all his afflictions**, and gave him favour and wisdom in the sight of Pharaoh king of Egypt; and he made him governor over Egypt and all his house.
- 1 Thessalonians 3:3
  That no man should be moved by these afflictions: for yourselves know that we are appointed thereunto.

If you are saved, do you know you have an appointment with *"affliction"*? I hope you are prepared to meet that appointment well.

- 2 Timothy 3:10-11
  But thou hast fully known my doctrine, manner of life, purpose, faith, longsuffering, charity, patience, **persecutions, afflictions, which came unto me at Antioch, at Iconium, at Lystra**; what persecutions I endured: but out of *them* all the Lord delivered me.
- 2 Timothy 4:5
  But watch thou in all things, **endure afflictions**, do the work of an evangelist, make full proof of thy ministry.

- 1 Peter 5:9
  Whom resist stedfast in the faith, knowing that **the same afflictions are accomplished in your brethren that are in the world.**
  Someone was talking to me just yesterday. He said that Satan enters into him at night yet this person claims to be a Christian. I said to this person that one of two things must be true. If you are a Christian the Holy Spirit is in your body and Satan cannot enter into that body. If you are lost, then Satan may enter into your body as he did in the body of Judas Iscariot.

2 Timothy 1:9

"Who hath saved us, and called us with an holy calling, not according to our works, but according to his own purpose and grace which was given us in Christ Jesus before the world began."

The Source Of Salvation
Salvation is of the Lord

- Jonah 2:9
  But I will sacrifice unto thee with the voice of thanksgiving; I will pay that I have vowed. **Salvation *is* of the LORD.**
  We are not saved or justified by works.
- Acts 13:39
  And **by him all that believe are justified from all things**, from which ye could not be justified by the law of Moses.

Works Won't Justify Us
Keeping the law will not justify us.

- Romans 3:20
  Therefore **by the deeds of the law there shall no flesh be justified in his sight**: for by the law *is* the knowledge of sin.

- **Romans 3:24**
  Being justified freely by his grace through the redemption that is in Christ Jesus:
- **Romans 3:28**
  Therefore **we conclude that a man is justified by faith** without the deeds of the law.
- **Romans 4:5**
  But to him that worketh not, but **believeth on him that justifieth the ungodly, his faith is counted for righteousness**.
- **Romans 5:1**
  Therefore **being justified by faith**, we have peace with God through our Lord Jesus Christ:
- **Romans 5:9**
  Much more then, **being now justified by his blood**, we shall be saved from wrath through him.

  John MacArthur doesn't believe that God can justify us through the blood of the Lord Jesus Christ. He only believes it is the death of Christ that justifies. Yes, the Lord Jesus Christ died for our sins, but He also shed his blood for the remission of our sins. Unfortunately, one of the pastors in our area agrees with John MacArthur now on all of this. Perhaps your pastor believes this same untruth.
- **Galatians 2:16**
  Knowing that **a man is not justified by the works of the law, but by the faith of Jesus Christ**, even we have believed in Jesus Christ, that we might be justified by the faith of Christ, and not by the works of the law: for by the works of the law shall no flesh be justified.
- **Galatians 3:11**
  But that **no man is justified by the law in the sight of God**, *it is* evident: for, The just shall live by faith.

The Way To Salvation
Faith in the Lord Jesus Christ is the way to salvation, not works.

- Ephesians 2:8-9
  For **by grace are ye saved through faith; and that not of yourselves**: *it is* the gift of God: **Not of works**, lest any man should boast.
- Titus 3:7
  That **being justified by his grace**, we should be made heirs according to the hope of eternal life.

The "Work" Of Calvary

We are saved by God's grace through faith, and no one can say that they saved themselves. God the Father will accept the work of God the Son and the work He accomplished on the Cross of Calvary. It does not apply if we don't accept it.

- Matthew 11:28
  Come unto me, all ye that labour and are heavy laden, and I will give you rest.

Only God's Grace Can Save Us

We are saved by God's grace.

Paul is writing this letter from Rome. He is in his second Roman imprisonment. He is writing to Timothy who is the pastor of the church over in Ephesus. This is located in present-day Turkey.

2 Timothy 1:10

"But is now made manifest by the appearing of our Saviour Jesus Christ, who hath abolished death and hath brought life and immortality to light through the gospel."

Now Paul is talking about the manifestation of the purpose and the grace of God.

- **2 Timothy 1:9**
  Who hath saved us, and called *us* with an holy calling, not according to our works, but according to his own purpose and grace, which was given us in Christ Jesus before the world began,

God's Grace Has Appeared

The manifestation of God's grace is *"by the appearing of our Saviour Jesus Christ."* When the Lord Jesus Christ came into this world God's grace appeared. Grace has been defined as *"getting something we do not deserve."* This grace appeared when He was born.

The world celebrates the birth of Christ on the 25th of December each year. They call it *"Christmas."*

The Incarnation Is Vital

I do not believe the Lord Jesus Christ was born on the 25th of December by any means, but I do believe that He was born by the miracle of the virgin birth. In His incarnation, He became both perfect Man and perfect God combined in one Person.

- **1 Timothy 6:14**
  That thou keep *this* commandment without spot, unrebukeable, **until the appearing of our Lord Jesus Christ**:
  He is going to appear in the rapture to the believers.

- 2 Timothy 4:1
  I charge *thee* therefore before God, and the Lord Jesus Christ, **who shall judge the quick and the dead at his appearing and his kingdom**;
- 2 Timothy 4:8
  Henceforth there is laid up for me a crown of righteousness, which the Lord, the righteous judge, **shall give me at that day: and not to me only, but unto all them also that love his appearing**.
- Titus 2:13
  Looking for that blessed hope, and the glorious appearing of the great God and our Saviour Jesus Christ;

Two Phases Of The 2nd Coming

The *"blessed hope"* is the rapture of the saved people. The *"glorious appearing"* is the return of the Lord Jesus Christ to earth to set up His millennial reign.

- 1 Peter 1:7
  That the trial of your faith, being much more precious than of gold that perisheth, though it be tried with fire, might be found unto praise and honour and glory **at the appearing of Jesus Christ:**

Paul then stated, about the Lord Jesus Christ, that He *"hath abolished death."*

The Meaning Of "Abolish"

The word *"abolish"* is KATARGEO which means:
"*1) to render idle, unemployed, inactivate, inoperative*
  1a) to cause a person or thing to have no further efficiency
  1b) to deprive of force, influence, power
2) to cause to cease, put an end to, do away with, annul, abolish
  2a) to cease, to pass away, be done away
  2b) to be severed from, separated from, discharged from, loosed from any one
  2c) to terminate all intercourse with one"

- John 5:24
  Verily, verily, I say unto you, He that heareth my word, and **believeth on him that sent me, hath everlasting life**, and shall not come into condemnation; but is passed from death unto life.
- John 11:25-26
  Jesus said unto her, I am the resurrection, and the life: he that believeth in me, **though he were dead, yet shall he live**: And whosoever liveth and believeth in me shall never die. Believest thou this?

In this passage, the Lord Jesus Christ is talking to Martha here. He is teaching that if you are a born-again Christian, you will never be separated from God. That is what *"death"* is referring to here.

Life and Immortality In The Gospel

Then Paul speaks of what the Lord Jesus Christ has brought: *"and hath brought life and immortality to light through the gospel."* The acceptance of the gospel of the Lord Jesus Christ is the only way any of us sinners can get this eternal life.

- John 3:16
  For God so loved the world, that he gave his only begotten Son, that **whosoever believeth in him should not perish, but have everlasting life**.
- John 10:27-28
  My sheep hear my voice, and I know them, and they follow me: And **I give unto them eternal life; and they shall never perish,** neither shall any *man* pluck them out of my hand.
- Romans 6:23
  For the wages of sin *is* death; but **the gift of God *is* eternal life through Jesus Christ our Lord**.
- John 3:36
  He that believeth on the Son hath everlasting life: and he that believeth not the Son shall not see life; but the wrath of God abideth on him.
- John 5:24
  Verily, verily, I say unto you, **He that heareth my word, and believeth on him that sent me, hath everlasting life**, and shall not come into condemnation; but is passed from death unto life.
- John 6:47
  Verily, verily, I say unto you, **He that believeth on me hath everlasting life.**

Gnostic Texts Leave Out "On Me"

Everlasting life is the life that Christ came to bring. It is important to notice that the new Bible versions based on the Gnostic critical Greek text leave out the two words, "*on me.*" They just translate it to read "*he that believes has everlasting life.*" Everyone in the world needs the Lord Jesus Christ. He is the only One Who has brought life and immortality to those who are saved.

2 Timothy 1:11

"Whereunto I am appointed a preacher, and an apostle, and a teacher of the Gentiles."

This *"gospel"* of the Lord Jesus Christ is good news. Yet, for a person to accept this *"gospel,"* they must also face some bad news. The bad news is that everyone in the world has sinned. Because of this, everyone in the world must go to Hell. That's bad news. The good news is the Lord Jesus Christ came into this world as perfect Man and perfect God in order to take the sins of the entire world in His own body on the cross. He died for the sins of everyone so that by the shedding of His blood and by their receiving the Lord Jesus Christ as their Saviour, they might have redemption. That's the good news. He paid for our sins so that we would not have to pay for them in Hell for all eternity. He was the perfect Substitute for us. Now we must believe that He died for us individually.

Concerning this *"gospel,"* Paul was appointed to be *"a preacher, and an apostle, and a teacher of the Gentiles."*

The Preacher As A "Herald"

A preacher is a KERUX. This word means

"a herald, a messenger vested with public authority who conveyed the official message of kings and magistrates, princes, and military commanders. He gave a public summons or demand and performed various other duties."

A *"preacher"* as a *"herald"* delivers the important messages of a king. The herald does not change the message. He just delivers it as it is. There are altogether too many preachers throughout the world who are changing the message of God.

Paul–An Apostle And Teacher

An *"apostle"* is one who has been sent forth like a missionary. Paul was also a *"teacher of the Gentiles."* If Paul had not taught Timothy, Titus and some of the others who were following with him on his various missionary journeys, we would not have the details in the Bible that we have today. Paul was a *"teacher."* If Paul were not a *"teacher"* he might not have written the book of Romans. If Paul were not a *"teacher"* he might not have written the books of 1 and 2 Corinthians to the church at Corinth; or the book of Galatians to the church at Galatia; or the book of Ephesians to the church at Ephesus; or the book of Colossians to the church at Colosse; or the books of 1 and 2 Thessalonians to the church at Thessalonica; or the books of 1 and 2 Timothy to Pastor Timothy; or the book of Titus to Pastor Titus if he were not "appointed" by the Lord Jesus Christ as a *"teacher."* He wanted his message that he learned from the Lord Jesus Christ to be perpetuated. That is what I want in our church. I want the message of the Words of God to be perpetuated faithfully by everyone who hears it.

2 Timothy 1:12

"For the which cause I also suffer these things nevertheless I am not ashamed for I know whom I have believed and am persuaded that he is able to keep that which I have committed unto him against that day."

"For the which cause" refers back to the cause of the gospel *"whereunto he was "appointed a preacher, and an apostle, and a teacher of the Gentiles."* It was because of the *"gospel"* that he was suffering these things. In certain ways to certain degrees every Christian suffers some things.

Paul Suffered Greatly For Christ

Paul suffered greatly. Very few of us suffer as greatly as Paul. You have only to look carefully at 2 Corinthians 11:21-33 for the details of Paul's suffering for the Lord Jesus Christ.

Yet, despite these suffering, Paul could say, "*I am not ashamed for I know whom I have believed.*" Paul knew the Lord Jesus Christ in Whom he had believed. Because of this knowledge of the Lord, he was "*persuaded that He is able to keep that which I have committed unto him against that day.*" Paul knew of Christ's keeping power throughout all of his sufferings. We see the suffering of Christians throughout the Bible.

- Acts 9:16
 For **I will shew him how great things he must suffer for my name's sake**.
- Romans 8:17
 And if children, then heirs; heirs of God, and joint-heirs with Christ; **if so be that we suffer with *him*, that we may be also glorified together**.

Christians are suffering all over the world. I know that the Christians in Liberia and Sierra Leone, West Africa, have been suffering. In China, Russia, Africa, and in many other countries Christians are suffering.

- Galatians 5:11
 And I, brethren, if I yet preach circumcision, **why do I yet suffer persecution?** then is the offence of the cross ceased.
- Galatians 6:12
 As many as desire to make a fair shew in the flesh, they constrain you to be circumcised; only **lest they should suffer persecution for the cross of Christ.**

"Politically Correct" Preachers

There are today what we might call "*politically correct*" preachers. They preach only that which is "*politically correct.*" If Paul had wanted to be "*politically correct*" in a Jewish culture, he would have preached that Gentile men had to be circumcised like the Jews in order to be saved. Paul was persecuted by the Jews for not being "*politically correct*" by not forcing Gentile men who were saved to be circumcised.

- Philippians 1:29
 For unto you it is given in the behalf of Christ, not only to believe on him, **but also to suffer for his sake**;

SUFFERING GOES ALONG WITH CHRISTIAN FAITH.

- 1 Thessalonians 3:4
  For verily, when we were with you, **we told you before that we should suffer tribulation;** even as it came to pass, and ye know.
- 2 Thessalonians 1:5
  Which is a manifest token of the righteous judgment of God, that ye may be counted worthy of the kingdom of God, **for which ye also suffer**:
- 2 Timothy 3:12
  Yea, and **all that will live godly in Christ Jesus shall suffer persecution.**

Are You Willing To Live Godly?

That word, "*will*," is not merely an indication of the future tense. It means those who have a strong will or desire to live a Christian life. They that really want to live "*godly in Christ Jesus shall suffer persecution.*" Living godly in Christ and suffering for Him go together.

- 1 Peter 3:14
  But and **if ye suffer for righteousness' sake, happy *are* ye:** and be not afraid of their terror, neither be troubled;

  MANY OF US WHO ARE SAVED DO SUFFER FOR RIGHTEOUSNESS SAKE.
- 1 Peter 2:20
  For what glory *is it*, if, when ye be buffeted for your faults, ye shall take it patiently? but if, **when ye do well, and suffer *for it*, ye take it patiently, this *is* acceptable with God.**

The Will of God In Suffering

It is not necessarily the will of God for every born-again Christian to suffer as Paul did, but if this is what God wills for our lives, we must be willing to suffer for well doing.

- 1 Peter 4:15
  But **let none of you suffer as a murderer, or *as* a thief, or *as* an evildoer, or as a busybody in other men's matters.**

  We should not want to suffer for doing the wrong thing, but only, if need be, for doing the right thing. Sometimes we suffer on our jobs just for being a Christian. Other people look the other way and might not want to talk with us. Sometimes they speak in wicked terms towards us. We must glorify God in all things.

- 1 Peter 4:19
  Wherefore **let them that suffer according to the will of God commit the keeping of their souls** *to him* in well doing, as unto a faithful Creator.

  Some believers suffer in pain and sickness. God is a faithful Creator, whatever the suffering is. If you are saved, you can look to Him, and He will help you.

  Paul also said in verse 12 of this 2 Timothy Chapter 1, that God is *"able to keep that which I've committed unto him against that day."* God is able to keep the souls which are led to Christ by Paul until the end.

The Meanings Of "Keep"

The word for "*keep*" is PHULLASSO. It means

"To keep guard over, to watch, to have an eye upon, to guard a person, to keep one from being snatched away, to reserve safe."

That's what our eternal life is. We don't have eternal life one day, and then we lose it.

2 Timothy 1:13

"Hold fast the form of sound words, which thou hast heard of me in faith and love, which is in Christ Jesus."

Hold Fast Sound Words

The word for *"hold fast"* is ECHO, which implies that Pastor Timothy is to take hold of the *"sound words"* and hold them fast. *"Sound words"* are *"healthy"* words. *"Sound words"* are Words that are in the Scripture. These are Words that God has given to us in the Bible. Paul was telling Timothy to *"hold fast"* these Words.

We have a whole group of fundamental Bible believing institutions that are against holding on to the Traditional Masoretic Hebrew and Greek *"sound words"* that underlie our King James Bible. The four leading institutions are: Bob Jones University, Detroit Baptist Seminary, Calvary Baptist Seminary and Central Baptist Seminary. To these four can be added Maranatha Baptist Bible College, Northland Baptist Bible College, International Baptist College, and others. These institutions are fundamentalists and professed *"friends"* of the Bible.

Fundamentalists And Gnostic Texts?

And because of the use of the Gnostic critical Greek text in these schools and the softness regarding the modern English Bible versions because of their position, I believe firmly that the Bible is undergoing more damage from its alleged *"friends"* then from its liberal *"enemies."* Did you know that? Everyone agrees that the modernist liberal apostates do not believe the Hebrew, Aramaic, and Greek Words of the Bible have been preserved until today.

"Friends" of Fundamentalism are doing the damage that is being done in our Fundamental churches today. Here are two verses that are subjects of debate about Bible preservation.

- **Psalm 12:6-7**
  The words of the LORD *are* **pure words:** *as* **silver tried in a furnace of earth, purified seven times. Thou shalt keep them, O LORD, thou shalt preserve them from this generation for ever.**

  I believe these verses teach clearly that God has promised both to *"preserve"* and *"keep"* the Hebrew, Aramaic, and (by extension) Greek *"Words of the Lord."* These above mentioned schools don't believe these verses apply to the Hebrew, Aramaic, and Greek Words. I believe that they do apply.

- **Psalm 119:89**
  For ever, O LORD, thy word is settled in Heaven."

  The Words of the Lord are not only *"settled in Heaven,"* but also they have been settled *"by Heaven."*

- **Matthew 4:4**
  But he answered and said, It is written, Man shall not live by bread alone, but **by every word that proceedeth out of the mouth of God**.

  The Lord Jesus Christ said this to the Devil when He was out in the wilderness without any food for forty days. The Lord Jesus Christ pointed out that **it was necessary for every Word to be** *"preserved"* **so that people could** *"live"* **by them.** It is impossible to live by Words that have not been preserved.

  The expression, *"it is written,"* is used eighty times in the King James Bible. Sixty-three of these times are in the New Testament. The Greek Word used is in the perfect tense. According to Greek grammatical authorities, the perfect tense differs from either the Greek aorist tense, or the Greek imperfect tense in the following way: It means that something has happened in the past, is *"preserved"* to the present and on into the future. This indicates verbal, plenary *"preservation"* of the original Hebrew, Aramaic, and Greek Words in the Bible.

Original Words Preserved

In this case, this verse (Matthew 4:4) was first written by Moses in Deuteronomy 8:3, it was *"preserved"* to the day that the Lord Jesus Christ quoted it to Satan, and it will continue to be *"preserved"* throughout the future. That is what that perfect tense of the Greek language means. It is proof of the verbal, plenary *"preservation"* of the original Hebrew, Aramaic, and Greek Words of the Bible.

- Matthew 5:17-18

    Think not that I am come to destroy the law, or the prophets: I am not come to destroy, but to fulfil.

    For verily I say unto you, **Till Heaven and earth pass, one jot or one tittle shall in <u>no wise</u> pass from the law, till all be fulfilled.**

    Has *"all been fulfilled"*? Of course not. Since that is true, the Lord Jesus Christ Himself promised that not even a *"jot"* or a *"tittle"* would *"pass from the law, till all be fulfilled."* The *"jot"* is the smallest Hebrew letter. It looks like our comma.

    According to Dr. Thomas Strouse, a specialist in the Hebrew language, the *"tittle"* is the *"hiriq"* which is the smallest Hebrew vowel. It looks like a dot or a period. The Lord Jesus Christ, the Author of every Word of the Bible guaranteed the verbal, plenary preservation of the original Hebrew, Aramaic, and Greek Words, including the smallest Hebrew consonant and the smallest Hebrew vowel until *"all be fulfilled."* The words *"no wise"* represent OU ME which is the strongest negative in the Greek language. It means *"never, never, never."* This is Bible preservation.

Denying Preservation Of Words

Shame on these Fundamental schools who do not believe these verses apply to the original Hebrew, Aramaic, and Greek Words. They believe that God has never promised to *"preserve"* His Words.

- Matthew 24:35

    Heaven and earth shall pass away, but **my words shall not pass away.**

    Some people don't believe that *"Heaven and earth will pass away."* The Lord said it, so it is the truth. The above-mentioned Fundamental schools should believe the Words of the Lord Jesus Christ as well. Jesus is the Author of all the New Testament Words and, by extension, all of the Old Testament Words. He is the Word, the Logos, and the Revelator. He says that His Words *"shall not pass away."*

Never, Never "Pass Away"

Again, as in Matthew 5:17-18, the negative used in this verse is OU ME which is the strongest negative in the Greek language. The Words of the Lord Jesus Christ shall never, never, never "*pass away.*"

Can there be any stronger teaching about the verbal, plenary preservation of the original Hebrew, Aramaic, and Greek Words? This verse is repeated exactly in two other New Testament verses: Mark 13:31, and Luke 21:33.

Paul says to Timothy, the preacher, to "*hold fast*" to the Words of the Lord Jesus Christ "*in faith and love which is in Christ Jesus.*"

- 1 Timothy 6:20

    O Timothy, **keep that which is committed to thy trust**, avoiding profane *and* vain babblings, and oppositions of science falsely so called:

If a pastor doesn't "*keep*" and guard the original Hebrew, Aramaic, and Greek Words found in the traditional manuscripts that underlie the King James Bible "*committed to his trust*" who is going to? Pastors must "*keep*" the Words committed to their trust. The Words that the pastors are taught in the Fundamentalist schools referred to above are false Words. They are from the Westcott and Hort false Gnostic critical Greek Text that has 8,000 differences from our Textus Receptus, which underlies our King James Bible. Dr. Jack Moorman has produced a tremendous volume showing the 8,000 Greek Words that are different from the Words of the Textus Receptus. Pastors must "*hold fast*" these "*sound words.*" Paul told Timothy to "*keep*" that which was "*committed to his trust.*"

- Jude 3

    Beloved, when I gave all diligence to write unto you of the common salvation, it was needful for me to write unto you, and exhort *you* that **ye should earnestly contend for the faith which was once delivered unto the saints** .

Contending For God's Words

Part of *"the faith"* for which pastors and all Christians are to generally *"contend for"* is *"the faith"* in the promises of God. One of God's promises is to preserve His original Hebrew, Aramaic, and Greek Words. These are Words from which our King James Bible has been translated. These Words must be the foundation for Bible versions in every language of the world. The battle for the Words of the Bible is part of *"the faith"* once *"delivered unto the saints."*

2 Timothy 1:14

"That good thing which was committed unto thee keep by the Holy Ghost which dwelleth in us."

I believe that the *"good thing"* which was *"committed"* to Pastor Timothy to *"keep"* was the Words of God. The way Timothy was to *"keep"* that which was *"committed"* to him was *"by the Holy Ghost which dwelleth in us"* who are Christians. If you are saved, the Holy Spirit of God dwells inside of your body.

- Psalm 51:11

  Cast me not away from thy presence; and **take not thy holy spirit from me.**

In the Old Testament the Holy Spirit came and went. It was not a permanent situation. In the New Testament times, this came to pass permanently.

- Romans 8:9

  But ye are not in the flesh, but in the Spirit, **if so be that the Spirit of God dwell in you.** Now if any man have not the Spirit of Christ, he is none of his.

The Indwelling Holy Spirit

If the Holy Spirit doesn't dwell in your body, you are *"none of his."* That's just as clear as anything. Every saved person does have the Spirit of God indwelling him.

- **Romans 8:11**
  But if the Spirit of him that raised up Jesus from the dead dwell in you, he that raised up Christ from the dead shall also quicken your mortal bodies **by his Spirit that dwelleth in you**.
- **Romans 8:15**
  For ye have not received the spirit of bondage again to fear; but **ye have received the Spirit of adoption**, whereby we cry, Abba, Father.
- **1 Corinthians 2:12**
  Now **we have received, not the spirit of the world, but the spirit which is of God**; that we might know the things that are freely given to us of God.
- **1 Corinthians 3:16**
  Know ye not that ye are the temple of God, and *that* **the Spirit of God dwelleth in you?**
- **1 Corinthians 6:19-20**
  What? know ye not that **your body is the temple of the Holy Ghost *which is* in you, which ye have of God**, and ye are not your own? For ye are bought with a price: therefore glorify God in your body, and in your spirit, which are God's.
- **2 Corinthians 1:22**
  Who hath also sealed us, and **given the earnest of the Spirit in our hearts**.
- **Galatians 3:2**
  This only would I learn of you, **Received ye the Spirit by the works of the law, or by the hearing of faith**?

  The Spirit of God is received by every person at the moment he is genuinely born-again.
- **Galatians 4:6**
  And because ye are sons, **God hath sent forth the Spirit of his Son into your hearts,** crying, Abba, Father.
- **Ephesians 1:13**
  In whom ye also *trusted*, after that ye heard the word of truth, the gospel of your salvation: in whom also after that ye believed, **ye were sealed with that holy Spirit of promise,**

> ## Sealed For Eternity
> Saved people are sealed for all eternity by the Spirit of God.

- Ephesians 4:30
  And grieve not **the holy Spirit of God, whereby ye are sealed unto the day of redemption**.
  A *"seal"* is a symbol of ownership. It is also something that is difficult to break. The Holy Spirit of God is Himself the Seal in the body of every saved Christian.
- 1 Thessalonians 4:8
  He therefore that despiseth, despiseth not man, but God, **who hath also given unto us his holy Spirit**.
- James 4:6
  Do ye think that the scripture saith in vain, **The spirit that dwelleth in us** lusteth to envy?
- 1 John 4:13
  Hereby know we that we dwell in him, and he in us, because **he hath given us of his Spirit**.

These are sixteen verses that show us and teach us carefully and clearly that the Holy Spirit of God dwells in every born-again Christian's body.

> ## God's Fruit In Houses Of Clay
> Our bodies are houses of clay. We are weak. Our physical natures die, but God says in His Word that if we have been saved by faith in the Lord Jesus Christ, the Holy Spirit has regenerated us. He wants to produce His fruit in us (Galatians 5:22-23).

The Lord Jesus Christ can be produced, and we can have this treasure in earthen vessels. The power and excellency cannot be in us, but in God.

2 Timothy 1:15

"**This thou knowest, that all they which are in Asia be turned away from me, of whom are Phygellus and Hermogenes.**"

As Paul is writing this letter to Pastor Timothy from a prison in Rome, he says that Timothy knows "*they which are in Asia*" are "*turned away*" from him. These people in Asia Minor were formerly with Paul but then "*turned away*" from him now that he is in prison.

Naming Names Is Biblical

Paul names two men who turned away from him: Phygellus and Hermogenes. Some people wonder if it is proper to name the names of people when you are preaching or writing. Here is a Pauline example of how it is Scriptural when needed and called for.

Some think Paul should have been nicer and shown more sweetness and not to mention any names. Paul wanted to warn believers about these turncoats who turned from the right army to the wrong army. Writing from prison, Paul felt led of the Lord to warn his fellow believers of these two, Phygellus and Hermogenes, who turned away from him and from the proper things of the Lord.

- Numbers 14:43
  For the Amalekites and the Canaanites *are* there before you, and **ye shall fall by the sword: because ye are turned away from the LORD**, therefore the LORD will not be with you.
- 1 Kings 11:4
  For it came to pass, **when Solomon was old, *that* his wives turned away his heart after other gods**: and his heart was not perfect with the LORD his God, as *was* the heart of David his father.
- 2 Chronicles 29:6
  For **our fathers have trespassed**, and done *that which was* evil in the eyes of the LORD our God, and have forsaken him, **and have turned away their faces from the habitation of the LORD**, and turned *their* backs.

Have you *"turned away"* from the things of the Lord? I hope not, and I trust that you will stay on target for the things of the Lord Jesus Christ and His Words. Don't be like Phygellus and Hermogenes. Paul was a prisoner of Rome who was about to be executed. Prisoners are often not very inviting. We know a prisoner with whom we have been corresponding. He came to know the Lord after he was in prison. He called me up a few days ago and asked me for some money to buy some soap.

When I was first saved I was involved in a prison ministry with Grace Bible Church in Ann Arbor, Michigan, when I was attending the University of Michigan. We had a prison ministry every Sunday and preached the gospel to the prisoners. Many of those prisoners were not appealing. As a Navy chaplain I went to the brigs at different times and visited the prisoners. They were not happy, but they needed to hear and accept the gospel of the Lord Jesus Christ.

Both Phygellus and Hermogenes were ashamed of Paul, the prisoner. I hope if you and I ever get sent to prison for our sound testimony for our Saviour that the rest of the Christians will not be ashamed to visit us, to comfort us, to write letters to us, or to see how they can help us. Don't *"turn away"* from the Lord's servants, especially when they fall on hard and difficult times.

2 Timothy 1:16

"The Lord give mercy unto the house of Onesiphorus, for he oft refreshed me and was not ashamed of my chain."

Now Paul names another name, but in a good sense. He had a good thing to say about Onesiphorus. Paul mentioned Phygellus and Hermogenes who were not good to him, but now he is pointing out Onesiphorus who was good to Paul. Paul was in chains during his first Roman imprisonment when he wrote Ephesians, Philippians, Colossians, and Philemon. Now, he is writing 2 Timothy in his second Roman imprisonment.

- Acts 21:33

    Then the chief captain came near, and took him, and **commanded** *him* **to be bound with two chains**; and demanded who he was, and what he had done.

    This is speaking of Paul's first Roman imprisonment

- Acts 28:20

    For this cause therefore have I called for you, to see *you*, and to speak with *you*: because that **for the hope of Israel I am bound with this chain.**

2 Timothy 1:16

Even today, you see prisoners chained when they come into the courthouse for trial. Paul was bound with a *"chain"* and Onesiphorus was not ashamed of Paul's *"chain."* Paul was not in jail because he robbed or killed somebody, or for doing any other evil doing. Paul was in prison because he loved and preached about the salvation provided by the Lord Jesus Christ. That is what might happen to some of us one of these days, as it has happened to persecuted Christians in other lands.

Onesiphorus was *"not ashamed"* of Paul's *"chain."* We must not be *"ashamed"* of the Lord Jesus Christ or of His people.

- **Romans 1:16**
  For **I am not ashamed of the gospel of Christ**: for it is the power of God unto salvation to every one that believeth; to the Jew first, and also to the Greek.
  We must never be ashamed of things that are right and godly.

- **Romans 9:33**
  As it is written, Behold, I lay in Sion a stumblingstone and rock of offence: and **whosoever believeth on him shall not be ashamed.**

- **Philippians 1:20**
  According to my earnest expectation and *my* **hope, that in nothing I shall be ashamed,** but *that* with all boldness, as always, *so* now also Christ shall be magnified in my body, whether *it be* by life, or by death.

- **2 Timothy 1:8**
  Be not thou therefore ashamed of the testimony of our Lord, nor of me his prisoner: but be thou partaker of the afflictions of the gospel according to the power of God;

Read God's Words Daily

- 2 Timothy 2:15
  Study to shew thyself approved unto God, a workman that needeth not to be ashamed, rightly dividing the word of truth.

That is why I urge everyone of you to read God's Words from Genesis through Revelation each year. This can be done at the rate of 85 verses per day. God does not want any saved person *"to be ashamed"* when it comes to knowing and understanding His Words.

- 1 John 2:28
  And now, little children, abide in him; that, when he shall appear, we may have confidence, and **not be ashamed before him at his coming.**
  This *"coming"* is speaking about the rapture of the saved people when the Lord Jesus Christ returns in the air.

The Meaning Of "Refreshing"

Paul mentions that Onesiphorus *"oft refreshed"* him. The word for refresh is ANAPSUCHO. This word has various meanings: *"to cool again and to cool off, to recover from the effects of heat, to recover breath, to take care."*

- Romans 15:32
  That I may come unto you with joy by the will of God, and **may with you be refreshed.**
  Are you and I *"refreshing"* to people? Can other people *"refresh"* you?
- 1 Corinthians 16:17-18
  I am glad of the coming of Stephanas and Fortunatus and Achaicus: for that which was lacking on your part they have supplied. **For they have refreshed my spirit and yours:** therefore acknowledge ye them that are such.
- 2 Corinthians 7:13
  Therefore we were comforted in your comfort: yea, and exceedingly the more joyed we for the joy of Titus, because **his spirit was refreshed by you all.**

Have you ever had a hot flash? I haven't, but I know some who have. My wife was fanning herself in a restaurant last night and a lady came and gave her a wet towel. It was very pleasant, refreshing, and needed.

2 Timothy 1:17

"But when he was in Rome, he sought me out very diligently and found me."

Onesiphorus left his place of residence and took the long journey to Rome where Paul was in prison. If you went to the big city of Rome would you have been able to find Paul? You would have to know what prison he was in. In order to find Paul in this strange city, you would have to be eager. That is why I believe it says in this verse, *"he sought me out very diligently and found me."*

2 Timothy 1:17

Onesiphorus was not ashamed of Paul at all. I am sure that Paul was thankful for this godly man who *"refreshed"* him often. Paul was in a very troublesome state and needed the Lord's deliverance.

- Psalm 34:4
  I sought the LORD, and he heard me, and delivered me from all my fears.

Audrey Sanborn's Favorite Verse

My wife's sister, Audrey, loved that verse. She was facing death from Hodgkin's disease. In that time Hodgkin's disease was a death sentence. The Lord finally *"delivered"* me in 1986 from this same disease. I am thankful for His *"deliverance."*

- Psalm 77:2
  In the day of my trouble I sought the Lord: my sore ran in the night, and ceased not: my soul refused to be comforted.
- Psalm 119:10
  With my whole heart have I sought thee: O let me not wander from thy commandments.

Because he sought the Lord, this man, Onesiphorus, he also sought out the apostle Paul, the servant of the Lord who was in prison in Rome. When you seek people out, you want to find them.

Coming To Seek & Save Sinners

If you are saved, the Lord Jesus Christ sought you out. He came into this world to seek sinners. He sought Zacchaeus up in that tree. Then the Lord invited Himself to his house and brought him to repentance and faith.

- Luke 19:10
  For the **Son of man is come to seek and to save that which was lost**.

The Lord Jesus Christ is a seeking Saviour. Praise God He sought me and found me, and I trusted Him and I'm saved. If you are saved, you can say this as well.

2 Timothy 1:18

"The Lord grant unto him that he may find mercy of the Lord in that day; and in how many things he ministered unto me at Ephesus, thou knowest very well."

Paul is still talking about Onesiphorus. When Paul used the phrase, *"in that day,"* I believe he was referring to the *"day"* when Onesiphorus would go Home to Heaven to be forever with the Lord Jesus Christ. Paul wanted the Lord to grant him *"mercy of the Lord."*

Then Paul reminded Pastor Timothy of the record of help that Onesiphorus had given to him. He wrote: *"in how many things he ministered unto me at Ephesus, thou knowest very well."* Timothy was with Paul during his ministry at Ephesus and was an eye witness of the *"ministry"* that Onesiphorus had toward Paul. I would hope that every Christian is able to *"minister"* to others as they have need.

The Meaning Of "Ministering"

The verb for *"ministered"* is DIAKONEO. It means to *"be an attendant, to wait upon someone, to serve."*

- Matthew 8:15
  And he touched her hand, and the fever left her: and she arose, **and ministered unto them**.

  This is speaking of Peter's wife's mother. Peter could not have been the first pope, or any pope at all. If he had a mother-in-law, and he did, he must have been married, thus disqualifying him from being even a Roman Catholic priest, much less a pope. When Peter's mother-in-law was healed, she ministered to those around her. We can, and should, minister to others as well.

- Luke 8:3
  And Joanna the wife of Chuza Herod's steward, and Susanna, and many others, **which ministered unto him of their substance**.

- **Acts 19:22**
  So **he sent into Macedonia two of them that ministered unto him,** Timotheus and Erastus; but he himself stayed in Asia for a season.

  Here are two people who helped and *"ministered"* unto Paul. Did Paul need some help? Yes. Do you sometimes need help? Yes. All of us need help and assistance from others from time to time, whether by prayer, or in other ways.

- **Hebrews 6:10**
  For God *is* not unrighteous to forget your work and labour of love, which ye have shewed toward his name, in that **ye have ministered to the saints, and do minister**.

  I hope that you and I can *"minister to the saints"* as well. We can *"minister"* by what we say to them, by letters, by helping them in any way we can.

Second Timothy
Chapter Two

2 Timothy 2:1

"Thou therefore, my son, be strong in the grace that is in Christ Jesus."

Timothy was called Paul's *"son"* because Paul, no doubt, led him to personal faith in the Lord Jesus Christ. Paul told Timothy to *"be strong in the grace that is in Christ Jesus."* The substance of that strength was God's *"grace,"* and the source of that strength is *"Christ Jesus."* It is important that those of us who are saved by faith in the Lord Jesus Christ be *"strong"* for the Lord. There are many things in Scripture about strength.

- **Romans 4:20**
  He staggered not at the promise of God through unbelief; **but was strong in faith**, giving glory to God;
- **1 Corinthians 16:13**
  Watch ye, stand fast in the faith, quit you like men, **be strong.**
  Timothy was to be *"strong in the grace of Christ Jesus."*
- **2 Corinthians 12:10**
  Therefore I take pleasure in infirmities, in reproaches, in necessities, in persecutions, in distresses for Christ's sake: for **when I am weak, then am I strong**.
  Weakness is strength in the Lord.
- **Ephesians 6:10**
  Finally, my brethren, **be strong in the Lord**, and in the power of his might.
- **Hebrews 11:34**
  Quenched the violence of fire, escaped the edge of the sword, **out of weakness were made strong**, waxed valiant in fight, turned to flight the armies of the aliens.

The early believers in the Old Testament were made *"strong"* out of weakness.

The Meanings Of "Grace"

Paul urges Pastor Timothy to *"be strong in the grace that is in Christ Jesus."* *"Grace"* has been defined as getting something you don't deserve. Here's another definition of *"grace"*:

"Grace is the merciful kindness by which God exercises and exerting His Holy influence upon souls, turns them to Christ, keeps, strengthens, increasing them in Christian faith, knowledge, affection, and kindles them to the exercise of the Christian virtues."

There are many verses on God's grace.
- Acts 20:32
 And now, brethren, **I commend you to God, and to the word of his grace**, which is able to build you up, and to give you an inheritance among all them which are sanctified.
- Romans 3:24
 Being justified freely by his grace through the redemption that is in Christ Jesus:
 We who are saved are justified by God's *"grace"* and not by any work of ours.
- 2 Corinthians 8:9
 For **ye know the grace of our Lord Jesus Christ**, that, though he was rich, yet for your sakes he became poor, that ye through his poverty might be rich.
 This is the key verse for *"grace."*
- 2 Corinthians 12:9
 And he said unto me, **My grace is sufficient for thee**: for my strength is made perfect in weakness. Most gladly therefore will I rather glory in my infirmities, that the power of Christ may rest upon me.
- Ephesians 1:7
 In whom we have redemption through his blood, **the forgiveness of sins, according to the riches of his grace;**
 God's grace can give us forgiveness when we trust Christ as our Saviour.

- Ephesians 2:8-9
  For **by grace are ye saved through faith**; and that not of yourselves: *it is* the gift of God:
  God's "*grace*" saves and keeps.

2 Timothy 2:2

"And the things that thou hast heard of me among many witnesses, the same commit thou to faithful men, who shall be able to teach others also."

Paul spoke of things that Timothy had "*heard*" from him "*among many witnesses.*" Timothy accompanied Paul on most of his journeys mentioned in the book of Acts. He heard Paul teach and preach to various groups of people. Paul is telling Timothy to "*commit*" the very same doctrines that he heard Paul teach "*to faithful men*" so they could "*teach others also.*" Paul did not want the doctrines taught to him by the Lord Jesus Christ Himself during his three years in Arabia (Galatians 1:18) to die out. He wanted them to be perpetuated for all the years to come. We have Paul's doctrines in the New Testament and some pastors have preached about them. Sadly, today, his doctrine is ignored on the part of many born-again Christians.

The Meanings Of "Commit"

The word for "*commit*" is PARATITHEMI. It means "*to place beside someone like food is placed on a table.*" That is what a pastor is to do. He is to place the spiritual food of the Words of God before his people. It also means "*to set before in teaching, set forth and explain.*" Timothy was to take Paul's sound doctrines and "*set them before*" those who were "*faithful.*"

The word for "*faithful*" is PISTOS. It refers to "*people who show themselves faithful in the transaction of business, the execution of commands, and the discharge of faithful duties.*"

Then these "*faithful men*" will "*be able to teach others also.*" These "*faithful men*" are to be teachers of others. This is what I am trying to do here in our 𝕭ible for 𝕿oday 𝕭aptist 𝕮hurch.

The Meanings Of "Teach"

The word for *"teach"* (DIDASKO) means *"to hold discourse with others in order to instruct them, to deliver didactic discourses, to impart instruction, to explain or expound a thing."* This should be the work of a pastor and a teacher rather than telling many stories and jokes from the pulpit.

In the phrase, *"teach others also,"* the word for *"others"* is HETEROS rather than the usual word, ALLOS. It means people of a different sort rather than of the same sort.

Teaching Those Who Disagree

We are to teach others who are not in agreement with us, as well as those who do agree. *"Teaching"* is a strong part of Scripture.

- Matthew 28:19
  Go ye therefore, and teach all nations, baptizing them in the name of the Father, and of the Son, and of the Holy Ghost:
- Matthew 28:20
  Teaching them to observe all things whatsoever I have commanded you: and, lo, I am with you alway, *even* unto the end of the world. Amen.

  That's why I preach and teach verse by verse so that we can try to *"observe all things."*
- Mark 6:34
  And Jesus, when he came out, saw much people, and was moved with compassion toward them, because they were as sheep not having a shepherd: and **he began to teach them many things.**

"Teaching" implies that the teacher knows something to teach and that he is able to set it forth clearly and forcefully. It implies that the people to whom the teacher teaches do not know this teaching but should know it.

- Acts 1:1
  The former treatise have I made, O Theophilus, **of all that Jesus began both to do and teach**,
  Jesus was a teacher.

By The Waters Of Galilee

"Behold a teacher went forth to teach
Some two thousand years ago.
Before the age of the car or the radio,
He had no books, and no magazines,
And he held no scholastic degree,
But men still ponder the things that he taught
By the waters of Galilee."
(Author Unknown)

I was given this poem by my high school janitor, Uncle Charlie Allen, who led me to the Lord Jesus Christ as my Saviour. I quoted this poem during my speech in my 1945 graduation ceremonies at Berea High School in Berea, Ohio. As the class salutatorian, I was permitted to give a salutatory speech. These were the days when students could talk about the Lord Jesus Christ in school without penalties. The Lord Jesus Christ was a teacher.

- 2 Timothy 2:24
  And **the servant of the Lord** must not strive; but be gentle unto all *men*, **apt to teach**, patient,
  These to whom Timothy taught Paul's doctrines were to be *"faithful."* He didn't want Timothy to teach those who were unfaithful people. They would not be able to communicate properly.
- Luke 16:10
  He that is faithful in that which is least is faithful also in much: and he that is unjust in the least is unjust also in much.

Be Faithful In "Least" And "Much"

Many people hear something about the Bible and then begin to scramble the meaning of what has been taught. We must not change what God has given to us. We must be faithful *"in that which is least"* as well as *"in much."*

- Luke 19:17
 And he said unto him, Well, thou good servant: **because thou hast been faithful in a very little**, have thou authority over ten cities.
- 1 Corinthians 4:2
 Moreover **it is required in stewards, that a man be found faithful.**
- Ephesians 6:21
 But that ye also may know my affairs, *and* how I do, Tychicus, **a beloved brother and faithful minister in the Lord**, shall make known to you all things:
- 1 Timothy 1:12
 And I thank Christ Jesus our Lord, who hath enabled me, for that **he counted me faithful, putting me into the ministry;**
 Ministers must be *"faithful."*
- Hebrews 3:5
 And **Moses verily *was* faithful in all his house**, as a servant, for a testimony of those things which were to be spoken after;

Faithful To The Saviour & His Words

Christians, of all people, young and old alike, must be *"faithful"* to the Lord Jesus Christ and to His Words. The unsaved world is looking at those professing to be born-again, and is very happy when they see hypocrisy. Let us disappoint them by being *"faithful"* to our Saviour.

2 Timothy 2:3
"Thou therefore endure hardness, as a good soldier of Jesus Christ."

Enduring "Hardness" Of Persecution

Pastor Timothy was to *"endure hardness."* This *"hardness"* speaks of persecution and afflictions.

He must be a *"good soldier of Jesus Christ."* Soldiers have great difficulties as they are engaged in battle with their enemy soldiers. If you don't believe that, you might go with the Marines as I did for a year with the ground troops out on maneuvers. You don't have a lot of food. You have to sleep whether it is dry or raining. You don't have any electricity. You don't have your family and former friends with you.

Timothy must be a *"good soldier."* The Lord wants us *"good."* A good [KALOS] soldier is excellent in his nature, well-equipped--not just any kind of soldier. He must be a champion for the cause of the Lord Jesus Christ.

- 2 Thessalonians 1:4
  So that we ourselves glory in you in the churches of God for your **patience and faith in all your persecutions and tribulations that ye endure**:
- 2 Timothy 4:5
  But watch thou in all things, **endure afflictions**, do the work of an evangelist, make full proof of thy ministry.

If you are a *"good soldier,"* you will have afflictions, but you must endure the things you can't do anything about.

- James 5:11
  Behold, **we count them happy which endure**. Ye have heard of the patience of Job, and have seen the end of the Lord; that the Lord is very pitiful, and of tender mercy.

ENDURE HARDNESS

Endure hardness!
As a soldier good.
Stand at your post
As a soldier should!

Eyes to the right!
With Sword out of sheath,
Ready to march
If the Leader should speak!

Endure hardness!
Tho' stern be your pace,
Serve without murmur
In the soldier's place!
(By Gertrude Grace Sanborn (1981)
From her book of poems, *With Tears in My Heart*

2 Timothy 2:4

"No man that warreth entangleth himself with the affairs of this life; that he may please him who hath chosen him to be a soldier."

If a soldier is warring [STRATEUOMAI], (*"making a military expedition"*), he must not "*entangle himself with the affairs of this life.*" As a soldier, he doesn't have "business as usual" as civilians have. He does not have an 8:00 a.m. to 5:00 p.m. schedule. He stays out where the troops are.

Pleasing Our Commanding Officer

The true and only real purpose of the Christian "soldier" is *"that he may please him who hath chosen him to be a soldier."* The Lord Jesus Christ is the One who has chosen every born-again Christian to be a faithful soldier for His cause in this wicked world. Sad to say, some Christians don't want to fight against the world, the flesh, and the Devil. They are Christian pacifists. If you are a spiritual pacifist as a redeemed Christian, you are not fit to be in the battle of the Lord Jesus Christ.

The Lord Jesus Christ is certainly not a pacifist in this spiritual battle. A battle implies that we have an enemy that is attacking us and seeking to defeat us. Our enemies are the world, the flesh, and the Devil. The Lord Jesus Christ is our Captain and our Commander-in-Chief. We must be willing to *"fight the good fight of faith"* (1 Timothy 6:12).

A good Christian soldier must not *"entangle himself in the affairs of this life."* The Bible has some illustrations of such *"entanglements."*

- Exodus 14:3
   For Pharaoh will say of the children of Israel, **They are entangled in the land,** the wilderness hath shut them in.
- Matthew 22:15
   Then went the Pharisees, and **took counsel how they might entangle him in** *his* **talk**.
   To *"entangle"* [EMPLEKO] means *"to interweave and to involve someone in something else."*
- Galatians 5:1
   Stand fast therefore in the liberty wherewith Christ hath made us free, and **be not entangled again with the yoke of bondage**.
- 2 Peter 2:20
   For if after they have escaped the pollutions of the world through the knowledge of the Lord and Saviour Jesus Christ, **they are again entangled therein, and overcome**, the latter end is worse with them than the beginning.

We can't be *"entangled"* with the things of this world.

Paul said that the Christian soldiers have been *"chosen"* to be "soldiers." Let's look at a few verses that speak of being *"chosen."*

- **Ephesians 1:4**
  According as **he hath chosen us in him** before the foundation of the world, that we should be holy and without blame before him in love

  The born-again Christians, as a group and as a body, have been chosen as a corporate body before the foundation of the world. As people repent (change their minds) concerning their sin and concerning their Saviour and genuinely accept the Lord Jesus Christ as their Saviour, they are brought into this pre-chosen body.

- **2 Thessalonians 2:13**
  But we are bound to give thanks alway to God for you, brethren beloved of the Lord, because **God hath from the beginning chosen you to salvation through sanctification of the Spirit and belief of the truth:**

  The "*belief of the truth*" means that people have accepted the Lord Jesus Christ Who is the "*truth*" and this personal faith makes that Christian a part of that previously and corporately chosen body.

- **James 2:5**
  Hearken, my beloved brethren, **Hath not God chosen the poor of this world rich in faith,** and heirs of the kingdom which he hath promised to them that love him?

Chosen To Be A Soldier

The soldier's battle has been a choice of the Lord. We did not choose that there would be a battle. In the Garden of Eden, Satan launched the first shot. He said, "*Yea, hath God said?*" This was an attack on the Words of God. God's soldiers have had a battle with the Devil ever since. God has chosen those who are saved "*to be a soldier.*"

---

2 Timothy 2:5

"And if a man also strive for masteries yet is he not crowned, except he strive lawfully."

Paul uses an illustration of a man who "*strives for masteries.*" This is a good picture for a pastor. The word "strive" (ATHLEO) means "*to engage in a contest, contend in public games, contend for a prize.*"

But the goal of the "*striving*" is to be "*crowned.*" The only way to be "*crowned*" is if the athlete "*strives lawfully.*" You were not given a crown unless you followed the rules. You can't cut corners.

The Five Crowns In The Bible

There are five crowns that are mentioned in Scripture. I have used the following letters to remember the crowns: **RGIRL.**

R–stands for the *"crown of rejoicing"*

- 1 Thessalonians 2:19

For what *is* our hope, or joy, or crown of rejoicing? *Are not even ye in the presence of our Lord Jesus Christ at his coming?*

G–stands for the *"crown of glory"*

- 1 Peter 5:4

And when the chief Shepherd shall appear, ye shall receive a crown of glory that fadeth not away.

I–stands for the *"incorruptible"* crown

- 1 Corinthians 9:25

And every man that striveth for the mastery is temperate in all things. Now they *do it* to obtain a corruptible crown; but we an incorruptible.

R–the *"crown of righteousness"*

- 2 Timothy 4:8

Henceforth there is laid up for me a crown of righteousness, which the Lord, the righteous judge, shall give me at that day: and not to me only, but unto all them also that love his appearing.

L–the *"crown of life"*

- James 1:12

Blessed *is* the man that endureth temptation: for when he is tried, he shall receive the crown of life, which the Lord hath promised to them that love him.

- Revelation 2:10

Fear none of those things which thou shalt suffer: behold, the devil shall cast *some* of you into prison, that ye may be tried; and ye shall have tribulation ten days: be thou faithful unto death, and I will give thee a crown of life.

These are the five *"crowns"* that God has given us in the Bible. The *"crown"* is the thing that the athlete would strive for. You might wonder why someone would work so hard in Paul's day for just a little *"crown"* of flowers. It is not the crown of flowers themselves for which they strive; it is for the honor of winning first place. That is what the Lord Jesus Christ will give those who are redeemed by faith in Him if they remain faithful. It tells us in Revelation 4:10 that we will *"cast our crowns"* before God's throne.

- **Revelation 4:10**
  The four and twenty elders fall down before him that sat on the throne, and worship him that liveth for ever and ever, and **cast their crowns before the throne**, saying,

2 Timothy 2:6

"The husbandman that laboureth must be first partaker of the fruits."

Here is the fourth illustration that Paul tells Timothy. It is a *"husbandman"* which refers to a farmer or a vinedresser. He is one who *"laboureth."* The word for "labour" [KOPIAO] means *"to grow weary, tired, exhausted (with toil or burdens or grief); to labour with wearisome effort, to toil."* I don't know if too many of us have had that kind of *"labour."* Farmers *"labour"* in just this way, especially the farmers who used to have to hoe everything by hand. Now that they have tractors, the farmers can just sit on these tractors in air-conditioned comfort. One of our farmer friends has a tractor that he runs for another man. He has a radio and air-conditioning in that tractor. Just think, in the heat of the summer, he is driving that tractor back and forth in total comfort. In the olden days a husbandman labored hard. If you toil and work that hard you must be a *"partaker of the fruits."* That is the purpose of all of the toiling

- **Genesis 9:20**
  And **Noah began *to be* an husbandman**, and he planted a vineyard:
- **John 15:1**
  I am the true vine, and **my Father is the husbandman**.
- **James 5:7**
  Be patient therefore, brethren, unto the coming of the Lord. Behold, **the husbandman waiteth for the precious fruit of the earth,** and hath long patience for it, until he receive the early and latter rain.

The Lord desires that every born-again Christian has spiritual fruit.

2 Timothy 2:7

Consider what I say; and the Lord give thee understanding in all things.

Paul wants Pastor Timothy to continue to *"consider"* what he is saying to him. God wants us to *"consider"* many things in His Words. *"Consider"* [NOEO] has various meanings, such as: *"to perceive with the mind, to understand, to have understanding; to think upon, heed, ponder, consider."* There are a number of verses that ask us to *"consider"* various things.

- Psalm 8:3-4
  When I consider thy Heavens, the work of thy fingers, the moon and stars, which thou hast ordained; What is man, that thou art mindful of him? and the son of man, that thou visitest him?
- Psalm 119:95
  The wicked have waited for me to destroy me: *but* **I will consider thy testimonies.**
- Proverbs 6:6-8
  Go to the ant, thou sluggard; **consider her ways, and be wise**: Which having no guide, overseer, or ruler, Provideth her meat in the summer, *and* gathereth her food in the harvest.
- Haggai 1:5
  Now therefore thus saith the LORD of hosts; **Consider your ways.**
  God is trying, through the Prophet Haggai, to get the attention of these Jews who were going from Babylon back to Jerusalem to rebuild the city. They were doing wrong.
- Matthew 6:28-30
  And why take ye thought for raiment? **Consider the lilies of the field, how they grow; they toil not, neither do they spin**: And yet I say unto you, That even Solomon in all his glory was not arrayed like one of these. Wherefore, if God so clothe the grass of the field, which to day is, and to morrow is cast into the oven, *shall he* not much more *clothe* you, O ye of little faith?
- Luke 12:24
  Consider the ravens: for they neither sow nor reap; which neither have storehouse nor barn; and God feedeth them: how much more are ye better than the fowls?

- Hebrews 3:1
  Wherefore, holy brethren, partakers of the heavenly calling, **consider the Apostle and High Priest of our profession, Christ Jesus;**
- Hebrews 10:24
  And **let us consider one another to provoke unto love and to good works:**

Paul asks that the Lord would give *"understanding in all things."* Consider these verses about *"understanding."*

- Psalm 119:130
  The entrance of **thy words giveth light; it giveth understanding unto the simple.**
- Proverbs 3:5-6
  Trust in the LORD with all thine heart; and **lean not unto thine own understanding.** In all thy ways acknowledge him, and he shall direct thy paths.
- Mark 12:33
  And to **love him with all the heart, and with all the understanding**, and with all the soul, and with all the strength, and to love *his* neighbour as himself, is more than all whole burnt offerings and sacrifices.

Love With Understanding

We who are saved must love the Lord with all of our *"understanding."* If we are saved, how can we love the Lord with all of our *"understanding"*? We must know and *"understand"* His Words by reading and studying it day by day throughout our lifetime.

- Luke 24:45
  Then opened he their understanding, that they might understand the scriptures,

When Mrs. Waite and I were in Jerusalem in the 1980's, we went to the town of Emmaus. We saw a church that was built there. In the front of that church was a picture of two people. I always assumed that these were two men, but the artist pictured them as husband and wife. This is very possible. The Lord Jesus Christ met these two on the road to Emmaus after He had been resurrected from the dead. The Lord spoke to these two people about the Law, the Psalms, and the Prophets concerning Himself. They didn't

know who He was until they asked the Lord to abide with them. As the Lord broke bread, they saw His Hands, and their understanding was opened. They knew it was the Lord Jesus Christ.
- Ephesians 5:17
Wherefore be ye not unwise, but understanding what the will of the Lord *is*.

God's Will Is In His Words

We don't know what the *"will of the Lord"* is unless we know His Words. As some have said, *"The full knowledge of His Will is found in the full knowledge of His Words."* That's why I encourage every born-again Christian to read God's Words year after year. This can be done at the rate of 85 verses each day. I never stop reading my King James Bible each year because I am a different person each year with different needs from God's Words.

2 Timothy 2:8

"Remember that Jesus Christ of the seed of David was raised from the dead according to my gospel."

Two Things to "Remember"

Paul wanted Pastor Timothy to *"remember"* something. There were two things to remember: (1) that the Lord Jesus Christ was *"of the seed of David"*; and (2) that He was *"raised from the dead according to* [Paul's] *gospel."* As the "seed of David," He had a human nature. By His virgin birth, that nature was perfect and sinless. He was also God the Son and was not only perfect humanity, but perfect Deity.

(1) The Lord Jesus Christ was of the "seed of David."

- Matthew 1:6

And Jesse begat **David the king**; and David the king begat Solomon of her *that had been the wife* of Urias;

I believe this genealogy in Matthew takes up the genealogy of Joseph. His line runs through King David. I believe that the following genealogy in Luke is the genealogy of Mary. Her genealogy also goes through David.

- Luke 3:23-31

And Jesus himself began to be about thirty years of age, being (as was supposed) the son of Joseph, which was *the son* of Heli, Which was *the son* of Matthat, which was *the son* of Levi, which was *the son* of Melchi, which was *the son* of Janna, which was *the son* of Joseph, Which was *the son* of Mattathias, which was *the son* of Amos, which was *the son* of Naum, which was *the son* of Esli, which was *the son* of Nagge, Which was *the son* of Maath, which was *the son* of Mattathias, which was *the son* of Semei, which was *the son* of Joseph, which was *the son* of Juda, Which was *the son* of Joanna, which was *the son* of Rhesa, which was *the son* of Zorobabel, which was *the son* of Salathiel, which was *the son* of Neri, Which was *the son* of Melchi, which was *the son* of Addi, which was *the son* of Cosam, which was *the son* of Elmodam, which was *the son* of Er, Which was *the son* of Jose, which was *the son* of Eliezer, which was *the son* of Jorim, which was *the son* of Matthat, which was *the son* of Levi, which was *the son* of Simeon, which was *the son* of Juda, Which was *the son* of Joseph, which was *the son* of Jonan, which was *the son* of Eliakim, W hich was *the son* of Melea, which was *the son* of Menan, which was *the son* of Mattatha, which was *the son* of Nathan, **which was *the son* of David**,

This is Mary's genealogy. It also goes through the line of David, but escapes the curse placed upon *"Jechonias"* or *"Coniah"* (Matthew 1:11-12; Jeremiah 22:24, 28). Even though Joseph was only the *"foster father"* of Jesus, his lineage went through David also.

- John 7:42

Hath not the scripture said, That **Christ cometh of the seed of David**, and out of the town of Bethlehem, where David was?

- Acts 13:22-23
  And when he had removed him, he raised up unto them **David to be their king**; to whom also he gave testimony, and said, I have found **David the** *son* **of Jesse**, a man after mine own heart, which shall fulfil all my will. **Of this man's seed hath God according to** *his* **promise raised unto Israel a Saviour, Jesus:**
- Romans 1:3
  Concerning his Son Jesus Christ our Lord, which was **made of the seed of David according to the flesh**;

Perfect God and Perfect Man

The Lord Jesus Christ was perfect God and perfect Man, and was of the lineage of David.

---

(2) The Lord Jesus Christ was "*raised from the dead according to* [Paul's] *gospel.*"

The second thing Paul wanted Pastor Timothy to "*remember*" was that the Lord Jesus Christ was "*raised from the dead according to* [Paul's] *gospel.*"

Christ Rose Bodily

The resurrection of the Lord Jesus Christ was a bodily resurrection. It was not that only His spirit was raised as the modernists and apostates believe.

Modernists and apostates do not believe that the body of the Lord Jesus Christ rose from the grave. In the book of Acts alone the bodily resurrection of Christ is mentioned twelve times.
- Acts 2:24
  Whom God hath raised up, having loosed the pains of death: because it was not possible that he should be holden of it.

- Acts 2:32
  This **Jesus hath God raised up**, whereof we all are witnesses.
- Acts 3:15
  And killed **the Prince of life, whom God hath raised from the dead;** whereof we are witnesses.
  People saw the resurrected Saviour.
- Acts 3:26
  Unto you first **God, having raised up his Son Jesus**, sent him to bless you, in turning away every one of you from his iniquities.
- Acts 4:10
  Be it known unto you all, and to all the people of Israel, that by the name of **Jesus Christ of Nazareth, whom ye crucified, whom God raised from the dead**, *even* by him doth this man stand here before you whole.
- Acts 5:30
  The God of our fathers raised up Jesus, whom ye slew and hanged on a tree.
- Acts 10:40
  Him God raised up the third day, and shewed him openly;
- Acts 13:30
  But **God raised him from the dead**:
- Acts 13:33
  God hath fulfilled the same unto us their children, in that **he hath raised up Jesus again**; as it is also written in the second psalm, Thou art my Son, this day have I begotten thee.
- Acts 13:34
  And as concerning that **he raised him up from the dead**, *now* no more to return to corruption, he said on this wise, I will give you the sure mercies of David.
- Acts 13:37
  But he, **whom God raised again**, saw no corruption.
- Acts 17:31
  Because he hath appointed a day, in the which he will judge the world in righteousness by *that* man whom he hath ordained; *whereof* he hath given assurance unto all *men*, in that **he hath raised him from the dead**.

Christ's Bodily Resurrection

The resurrection of the Lord Jesus Christ was a part of Paul's gospel. The fearless declaration of Christ's bodily resurrection was one of the major things that caused Paul to be put in prison. The Jews didn't believe in the resurrection, but Paul kept preaching the bodily resurrection of the Lord Jesus Christ. This is important.

Importance of Bodily Resurrection

If the Lord Jesus Christ has not been bodily raised from the dead, He has not ascended into Heaven. If He has not ascended into Heaven, then He is not seated at the right hand of God the Father's right hand. If He is not seated at the Father's right hand, He is not interceding for the born-again Christians. If He is not seated at the Father's right hand, he will not be able to fulfill his promise to come back first in the rapture in the air and then, after the seven-year Tribulation, to earth to set up his thousand-year millennial-reign.

Good News and Bad News

The bad news when you tell people about the gospel is that you must remind them that they are sinners in the sight of God, they are lost, and they are deserving of Hell's everlasting fire. The good news is that the Lord Jesus Christ took the punishment due every sinner at the cross of Calvary. We have been commanded, in the Lord's supper service, to remember His death until He comes back.

2 Timothy 2:9
"Wherein I suffer trouble, as an evil doer, even unto bonds, but the word of God is not bound."

The Reason For Paul"s "Trouble"

The *"wherein"* refers back to the fact that the Lord Jesus Christ was *"raised from the dead"* according to Paul's *"gospel."*

Paul was first arrested by the Romans because the Jewish leaders did not believe in the bodily resurrection that Paul was preaching. Because of this preaching he *"suffered trouble as an evil doer, even unto bonds."* The ultimate *"trouble"* was the *"bonds"* of a Roman prison for the second time. Notice all of the other "troubles" and persecutions Paul suffered because of his faithfulness to his Saviour.

- **2 Corinthians 11:23-28**
  23 Are they ministers of Christ? (I speak as a fool) I *am* more; in labours more abundant, in stripes above measure, in prisons more frequent, in deaths oft. 24 Of the Jews five times received I forty *stripes* save one. 25 Thrice was I beaten with rods, once was I stoned, thrice I suffered shipwreck, a night and a day I have been in the deep; 26 *In* journeyings often, *in* perils of waters, *in* perils of robbers, *in* perils by *mine own* countrymen, *in* perils by the heathen, *in* perils in the city, *in* perils in the wilderness, *in* perils in the sea, *in* perils among false brethren; 27 In weariness and painfulness, in watchings often, in hunger and thirst, in fastings often, in cold and nakedness. 28 Beside those things that are without, that which cometh upon me daily, the care of all the churches.

Paul was thought of as an *"evil doer"* yet he had done no *"evil"* except to preach the gospel of the Saviour. Perhaps people have thought of born-again Christians as *"evil"* in the days in which we live. If we expose the liberals, the modernists, the unbelievers, and the ones who are heretics in churches of all denominations we might be thought of as *"evil."* If we preach that those who refuse the Lord Jesus Christ are lost and will go to the lake of fire when they die, we might be thought of as *"evil."* In fact, if we believe God has preserved His original Hebrew, Aramaic, and Greek Words to this day, even Fundamentalists have thought of us as "*evil*." But we, in this country, have not yet suffered "*bonds*" and chains as Paul did.

But Paul contrasted the Words of God to his own bondage. He said that "*the Word of God is not bound*." Those Words were still able to be preached with God's power freely, even though His servant was "*bound*." Many Bible verses speak of this.

- Acts 6:7
  And **the word of God increased**; and the number of the disciples multiplied in Jerusalem greatly; and a great company of the priests were obedient to the faith.
- Acts 12:24
  But **the word of God grew and multiplied**.
- Acts 19:20
  So **mightily grew the word of God and prevailed**.
- Ephesians 6:17
  And take the helmet of salvation, and **the sword of the Spirit, which is the word of God**:
- 1 Thessalonians 2:13
  For this cause also thank we God without ceasing, because, when **ye received the word of God which ye heard of us**, ye received *it* not *as* the word of men, but as it is in truth, the word of God, **which effectually worketh also in you that believe.**
- Hebrews 4:12
  For **the word of God *is* quick, and powerful**, and sharper than any twoedged sword, piercing even to the dividing asunder of soul and spirit, and of the joints and marrow, and *is* a discerner of the thoughts and intents of the heart.
- 1 Peter 1:23
  Being born again, not of corruptible seed, but of incorruptible, **by the word of God, which liveth and abideth for ever.**

We are "*born-again*" only "*by the Word of God*." The Word of God "*is not bound*." Even though Paul was in prison, the Word of God was continuing through Timothy the preacher, and others, who knew the Scriptures. Paul had laid a good foundation. Paul had founded the church at Rome, the church at Galatia, the Church at Thessalonica, the Church at Corinth, the Church at Ephesus, the Church at Colosse, the Church at Philippi, and many other local churches. Timothy was preaching the Words of God at Ephesus as its pastor.

Paul's Two Imprisonments

Paul was going to be martyred for his faith in the Lord Jesus Christ. This was his last letter. He was enslaved. He was in his second Roman imprisonment. In the first Roman imprisonment he wrote the four books of Ephesians, Philippians, Colossians, and Philemon. Here in his second Roman imprisonment he is writing the books of 1 and 2 Timothy.

The Word of God is not bound. It is not bound today. Though we are a small church here, we have a worldwide outreach through the miracle of radio and the Internet. When I first preached the book of 2 Timothy in our church, we had people who downloaded our messages from every one of the 50 States and 21 foreign countries. As this book is being written, we still hear from all 50 States, but in our last month people from 62 foreign countries downloaded our messages. In May, 2008, our Bible For Today ministry had a record month of **20,470 downloads** at the present time and have had **2,124 messages** on the Internet. The Word of God is not bound.

Preserved Original Bible Words

Even while Paul was in prison God's Word was not bound. That is why we are most intent on having the right Words of God. It is important that we have the preserved original Hebrew, Aramaic, and Greek Words which we have that underlie the King James Bible. We must also have accurate translations of these preserved Words in every language of the world like we have in the English King James Bible. In our church, we use and defend the King James Bible. Some pastors use the King James Bible, but do not defend it.

I remember a pastor in a church in this area who used the King James Bible in every one of his sermons, but he never defended it or told the people why it was the best English translation in print. The people in the congregation used many of the modern English versions. Eventually, when a new pastor came, he changed the entire church to the New King James Version because the church had no conviction about the King James Bible.

The Battle For God's Words

The Words of God are not bound. Men bind them when they use the NIV, the NASV, the ESV and other modern versions that are based on a Gnostic Greek text that differs from the Received Greek text of the King James Bible in 8,000 places in the New Testament alone. We have a battle on our hands for the Words of the Living God.

2 Timothy 2:10

"Therefore I endure all things for the elect's sakes, that they may also obtain the salvation which is in Christ Jesus with eternal glory."

Paul says that he *"endures"* and puts up with prison, bonds, or whatever may come his way. Why does he say he *"endures"* this? It was *"for the elect's sakes."* I believe the *"elect"* are those who have been saved by God's grace through genuine faith in the Lord Jesus Christ. My understanding of Biblical *"election"* is that of *"corporate election."* I believe Israel is a *"chosen body"* which has been *"chosen"* by the Lord. I also believe that the *"Church which is His body"* (Ephesians 1:22-23) consists of every born-again person from the Day of Pentecost to the rapture of the Church. I believe that this *"corporate body"* was a *"chosen"* and *"elect body"* from before the foundation of the world. When a person is born-again by genuine faith in the Lord Jesus Christ he becomes a part of that *"elect body."* This is what *"corporate election"* means to me.

What is Paul's desire for those saved people? It is *"that they may also obtain the salvation which is in Christ Jesus with eternal glory."* He wants these saved people to have *"eternal glory"* rather than to be *"saved, yet so as by fire"* (1 Corinthians 3:15) at the *"judgment seat of Christ"* (2 Corinthians 5:10). They have built upon Christ the foundation, but they have not built with *"gold, silver, and precious stones"* (1 Corinthians 3:12). They have built upon Christ with *"wood, hay, and stubble"* (1 Corinthians 3:12). The latter group will not receive a reward with *"eternal glory."* Paul was willing to suffer or do anything else to help these saints to live for the Lord Jesus Christ.

2 Timothy 2:11

"It is a faithful saying, For if we be dead with him, we shall also live with him."

There are a number of things theologically that God considers saved people to be. One of them is that we are *"with"* Christ. First of all, the redeemed people were *"with Christ"* in His death. God tells us we were *"crucified with Christ."*

- Galatians 2:20
  I am crucified with Christ: nevertheless I live; yet not I, but Christ liveth in me: and the life which I now live in the flesh I live by the faith of the Son of God, who loved me, and gave himself for me.

Believers Identified with Christ

We who are saved were buried with Christ. We were raised with Christ, and we are seated with Christ. One day we will reign with Christ. This is the way that God sees us if we are born again. Notice the various verses that show these truths.

- Romans 6:4
  Therefore **we are buried with him** by baptism into death: that like as Christ was raised up from the dead by the glory of the Father, even so we also should walk in newness of life.
- Colossians 2:12
  Buried with him in baptism, wherein also ye are risen with *him* through the faith of the operation of God, who hath raised him from the dead.
- Ephesians 2:6
  And **hath raised** *us* **up together**, and **made** *us* **sit together** in heavenly *places* in Christ Jesus:
- Romans 5:17
  For if by one man's offence death reigned by one; much more they which receive abundance of grace and of the gift of righteousness **shall reign in life by one, Jesus Christ**.)

- **2 Timothy 2:12**
  If we suffer, **we shall also reign with *him***: if we deny *him*, he also will deny us:
- **Revelation 20:6**
  Blessed and holy *is* he that hath part in the first resurrection: on such the second death hath no power, but they shall be priests of God and of Christ, and **shall reign with him a thousand years**.
- **Revelation 22:5**
  And there shall be no night there; and they need no candle, neither light of the sun; for the Lord God giveth them light: and **they shall reign for ever and ever**.

There are a number of verses that contrast death with life. This follows the thought that Paul mentions when he wrote *"If we be **dead** with him, we shall also **live** with him."*

- **Romans 8:13**
  For if ye **live** after the flesh, ye shall **die**: but if ye through the Spirit do **mortify** the deeds of the body, ye shall **live**.

We Are The Lord's

- **Romans 14:8**
  For whether we live, we live unto the Lord; and whether we die, we die unto the Lord: whether we live therefore, or die, we are the Lord's.

- **2 Corinthians 4:11**
  For we which **live** are alway delivered unto **death** for Jesus' sake, that the **life** also of Jesus might be made manifest in our **mortal** flesh.
- **2 Corinthians 5:15**
  And *that* he **died** for all, that they which **live** should not henceforth **live** unto themselves, but unto him which **died** for them, and rose again.
- **2 Corinthians 6:9**
  As unknown, and *yet* well known; as **dying**, and, behold, we **live**; as chastened, and not killed;

- 2 Corinthians 13:4
  For though he was **crucified** through weakness, yet he **liveth** by the power of God. For we also are weak in him, but we shall live with him by the power of God toward you.

Crucified With Christ

- Galatians 2:20
  I am crucified with Christ: nevertheless I live; yet not I, but Christ liveth in me: and the life which I now live in the flesh I live by the faith of the Son of God, who loved me, and gave himself for me.

Paul was not a Christian when Christ was crucified physically, but in God's eyes Paul was crucified with Christ. All believers were crucified with Christ. We partake of His death, His burial, His resurrection, ascension, and His "*session*" (a theological term for the Lord Jesus Christ who is seated at the right hand of God the Father) in Heaven. How can you be crucified yet live? This is God's viewpoint.

Christ Bare All People's Sins

- 1 Peter 2:24
  Who his own self bare our sins in his own body on the tree, that we, being dead to sins, should live unto righteousness: by whose stripes ye were healed.

2 Timothy 2:12

"If we suffer, we shall also reign with him: if we deny him, he also will deny us."

The "*we suffer*" means Paul and all of the apostles and leaders who suffered greatly for their stand on the gospel of the Lord Jesus Christ. Many of them were condemned and crucified as martyrs. The Apostle Paul suffered especially. Tradition says that Peter was crucified upside down.

Paul combines *"suffering"* with *"reigning"* as he wrote, *"we shall also reign with him."* There are other verses that speak of the *"reigning"* of saved people.

- **Romans 5:17**
  For if by one man's offence death reigned by one; much more they which receive abundance of grace and of the gift of **righteousness shall reign in life** by one, Jesus Christ.)
- **Romans 5:21**
  That as sin hath reigned unto death, even **so might grace reign through righteousness unto eternal life** by Jesus Christ our Lord.
- **Revelation 5:10**
  And hast made us unto our God kings and priests: and **we shall reign on the earth**.

The Millennial Reign Of Christ

The millennial reign of the Lord Jesus Christ will also be the millennial reign of all born-again Christians.

- **Revelation 20:6**
  Blessed and holy *is* he that hath part in the first resurrection: on such the second death hath no power, but they shall be priests of God and of Christ, and **shall reign with him a thousand years**.

Paul also mentioned that *"if we deny him, he also will deny us."* This is a truth that is a warning to Christians who refuse to speak up in defense of the Lord Jesus Christ. There are other verses on *"denial"* as well.

- **Matthew 10:33**
  But **whosoever shall deny me before men, him will I also deny before my Father which is in Heaven**.

Peter denied the Lord Jesus Christ three times. One time he cursed and swore. We who know Him as our Saviour must never deny the Lord Jesus Christ, even if it means our death.

2 Timothy 2:13
"If we believe not, yet he abideth faithful: he cannot deny himself."

God Is Faithful

No matter how Christians might not *"believe"* the things of our God, *"He abideth faithful he cannot deny Himself."* God is "faithful" in everything He has promised to do. I am thankful that God has that wonderful attribute.

- Deuteronomy 7:9
  Know therefore that the LORD thy God, he *is* God, the faithful God, which keepeth covenant and mercy with them that love him and keep his commandments to a thousand generations;
  That means that our God will keep all of His promises.
- 1 Corinthians 1:9
  God *is* faithful, by whom ye were called unto the fellowship of his Son Jesus Christ our Lord.
- 1 Corinthians 10:13
  There hath no temptation taken you but such as is common to man: but **God *is* faithful**, who will not suffer you to be tempted above that ye are able; but will with the temptation also make a way to escape, that ye may be able to bear *it*.
- 1 Thessalonians 5:24
  Faithful *is* he that calleth you, who also will do *it*.
- 2 Thessalonians 3:3
  But **the Lord is faithful**, who shall stablish you, and keep *you* from evil.
- Hebrews 10:23
  Let us hold fast the profession of *our* faith without wavering; (for **he *is* faithful that promised**;)

God Promised Words Preservation

God has promised to keep His original Hebrew, Aramaic, and Greek Words. I believe He has kept that promise in the Words underlying the King James Bible. He has kept that important promise and all others.

- 1 Peter 4:19
  Wherefore let them that suffer according to the will of God commit the keeping of their souls *to him* in well doing, as unto **a faithful Creator**.
- 1 John 1:9
  If we confess our sins, **he is faithful** and just to forgive us *our* sins, and to cleanse us from all unrighteousness.

2 Timothy 2:14

"Of these things put them in remembrance, charging them before the Lord that they strive not about words to no profit, but to the subverting of the hearers."

Paul is telling Pastor Timothy to put his congregation *"in remembrance."* One of the things they are to remember was Paul's words: *"strive not about words to no profit."* Since *"strive not"* is in the present tense and is a prohibition in Greek, it means to stop an action that is already in progress. They had strivings, and fights and battles, and Paul told Timothy to stop it.

Striving About Words

The word for *"strive about words"* [LOGOMACHEO] means *"to contend about words, to wrangle about empty and trifling matters."* This does not mean we are not to stand for truth and good, sound, and important doctrines of the faith.

These *"words"* are not only of *"no profit,"* but they also *"subvert the hearers."* Some of these things do *"subvert"* [KATASTROPHE, meaning *"to overthrow or destroy"*] the people who hear these strivings. This is dangerous and Paul charges them *"before the Lord"* that they stop it. There are many references to *"striving"* in the Scripture.

- Proverbs 3:30
  Strive not with a man without cause, if he have done thee no harm.

> ## When Not To "Strive"
> Sometimes there are causes to *"strive"* and to argue about, but if there is no real *"cause,"* we should not do it.

- Proverbs 25:8
  Go not forth hastily to strive, lest *thou know not* what to do in the end thereof, when thy neighbour hath put thee to shame. What if you make a mistake about this? You would go forward about a matter and if you are in error, you will be *"put to shame."*
- Matthew 12:19
  He shall not strive, nor cry; neither shall any man hear his voice in the streets.
  This verse is speaking about the Lord Jesus Christ.
- Titus 3:9
  But **avoid** foolish questions, and genealogies, and contentions, and **strivings about the law**; for they are unprofitable and vain.

2 Timothy 2:15

"Study to shew thyself approved unto God, a workman that needeth not to be ashamed, rightly dividing the word of truth."

Paul was telling Pastor Timothy to *"study to show himself approved unto God."* The word for *"study"* [SPOUDAZO] means *"to hasten, make haste; to exert one's self, endeavour, give diligence."* It implies that Timothy is to really roll up his sleeves to learn about the Lord that he might be *"approved"* by Him. This is a gigantic order. It is the most difficult thing any Christian could undertake. Some have questioned the King James Bible's use of the word, *"study"* for SPOUDAZO.

The 1611 Meaning Of "Study"

In the Oxford English Dictionary, the most exhaustive in print, there are no less than fifteen distinct meanings listed by dates of usage for "*study*." The very first meaning (out of fifteen different meanings) of the English word, "*study*," from about 1300 to 1769 A.D. is this:

"1.a. *To apply the mind to the acquisition of learning, whether by means of books, observation, or experiment. Const. in, on, upon (a book, a branch of learning). See also sense 1 d.*"

The meaning 1 d is as follows:

"*d. To make a close study of (a subject), to 'bone' up (on, in), esp. in preparation for some display of knowledge (intr. use of sense 7 b). U.S. colloq.*"

The meaning of 7b is as follows:

"*b. colloq. to study up: to study (a subject) in view of some special emergency, e.g. an examination; to 'get up'.*"

I maintain that this is the precise sense of "*study*" used by our King James translators in 1611 in this verse.

Part of the diligent study process involves, to my mind, a daily reading of God's Words, going from Genesis through Revelation. I want those in our church to read and re-read the Scriptures over and over again throughout their lives. I want the same thing for Christians everywhere. I want them to know the Words of God and to love them. There are some things we don't understand that are found in the Scriptures. There is no question about that. We must keep reading them and apply the things that we do understand that we find therein.

Yearly Bible Reading Needed

I have been reading the Bible through every year at 85 verses per day ever since I was saved in 1944. That is sixty-four years ago as this book is being written. If there is something I don't understand I read it anyway. Sometimes the next year when I read it again, I do understand that part. Each year I have a different need in my life. God says that we are to continue to study in order to show ourselves *"approved unto God,"* not unto men. We must not be arrogant and boasting in front of people about our knowledge of the Bible. That's not the purpose for our studying.

The result of this diligent study is that we might be *"a workman that needeth not to be ashamed, rightly dividing the word of truth."* There should be no *"shame"* in the work of a *"workman."* He should not do a shoddy job. When it comes to the Words of God, he must *"rightly divide"* them. The word for *"rightly dividing"* is ORTHOTOMEO which has various meanings:

" to cut straight, to cut straight ways; to proceed on straight paths, hold a straight course, equiv. to doing right; to make straight and smooth, to handle aright, to teach the truth directly and correctly."

ORTHO means *"straight"* like an orthodontist who straightens teeth. TOMEO means *"to cut."* We must *"rightly divide the Word of truth."*

The Need Of Dispensationalism

I believe that a person must believe in some form of dispensationalism to *"rightly divide"* the Bible. This means that God has dealt differently at different times throughout the Bible. We do not have a Garden of Eden. We are not told, as was Noah, to build an ark before a universal flood. We were not given the law of Moses from Mount Sinai. But we're living in the age of grace and there will one day be a millennial reign of the Lord Jesus Christ. Distinguish the dispensations and God's dealing with man in the Bible, and you can understand it, because it can then be *"rightly divided."*

The word *"study"* is used in various places in the Bible.
- **Ecclesiastes 12:12**
And further, by these, my son, be admonished: of making many books *there is* no end; and **much study *is* a weariness of the flesh.**
- **1 Thessalonians 4:11**
And **that ye study to be quiet**, and to do your own business, and to work with your own hands, as we commanded you;
Sometimes being quiet is a very difficult *"study."*

When Paul told Timothy about being *"approved"* of God, this word is used elsewhere in the Bible as well. The Lord Jesus Christ Himself was *"approved of God."*
- **Acts 2:22**
Ye men of Israel, hear these words; **Jesus of Nazareth, a man approved of God** among you by miracles and wonders and signs, which God did by him in the midst of you, as ye yourselves also know:
God blessed Him and sanctified Him, and that's what we need to do.
- **Romans 16:10**
Salute **Apelles approved in Christ**. Salute them which are of Aristobulus' *household*.

Approved By The Lord Jesus Christ

We might not be *"approved"* by the neighbors or others, but if we are saved, we have been *"approved"* by the Lord Jesus Christ.

- **2 Corinthians 10:18**
For **not he that commendeth himself is approved**, but whom the Lord commendeth.
We must look to the Lord. Does the Lord agree with what we are doing, what we are saying, where we are going? Is He on our side, and does God approve us? That is why we who are redeemed by our Saviour must diligently *"study to show ourselves approved unto God."*

2 Timothy 2:16

"But shun profane, and vain babblings, for they will increase unto more ungodliness."

By using the word, *"shun,"* in the present tense, Paul is telling Pastor Timothy to continue to *"shun"* these *"profane, and vain babblings."*

The Meanings Of "Shun"

The word for *"shun"* is PERIISTEMI which means various things such as: *"to turn one's self about for the purpose of avoiding something; to avoid, shun."* The reason for this *"shunning"* is that *"they will increase unto more ungodliness."* Paul is saying for Timothy to stay right away from any of these *"babblings"* and have nothing to do with them.

"Profane" [BEBELOS] means things that are *"unhallowed, common, public place; of men, ungodly."* These are things that are filthy, ungodly, and secular. The second things Pastor Timothy (and every Christian) should "shun" are *"vain babblings"* [KENOPHONIA] which means: *"empty discussion, discussion of vain and useless matters."* We must discuss, preach about, and contend for matters that are Biblical, we must *"shun"* these *"profane and vain babblings."* Paul has repeated similar warnings in his first letter to Timothy.

- 1 Timothy 6:20

  O Timothy, keep that which is committed to thy trust, **avoiding profane *and* vain babblings, and oppositions of science falsely so called**:

If we who are pastors and others do not continue to *"shun"* these *"profane and vain babblings,"* it will increase to further *"ungodliness."* This *"ungodliness"* is warned against in a number of Scripture passages.

- Romans 1:18

  For **the wrath of God is revealed from Heaven against all ungodliness** and unrighteousness of men, who hold the truth in unrighteousness;

- Romans 11:26

  And so all Israel shall be saved: as it is written, There shall come out of Sion **the Deliverer, and shall turn away ungodliness from Jacob**:

One day the Jews will turn to their Messiah and be saved. I believe Isaiah 66:8

refers to this miraculous event.
- **Isaiah 66:8**
Who hath heard such a thing? who hath seen such things? **Shall the earth be made to bring forth in one day? or shall a nation be born at once?** for as soon as Zion travailed, she brought forth her children.
- **Titus 2:12**
Teaching us that, **denying ungodliness** and worldly lusts, we should live soberly, righteously, and godly, in this present world;

The Saved Should Not Live Ungodly
God does not want the saved ones to live in an ungodly fashion.

---

2 Timothy 2:17
"And their word will eat as doth a canker of whom is Hymenaeus and Philetus;"

Paul is continuing his remarks about people who have followed *"profane and vain babblings"* who have gone into *"ungodliness."* The *"word"* of these people *"will eat as doth a canker."* That word to *"eat"* [NOME] means *"growth, increase; of evils spreading like a gangrene; of ulcers; of a conflagration; to grow and to increase."*

The result of this *"eating"* or increasing is as a *"canker"* [GAGGRAINA] which is defined as:

"a gangrene, a disease by which any part of the body suffering from inflammation becomes so corrupted that, unless a remedy be seasonably applied, the evil continually spreads, attacks other parts, and at last eats away the bones."

False Teaching Is Like Cancer
From this definition, we can see that this is a very serious disease, far greater than a mere ulcer that might cause bleeding and other damage. This refers to the words of those who are ungodly that eat, like a great burning, as a forest fire will gobble away a forest.

Two Heretics Named By Paul

Paul names two individuals to illustrate those who are spreading the gangrene of false teachings. The names of these heretics and purveyors of perverted theology are Hymenaeus and Philetus. These two men have used words that eat away *"as a canker."* Since Paul named these two false teachers, I believe it is a principle that pastors today should follow in the naming of the names of those who teach false doctrines.

- 1 Timothy 1:19
  Holding faith, and a good conscience; **which some having put away concerning faith have made shipwreck :**

False Teachers Ruin Others

False teachers such as the two mentioned and many others today are not satisfied to just ruin their own faith, but sadly, they must also ruin the faith of many others.

2 Timothy 2:18

"Who concerning the truth have erred saying that the resurrection is past already; and overthrow the faith of some."

The two heretics Paul just named *"have erred"* in the area of *"the truth"* of God's Words and doctrine. The specific *"truth"* involved concerns the *"resurrection"* of saved people. They taught that this was *"past already"* so that some living Christians had missed the coming of the Lord Jesus Christ.

There is one of these false teachers right in our area. His name is Arthur Melansen who broadcasts on WTMR Radio. He believes in Preterism which puts in the past most of the events that we hold to be in the future. I heard him say the other day that when the Lord Jesus Christ came from Heaven that He gave up all of the Divine attributes. This is also a false doctrine. The Lord Jesus Christ gave up none of His Divine attributes when He came to earth. He was perfect Man and perfect God.

The Goal Of False Teachers

The result of these false teachers in Paul's day is that they are said to *"overthrow the faith of some."* That is the chief goal of any false teacher. He wants to cause people to depart from the clear teachings of the Bible. It was not enough that Hymenaeus and Philetus were in error in their own doctrines, but they want to make converts.

If you have ever been around a real five point hyper-Calvinist you will observe that the chief thing they want to talk about is that Christ died only for the elect rather than, as the Bible clearly teaches, for the sins of the whole world. I remember when Mrs. Waite and I were visiting a pastor's home in Michigan, a few years ago, that the first thing this pastor began talking about was his hyper-Calvinist beliefs. We couldn't get him off that subject with which I strongly disagree.

We must be sure that false teaching and doctrines do not influence adversely the faith of others. We have some clones of Harold Camping. He is such a false teacher on many fronts. Harold Camping of Family Radio is one of these false teachers. He said that the return of the Lord Jesus Christ was to take place in 1984, but this did not happen. He also teaches that right now we are in the Tribulation. He teaches that the church is no longer in the world and that the church is finished.

2 Timothy 2:19

"Nevertheless the foundation of God standeth sure, having this seal, The Lord knoweth them that are his. And, let every one that nameth the name of Christ depart from iniquity."

Regardless of how much damage the false teachings of either Hymenaeus or Philetus had caused in the lives of the believers in Paul's day, *"the foundation of God standeth sure."* God's Words never change. They are *"sure."* The word for *"sure"* is STEREOS which means: *"strong, firm, immovable, solid, hard, rigid; in a bad sense, cruel, stiff, stubborn, hard; in a good sense, firm, steadfast."*

False Teachings Are Unsure

On the other hand, the teachings of these heretics are unsure.

- 1 Corinthians 3:11
  For **other foundation can no man lay than that is laid, which is Jesus Christ**.

Christ The Only True Foundation

The only true Foundation that you and I can have for all eternity is the Lord Jesus Christ. If we are not on His foundation, we are lost and without hope.

There is a *"seal"* [SPHRAGIS] that guarantees God's *"foundation."* That word has various meanings:
"a seal; the seal placed upon books; a signet ring; the inscription or impression made by a seal; of the name of God and Christ stamped upon their foreheads; that by which anything is confirmed, proved, authenticated, as by a seal (a token or proof)."

God Knows Who Are Saved

Paul wrote a very important truth to Timothy when he said *"The Lord knoweth them that are his."* We as human beings do not know the ones who are really saved, only the Lord does.

The Saved Must Depart From Sin

One thing is true, however, for those who are genuinely saved. Paul put it this way: *"let every one that nameth the name of Christ depart from iniquity."* Some people claim that they are Christians, but they continue living in open or secret *"iniquity."* According to this verse, saved people are commanded to *"depart from iniquity."* God doesn't want to have any dealings with *"iniquity,"* He hates it. We who are saved should hate it also. Though we don't know who are the Lord's people, we are told *"by their fruits ye shall know them"* (Matthew 7:20). Obviously, if a person is picking pears, he's not picking them off of an apple tree. He is picking them off of a pear tree.

2 Timothy 2:20

"But in a great house there are not only vessels of gold and of silver, but also of wood and of earth, and some to honour, and some to dishonour."

This is an important illustration. I am sure you have different *"vessels"* in your house. You may even have some gold and silver vessels, though these are rare in most of our homes. You may have some vessels made of wood or terra cotta. What is the great house? I think it is an illustration of born-again Christians

- 1 Corinthians 3:11-12
  For other foundation can no man lay than that is laid, which is Jesus Christ. Now <u>if any man build upon this foundation gold, silver, precious stones, wood, hay, stubble</u>;

I believe this *"great house"* speaks of the saved people. Some people teach that the ones who are *"of gold and of silver"* are saved, but that the *"vessels"* of *"wood and earth"* are unsaved people. This is one interpretation.

This might be true. But I also believe that this house might refer to saved people, some of whom are living for the Lord whose *"vessels"* are *"of gold and of silver."* These are the good *"vessels"* to *"honour."*

On the other hand, there are some born-again Christians who are carnal and not living as close to the Lord as they should. These are *"vessels"* of *"wood and of earth."* These are much easier to break than the others. These are *"to dishonour."* These people manifest the *"works of the flesh"* rather than the fruit of the Spirit.

- Galatians 5:19-20
  Now <u>the works of the flesh are manifest</u>, which are *these*; Adultery, fornication, uncleanness, lasciviousness, Idolatry, witchcraft, hatred, variance, emulations, wrath, strife, seditions, heresies,

The People In The "Great House"

Both of these Christians are in this *"great house."* Believers have two natures. They have a daily choice of either following the *"works of the flesh"* or the *"fruit of the Spirit."* God wants every born-again Christian to follow the dictates of their new nature and the leadership of God the Holy Spirit Who indwells them.

2 Timothy 2:21

"If a man therefore purge himself from these, he shall be a vessel unto honour, sanctified, and meet for the master's use, and prepared unto every good work."

What should a Christian *"purge himself from"*? It is obvious that it is from the *"vessels"* which are *"of wood and of earth."* Here are some verses that deal with *"purging."*

- Isaiah 1:25
  And I will turn my hand upon thee, and **purely purge away thy dross**, and take away all thy tin:

In this verse, purging implies burning up the things that are impurities.

- Ezekiel 43:26
  Seven days shall they purge the altar and purify it; and they shall consecrate themselves.

- 1 Corinthians 5:7
  Purge out therefore the old leaven, that ye may be a new lump, as ye are unleavened. For even Christ our passover is sacrificed for us:

There are verses also that speak of "honour" and "dishonour" which give us some background for this verse in 2 Timothy.

- Romans 9:21
  Hath not the potter power over the clay, of the same lump to make **one vessel unto honour, and another unto dishonour**?

- 1 Peter 3:7
  Likewise, ye husbands, dwell with *them* according to knowledge, **giving honour unto the wife**, as unto the weaker vessel, and as being heirs together of the grace of life; that your prayers be not hindered.

Stay Clear Of Carnal Christians

Paul wants Pastor Timothy and all Christians to *"purge himself"* from dishonorable Christians and evil of all kinds that would work against the things of the Lord. We cannot have very close fellowship with Christians who are not living for the Lord and not expect that some of their habits and carnality might be absorbed by us. That is the way things generally go. God wants every born-again Christian to be *"unto honour"* and *"sanctified"* for His *"use,"* being *"prepared unto every good work."*

2 Timothy 2:22
"Flee also youthful lusts: but follow righteousness, faith, charity, peace with them that call on the Lord out of a pure heart."

Flee Youthful Lusts

If you love flowers you must hate the weeds. Paul told Timothy to *"flee youthful lusts."* He also told him to *"follow righteousness, faith, charity, and peace."* Joseph fled from Potiphar's wife's sexual advances (Genesis 39:5-20).

There are various *"lusts"* which should be avoided by Pastor Timothy and every Christian.
- John 8:44
  Ye are of *your* father the devil, and **the lusts of your father ye will do.** He was a murderer from the beginning, and abode not in the truth, because there is no truth in him. When he speaketh a lie, he speaketh of his own: for he is a liar, and the father of it.
  Lust is the desire, the craving, the longing for what is forbidden.
- Romans 6:12
  Let not sin therefore reign in your mortal body, that ye should obey it in the lusts thereof.
  Satan has his brand of lusts, and our bodies have lusts also. Don't obey any of these lusts.
- Romans 13:14
  But put ye on the Lord Jesus Christ, and **make not provision for the flesh, to *fulfil* the lusts *thereof*.**
  The one who is trying not to obey the lust of alcoholism should not hide a couple of bottles in his house to make provision for that lust. We should not make provision for any evil lusts.
- Ephesians 4:22
  That ye put off concerning the former conversation **the old man, which is corrupt according to the deceitful lusts**;
  The flesh has lusts that are deceitful and wicked.

- Titus 2:12
  Teaching us that, **denying** ungodliness and **worldly lusts**, we should live soberly, righteously, and godly, in this present world;   You have the satanic lusts and the worldly lusts drawing you in. You must *"deny"* these.
- 1 Peter 2:11
  Dearly beloved, I beseech *you* as strangers and pilgrims, **abstain from fleshly lusts**, which war against the soul;

The Christian's Three Enemies
Every Christian has three enemies:
1. the world (John 2:15-17)
2. the flesh, (Galatians 5:19-21; Romans 13:14), and
3. the Devil (1 Peter 5:8-9; James 4:7)

Paul tells Timothy to *"flee also youthful lusts."* Does this mean that only the youth have these lusts? No. The lusts are *"youthful,"* but the lusters can be old rather than *"youthful."* Don't think because you have reached a certain age that you will be automatically free from *"lusts."*

The Old Nature & The New Nature
The *"lusts"* will follow us as long as we have the old nature. All those works of the flesh from Galatians 5:19-21 are possible for believers if they don't walk by means of the Holy Spirit (Galatians 5:16). We have to *"flee"* away from these lusts so we can *"follow righteousness, faith, charity, and peace."* This following action must be *"out of a pure heart."* This means a heart which does not have any corrupt desire. Our hearts must be pure from any false mixture. We must have a sincere and genuine heart.

2 Timothy 2:23
"But foolish and unlearned questions avoid, knowing that they do gender strifes."

The *"unlearned questions"* mentioned here are *"uneducated, ignorant, and rude."* They are to be pushed aside completely because they *"gender strifes."*

The word for "strifes" is MACHE, meaning "*a fight or combat; of those in arms, a battle; of persons at variance, disputants etc., strife, contention; a quarrel.*" As you know, sometimes questions lead to battles with the fists.

One evening on the TV news, I saw the police parading around an Eagle's football game. It was very orderly. One of the things that the TV said was that the police were surrounding the field so that everything would stay orderly. As soon as people begin arguing with their mouths, sometimes they begin using their fists. God tells us not to get involved with these "*foolish and unlearned questions*" because they will begin "*strifes.*"

2 Timothy 2:24

"And the servant of the Lord must not strive, but be gentle unto all men, apt to teach, patient."

Paul tells Pastor Timothy that, as a "*servant of the Lord,*" he must not "*strive.*" That word for strive is MACHOMAI. Here are the various meanings: "*to fight of armed combatants, or those who engage in a hand to hand struggle; of those who engage in a war of words, to quarrel, wrangle, dispute; of those who contend at law for property and privileges.*"

One of these meanings refers to "*those who engage in a hand to hand struggle.*" One of the qualifications of a pastor is that he can not be a striker. That means fighting with your fist.

- **1 Timothy 3:3**
  Not given to wine, **no striker**, not greedy of filthy lucre; but patient, not a brawler, not covetous;
- **Titus 1:7**
  For a bishop must be blameless, as the steward of God; not selfwilled, not soon angry, not given to wine, **no striker**, not given to filthy lucre;

Sometimes a pastor might want to strike somebody, but if he is a "*striker,*" he cannot be a pastor. Should pastors be "*servants of the Lord*"? Certainly they should. The word for "*servant*" is DOULOS. The word has various meanings: "*a slave, bondman, man of servile condition; a slave; metaph., one who gives himself up to another's will; those whose service is used by Christ in extending and advancing His cause among men; devoted to another to the disregard of one's own interests; a servant, attendant*"

Warring With Words

Someone sent me an E-mail recently asking what I thought about a certain Internet site. I saw that this site was just arguing about foolish contentions. I would not bother going to that site. There are all kinds of people who want to engage in wrangling and warring with words.

One of the men on that site I asked to speak to our Dean Burgon Society many years ago. He was going to speak against Peter Ruckman and the false views that he holds about the King James Bible. Though this man signed the Dean Burgon statement that he agreed with us, as soon as he left that meeting, he went out and changed his position. He has been fighting and battling against the Textus Receptus ever since. He writes me letters and tries to get me in on this fighting, but I don't even waste my time by answering. All he is trying to do is to get some words from me so he can tear them apart.

I know another man, James White. Several years ago, I debated him for two hours on the radio. I could tell from those two hours of debating on the radio that James White did not listen to what I said and was not fair and honest in his replies. He wanted to get me into a debate again. I don't answer him. When you meet certain people you know they only want to cause strife. When someone writes me with an honest question I usually answer him or her. Everyday I get questions from people. My wife has suggested I write a QUESTION AND ANSWER BOOK, but this is coming slowly and is not on my high priority list at this time. Every time someone asks me a question that I answer, I also copy it for the Website. As of this writing, I am up to over 784 rough pages of questions and answers. If a person has a genuine question I will answer it. People who have striving questions I don't bother replying.

In addition to the above, Timothy (and every pastor, even today) was to be "*gentle unto all men, apt to teach, and patient.*" These are qualities that seem to be absent in many pastors today.

Pastors Should Be "Apt To Teach"

As for the need to be "*apt to teach,*" it points out that pastors should have a teaching ministry in order to edify and build up their flock in the teachings and doctrines of the Bible.

- **1 Timothy 3:2**
  A bishop then must be blameless, the husband of one wife, vigilant, sober, of good behaviour, given to hospitality, **apt to teach**;

2 Timothy 2:25

"In meekness instructing those that oppose themselves; if God peradventure will give them repentance to the acknowledging of the truth;"

Pastor Timothy was to exemplify the attitude of *"meekness"* throughout his ministry. This is not to be confused with "weakness." He was to be *"strong in the Lord and in the power of His might"* (Ephesians 6:10). Meekness is listed in many New Testament verses.

- **2 Corinthians 10:1**
  Now **I Paul myself beseech you by the meekness and gentleness of Christ**, who in presence *am* base among you, but being absent am bold toward you:
- **Galatians 5:22-23**
  But **the fruit of the Spirit is** love, joy, peace, longsuffering, gentleness, goodness, faith, **Meekness**, temperance: against such there is no law.
- **1 Peter 3:15**
  But sanctify the Lord God in your hearts: and **be ready always to *give* an answer** to every man that asketh you a reason of the hope that is in you **with meekness** and fear:

Timothy was to be *"instructing"* those who opposed him and who opposed themselves. This is not an easy task. His goal was to see if God would give these people *"repentance to the acknowledging of the truth."*

There are many verses that deal with *"repentance"* in the New Testament. Various Bible teachers do not agree on the definition of this term.

- **Matthew 9:13**
  But go ye and learn what *that* meaneth, I will have mercy, and not sacrifice: for **I am not come to call the righteous, but sinners to repentance**.
- **Luke 24:47**
  And **that repentance and remission of sins should be preached in his name among all nations, beginning at Jerusalem**.

- Acts 5:31
  <u>Him hath God exalted with his right hand</u> *to be* <u>a Prince and a Saviour, for to give repentance to Israel, and forgiveness of sins</u>.
- 2 Corinthians 7:10
  For <u>godly sorrow worketh repentance to salvation</u> not to be repented of: but the sorrow of the world worketh death.
- 2 Peter 3:9
  The Lord is not slack concerning his promise, as some men count slackness; but is longsuffering to us-ward, **<u>not willing that any should perish, but that all should come to repentance</u>**.

The Meaning Of "Repentance"

The Greek word for *"repentance"* is METANOIA. It means *"a change of the mind."* Regarding salvation, I define the word as the need of every one in the world to change his or her mind regarding two things: (1) regarding sin, that is, to admit that they are sinners and condemned to Hell. (2) regarding the Saviour, that is, to realize that the Lord Jesus Christ is able to forgive their sins. After these two phases of *"repentance"* or a *"change of mind,"* the person must genuinely believe in and trust the Lord Jesus Christ as the One Who died for them and can give them everlasting life. Genuine faith in the Saviour and these two phases of *"repentance"* are combined to achieve the salvation of the person's soul.

2 Timothy 2:26

"And that they may recover themselves out of the snare of the devil, who are taken captive by him at his will."

We Are Born Into Satan's Kingdom

All the people in the world are born into Satan's kingdom by their physical birth. You were born that way. I was born that way. We were Satan's children from the day that we were born. Satan does not want to give up any of his children.

By *"meekness"* and *"instructing"* them by preaching the Biblical gospel of the Lord Jesus Christ, these people can be saved if they have genuine faith in Him. These people, who are his *"captives,"* can *"recover themselves out of the snare of the devil."* Satan wants to keep his children *"captives."* He has these *"children"* of his in a *"snare."* That word for snare is PAGIS. It has some very important meanings:

"a snare, trap, noose; of snares in which birds are entangled and caught; implies unexpectedly, suddenly, because birds and beasts are caught unawares; a snare, i.e. whatever brings peril, loss, destruction; of a sudden and unexpected deadly peril; of the allurements and seductions of sin; the allurements to sin by which the devil holds one bound; the snares of love"

It is a *"snare"* by which birds are entangled and caught. It implies *"unexpectedly and suddenly."* You don't see it. It snaps you right up. How can a person who is bound by Satan get unbound? Satan has them *"captive."* What will free them? Only the genuine acceptance of the gospel of the Lord Jesus Christ will free them.

- **Romans 1:16**
  For I am not ashamed of **the gospel of Christ: for it is the power of God unto salvation to every one that believeth;** to the Jew first, and also to the Greek.

That gospel will free even the *"captives"* that have been in Satan's *"snare"* for many years.

Giving The Gospel In Meekness

Those who are bound, and don't want to know the Lord Jesus Christ as Saviour and Redeemer are fighting this gospel message. What about people who are not interested in accepting the Lord Jesus Christ? You just give them the gospel in *"meekness"* and in kindness, then go on to someone else if there is opposition. It does not help to beat them on the head with the gospel. Pray for them.

You must agree to disagree and then go on to someone else who is receptive to the gospel message. There are all kinds of people who are receptive to the gospel. They are the ones in whom we should seek to lead to salvation by genuine faith in the Lord Jesus Christ. It is often a waste of your time to argue and debate with those who only want to fight. That is why I don't spend a lot of time with the Jehovah Witnesses when they come to the door.

Second Timothy
Chapter Three

2 Timothy 3:1

"This know also, that in the last days perilous times shall come."

The "*last days*," as mentioned in the Bible, cover a great number of years. How did Paul know these signs were going to appear in the "*last days*"? Because the Lord Jesus revealed them to him. Here are a few verses on these "*last days*."

- Hebrews 1:2
  Hath **in these last days spoken unto us by _his_ Son**, whom he hath appointed heir of all things, by whom also he made the worlds;
  This refers to the "*last days*" when the Lord Jesus Christ came to this world at His first advent.
- 2 Peter 3:3
  Knowing this first, that **there shall come in the last days scoffers**, walking after their own lusts,
  I personally believe, though I do not set dates, that we are now living in the "*last days*" of the "*last days*." This word for "*perilous times*" is CHALEPOS. Here are a few meanings:

"*hard to do, to take, to approach; hard to bear, troublesome, dangerous; harsh, fierce, savage.*"

Last Days And "Perilous Times"

These days will be "*troublesome, dangerous, harsh, fierce, and savage.*" I believe that Paul was given the information about these "*last days*" by the Lord Jesus Christ Himself during his three years in the desert (Galatians 1:16-18) where the Lord Jesus was his Teacher. The Lord Jesus Christ told Paul of at least twenty-three different signs of the "*last days*." I believe every one of these will happen

2 Timothy 3:2

"For men shall be lovers of their own selves, covetous, boasters, proud, blasphemers, disobedient to parents, unthankful, unholy."

> ✔ #1 The first sign of the *"last days"* is a selfish attitude, *"For men shall be lovers of their own selves"* (2 Timothy 3:2).

Men want to know what is in it for them. They are selfish. The Greek Word used here is PHILAUTOS which consists of two parts, PHILOS (*"love"*) and AUTOS (*"self"*). It means literally *"love self."*

> ✔ #2 Notice the second sign of the *"last days."* People will be *"covetous"* (2 Timothy 3:2).

We have had that for years, but in the *"last days"* it will even be worse.
- Exodus 20:17
  Thou shalt not covet thy neighbour's house, thou shalt not covet thy neighbour's wife, nor his manservant, nor his maidservant, nor his ox, nor his ass, nor any thing that *is* thy neighbour's.

> ## The Meaning of "Covetousness"
> Covetousness has been defined as "*the itch for more.*"

- Psalm 10:3
  For **the wicked** boasteth of his heart's desire, and **blesseth the covetous**, *whom* the LORD abhorreth.

Are you and I ever content with anything? We must ask ourselves that question. Paul said:

- **Philippians 4:11** . . . for I have learned, in whatsoever state I am, *therewith* **to be content**

  Being content does not mean you are not trying to continue doing the best you can. Are we content and happy with what the Lord has given to us, and what he has done for us? That is important.

- **Luke 16:14**

  And **the Pharisees also, who were covetous**, heard all these things: and they derided him.

- **1 Corinthians 5:11**

  But now I have written unto you not to keep company, if any man that is called **a brother be** a fornicator, **or covetous**, or an idolater, or a railer, or a drunkard, or an extortioner; **with such an one no not to eat**.

  I have been told that, in the Brazilian culture, if a Brazilian sees something in your house that he likes, he takes it. We don't have anything like that in our country. We call those people kleptomaniacs.

- **1 Timothy 3:3**

  Not given to wine, no striker, not greedy of filthy lucre; but patient, not a brawler, **not covetous**;

  One of the qualifications of the pastor/bishop/elder of a church is to not be *"covetous."* A pastor who is *"covetous"* might steal from the church. Some pastors have done this. If you are a fundamental Bible believing pastor, you probably do not make a lot of money. To make up for it these pastors sometimes are tempted to steal from the church. The first church I went to after the chaplaincy was a church where there had been a thief who was the church treasurer. In another instance, one of our friends, who was a pastor, borrowed from money from one of the friends in the church. He never was able to pay that fund back.

✔ **#3 Notice the third sign of the *"last days"* is *"boasters"* (2 Timothy 3:2).**

Among other references in the Bible are the following verses:
- **Romans 1:30**

  Backbiters, haters of God, despiteful, proud, **boasters**, inventors of evil things, disobedient to parents,

- **Ephesians 2:9**

  Not of works, lest any man should **boast**.

- Proverbs 27:1
  Boast not thyself of to morrow; for thou knowest not what a day may bring forth.
- Psalm 49:6
  They that trust in their wealth, and **boast themselves in the multitude of their riches**;
- 1 Kings 20:11
  And the king of Israel answered and said, Tell *him*, **Let not him that girdeth on** *his harness* **boast himself as he that putteth it off.**

> ✔ **#4 Notice, the fourth sign of the *"last days"* is *"pride"* (2 Timothy 3:2).**

This Greek Word is HYPEREPHANOS which means:
"showing one's self above others, overtopping, conspicuous above others, pre-eminent; with an overweening estimate of one's means or merits, despising others or even treating them with contempt, haughty."

There are many verses that speak of *"pride."*
- Proverbs 13:10
  Only by pride cometh contention: but with the well advised *is* wisdom.
- Proverbs 16:18
  Pride *goeth* before destruction, and an haughty spirit before a fall.
- James 4:6
  But he giveth more grace. Wherefore he saith, **God resisteth the proud**, but giveth grace unto the humble.
- 1 Peter 5:5
  Likewise, ye younger, submit yourselves unto the elder. Yea, all *of you* be subject one to another, and be clothed with humility: for **God resisteth the proud**, and giveth grace to the humble.

Keep Away From "Pride"

No born-again Christian should have a prideful spirit. We are seeing it in every walk of life today—including the ministry!

> ✔ **#5 The fifth sign of the *"last days"* is *"blasphemy."* (2 Timothy 3:2).**

There are warning signs throughout the New Testament about this sin of *"blasphemy."*
- Acts 26:11
And I punished them oft in every synagogue, and **compelled them to blaspheme**; and being exceedingly mad against them, I persecuted *them* even unto strange cities.
- James 2:7
Do not they blaspheme that worthy name by the which ye are called?

TV Blasphemy Is Common

There are *"blasphemers"* and *"blasphemies"* spoken even on the *"regular"* TV channels. We hear God's Name taken *"in vain"* on a regular basis. You cannot turn the TV on anymore without sooner or later hearing *"blasphemy."* It's a sad thing.

> ✔ **#6 The sixth sign of the *"last days"* is *"disobedience to parents"* (2 Timothy 3:2).**

There are a number of verses that teach us the need to have children under obedience to their parents and other proper authority.
- Romans 1:30
Backbiters, haters of God, despiteful, proud, boasters, inventors of evil things, **disobedient to parents**,
- Ephesians 6:1
Children, obey your parents in the Lord: for this is right.
- Colossians 3:20
Children, obey *your* parents in all things: for this is well pleasing unto the Lord.
- 1 Timothy 3:4
One that ruleth well his own house, **having his children in subjection with all gravity;**
This is a prerequisite for pastors/bishops/elders.

Pastors' Children Must Behave

I told my four sons and my daughter when I was a pastor in Newton, Massachusetts that since I was a pastor and had to meet this qualification, if any of them got out of line I could not be a pastor anymore. I am not talking about pastors' children who are not under his roof. A pastor has no control over his children who don't live with him anymore. If a pastor's children do not obey him, then, according to God's Word he should resign from the ministry. Sometimes such a pastor resigns and the deacons talk him into staying. The pastor should obey the Lord and not listen in this matter to other people, including his deacons.

- 1 Timothy 3:12
  Let the deacons be the husbands of one wife, **ruling their children and their own houses well.**

Wild Deacons' Children?

Deacons who have children who are wild should not be deacons. I've seen some of them in this situation.

- Titus 1:6
  If any be blameless, the husband of one wife, **having faithful children not accused of riot or unruly**.

✔ #7 The seventh sign of the "*last days*" is "*unthankful*" (2 Timothy 3:2).

Very few people are thankful for things in the days in which we live. It will get more pronounced as the last of the "*last days*" arrive. God encourages saved people to be "*thankful.*"
- **Colossians 3:15**
  And let the peace of God rule in your hearts, to the which also ye are called in one body; and **be ye thankful**.

- 1 Thessalonians 5:18
  In every thing give thanks: for this is the will of God in Christ Jesus concerning you.

  When our children were growing up, we read to them the story of Farmer Jones and his various barnyard animals. Farmer Jones fed his chickens and the chickens said *"Thank you Farmer Jones."* Farmer Jones fed his horses and the horses said *"Thank you Farmer Jones."* Farmer Jones fed the cows and the cows said *"Thank you Farmer Jones."* After feeding all the other animals, Farmer Jones fed the pigs, but the pigs did not say *"Thank you Farmer Jones."* The pigs didn't say anything. They were much too busy eating. We have a lack of *"thankfulness"* today, and we will have even more in the last of the *"last days."*

✔ **#8 The eighth sign of the *"last days"* is *"unholy"* (2 Timothy 3:2).**

People don't even have a pretense of the holy things of God. This is a sad thing indeed. Secularism is rampant now and will be much worse in the last of the *"last days"* before the rapture of the *"church which is His Body"* (Ephesians 1:22-23). Wickedness and sinfulness of all sorts is the essence of being *"unholy."* Review the mounting crime statistics and you will have a measure of the *"unholiness"* of our days.

- 1 Timothy 1:9
  Knowing this, that the law is not made for a righteous man, but for the lawless and disobedient, for the ungodly and for sinners, for **unholy** and profane, for murderers of fathers and murderers of mothers, for manslayers,

2 Timothy 3:3

"Without natural affection, trucebreakers, false accusers, incontinent, fierce, despisers of those that are good."

✔ **#9 The ninth sign of the *"last days"* is *"without natural affection"* (2 Timothy 3:3).**

This sin is mentioned in the catalog of sins which were prominent among the heathen.

- Romans 1:31
  Without understanding, covenantbreakers, **without natural affection**, implacable, unmerciful:

> ### Things "Without Natural Affection"
> There are a number of possible things that might be defined as "*without natural affection.*"
> (1) Homosexuality is not "*natural affection.*"
> (2) Abortion is not "*natural affection.*"
> (3) Incest is not "*natural affection.*"
> (4) Bestiality is not "*natural affection.*"
> All of these things, and many others, are signs of the last days. We certainly are the "*last days.*"

✔ #10   The tenth sign of the "*last days*" is "*trucebreakers*" (2 Timothy 3:3).

The Greek term for this is ASPONDOS which has various meanings:
   "*without a treaty or covenant; of things not mutually agreed upon e.g. abstinences from hostilities; that cannot be persuaded to enter into a covenant, implacable.*"

> ### "Covenant Breaking" Divorce Data
> This word means either breaking a covenant, or not even being willing to enter into a covenant or agreement. Look at the marriages that break up.
>
> Here are some statistics on percentages of divorces for first, second, and third marriages:
>
> "*The divorce rate in America for first marriage, vs second or third marriage <u>50% percent of first marriages, 67% of second and 74% of third marriages end in divorce</u>, according to Jennifer Baker of the Forest Institute of Professional Psychology in Springfield, Missouri.*"
>
> This certainly is a measure of "*trucebreaking*" in the U.S.A.

Lenin and Stalin had this to say about truces and agreements in the form of national treaties: *"Treaties are like pie crusts, made to be broken."*

> ✔ **#11 The eleventh sign of the "*last days*" is "false accusers." (2 Timothy 3:3).**

The Greek word for this is DIABOLOS often translated "*Devil.*" Some of the meanings of this word are as follows:
"prone to slander, slanderous, accusing falsely; a calumniator, false accuser, slanderer; metaph. applied to a man who, by opposing the cause of God, may be said to act the part of the devil or to side with him; Satan the prince of the demons, the author of evil, persecuting good men, estranging mankind from God and enticing them to sin, afflicting them with diseases by means of demons who take possession of their bodies at his bidding."

> ## "False Witness" A Popular Sin
> The Bible speaks out against bearing "*false witness*" against people yet this is a popular sin now and will be much greater in the "*last days.*"

- Exodus 20:16
  Thou shalt not bear false witness against thy neighbour.
- Proverbs 14:5
  A faithful witness will not lie: but **a false witness will utter lies**.
- Matthew 26:59
  Now the chief priests, and elders, and **all the council, sought false witness against Jesus, to put him to death** ;

> ✔ **#12 The twelfth sign of the "*last days*" is "incontinent" (2 Timothy 3:3).**

The Greek word for this is AKRATES which means "*without self-control, intemperate.*" It refers to people who can't control themselves. Sometimes, at sports events, some people are "*incontinent*" and uncontrolled in their actions. This leads into all sorts of sins, including murder and many others.

> ✔ **#13 The thirteenth sign of the "last days" is "fierce" (2 Timothy 3:3).**

The Greek word is ANEMEROS which means: " *not tame, savage, fierce.*"
- Matthew 8:28
And when he was come to the other side into the country of the Gergesenes, **there met him two possessed with devils, coming out of the tombs, exceeding fierce,** so that no man might pass by that way.
- Luke 23:5
And they were the more fierce, saying, He stirreth up the people, teaching throughout all Jewry, beginning from Galilee to this place.

Current USA Murder Statistics
According to recent FBI records:
   1 murder occurs every 24 minutes.
   1 robbery occurs every 54 seconds.
   1 assault occurs every 29 seconds.
   1 missing child occurs every 24 seconds.
   Larceny occurs every 4 seconds.

> ✔ **#14 The fourteenth sign of the "last days" is "despisers of those that are good." (2 Timothy 3:3).**

The Sin of Despising Good People
This sin of despising good people was one of the reasons the Pharisees and chief priests wanted to crucify the Lord Jesus Christ. He was truly "*good*" in all areas being perfect God and perfect Man, and yet He was "*despised.*"

- Proverbs 15:20
  A wise son maketh a glad father: but **a foolish man despiseth his mother.**
- Luke 10:16
  He that heareth you heareth me; and **he that despiseth you despiseth me; and he that despiseth me despiseth him that sent me.**

The Saviour Was "Good" But Hated

The Lord Jesus Christ was good, but He was "*despised*."

- 1 Corinthians 1:28
  And base things of the world, and **things which are despised, hath God chosen**, *yea*, and things which are not, to bring to nought things that are:
- 1 Corinthians 4:10
  We *are* fools for Christ's sake, but ye *are* wise in Christ; we *are* weak, but ye *are* strong; ye *are* honourable, but **we *are* despised**.
- 1 Timothy 4:12
  Let no man despise thy youth; but be thou an example of the believers, in word, in conversation, in charity, in spirit, in faith, in purity.

2 Timothy 3:4

"**Traitors, heady, highminded, lovers of pleasures more than lovers of God.**"

✔ **#15 The fifteenth sign of the "*last days*" is "*traitors*" (2 Timothy 3:4).**

A "*traitor*" is a person who betrays someone.
- Matthew 10:4
Simon the Canaanite, and **Judas Iscariot, who also betrayed him.**
- Matthew 24:10
And then shall many be offended, and **shall betray one another**, and shall hate one another.
- Matthew 26:16
And from that time **he sought opportunity to betray him.**
- Matthew 26:48
Now **he that betrayed him** gave them a sign, saying, Whomsoever I shall kiss, that same is he: hold him fast.

In these "*last days*" we are going to have some traitors who will turn us in. In some states, there are new laws either in place or proposed that if preachers preach the Bible truth against homosexuality he will be have to pay a fine, be thrown in jail, or both. That law could come to New Jersey as well. If it does come here to New Jersey, there might be a "*traitor*" who will turn me in as a pastor for preaching about the Bible's opposition to homosexuality. I must "*obey God rather than men*" (Acts 5:29).
- Acts 7:52
Which of the prophets have not your fathers persecuted? and they have slain them which shewed before of the coming of the Just One; **of whom ye have been now the betrayers** and murderers:
- 1 Corinthians 11:23
For I have received of the Lord that which also I delivered unto you, That **the Lord Jesus the** *same* **night in which he was betrayed took bread**:

It was at the last supper with the Lord Jesus Christ and His disciples where Judas Iscariot decided to betray the Saviour.

✔ **#16 The sixteenth sign of the "*last days*" is "*heady*" (2 Timothy 3:4).**

The Greek word is PROPETES which has various meanings.
"*to fall forwards, headlong, sloping, precipitously; precipitate, rash, reckless*"

The Meaning of Being "Heady"

If a person is *"falling forwards,"* he is so fast that he cannot stop. He thinks he knows what he is doing and doesn't care about listening to any others who are noticing what he is doing and are trying to stop him. He will not listen to these detractors because he is *"heady"* and has a "k*now-it-all"* attitude.

✔ **#17   The seventeenth sign of the *"last days"* is *"highminded"* (2 Timothy 3:4).**

The Greek word is TUPHOO. It brings out many pictures with many meanings such as the following:
"to raise a smoke, to wrap in a mist; metaph. to make proud, puff up with pride, render insolent; to be puffed up with haughtiness or pride; to blind with pride or conceit, to render foolish or stupid; beclouded, besotted."

The Meaning of Being "Highminded"

The people who are *"highminded"* think they are wrapped in a mist that makes them special and sets them apart from everyone else. This is a sad state of affairs. This arrogant trait will increase more and more as we approach the last of the *"last days."* The Bible speaks against this sin.

- Romans 11:20
  Well; because of unbelief they were broken off, and thou standest by faith. **Be not highminded**, but fear:
- 1 Timothy 6:17
  Charge them that are rich in this world, **that they be not highminded**, nor trust in uncertain riches, but in the living God, who giveth us richly all things to enjoy;
  We have to keep our minds down to earth.

> ✔ **#18 The eighteenth sign of the "*last days*" is "*lovers of pleasures more than lovers of God*" (2 Timothy 3:4).**

- Proverbs 21:17
  He that loveth pleasure *shall be* a poor man: he that loveth wine and oil shall not be rich.

> ## The High Cost of "Pleasure"
> Worldly "*pleasures*" have high price tags.

- Ecclesiastes 2:1
  I said in mine heart, Go to now, I will prove thee with mirth, therefore **enjoy pleasure: and, behold, this also *is* vanity.**
- Isaiah 47:8
  Therefore hear now this, **thou that art given to pleasures**, that dwellest carelessly, that sayest in thine heart, I *am*, and none else beside me; I shall not sit *as* a widow, neither shall I know the loss of children:
- Luke 8:14
  And that which fell among thorns are they, which, when they have heard, go forth, and are **choked with cares and riches and pleasures of *this* life**, and bring no fruit to perfection.

> ## "Pleasure" Brings No Spiritual Fruit
> If we are involved with worldly "*pleasures*" we will have no spiritual fruit.

- 1 Timothy 5:6
  But **she that liveth in pleasure is dead while she liveth**.
- Titus 3:3
  For we ourselves also were sometimes foolish, disobedient, deceived, **serving divers lusts and pleasures**, living in malice and envy, hateful, *and* hating one another.

- Hebrews 11:25
  Choosing rather to suffer affliction with the people of God, than to enjoy the pleasures of sin for a season;

Sinful "Pleasures" Only Temporary
There are pleasures in sin, but it is only for a season.

- James 5:5
  Ye have lived in pleasure on the earth, and been wanton; ye have nourished your hearts, as in a day of slaughter.

2 Timothy 3:5
"Having a form of godliness, but denying the power thereof: from such turn away."

✔ #19 The nineteenth sign of the "last days" is "having a form of godliness" (2 Timothy 3:5)

It takes more than a mere "form" to be genuine. A "form" is just an outward show. The Roman Catholic Church has a religious "form," but lacks genuine Biblical standards. A few years ago, Pastor Joshua Wallnofer visited many churches in our area in order to find out what they believed and what "form" of Christianity they followed. He told me that, in his opinion, there were great defects in what he observed in these churches. They all had various "forms."

✔ #20 The twentieth sign of the "last days" is "denying the power thereof" (2 Timothy 3:5).

God's "power" is vital if there are to be any genuine blessings from Heaven to be gained for the Lord.
- Romans 1:16
  For I am not ashamed of the gospel of Christ: for it is the power of God unto salvation to every one that believeth; to the Jew first, and also to the Greek.
  These who exhibit this sign deny the "power of God."

- 1 Corinthians 1:18
  For the preaching of the cross is to them that perish foolishness; but **unto us which are saved it is the power of God.**

2 Timothy 3:6

"For of this sort are they which creep into houses, and lead captive silly women laden with sins, led away with divers lusts."

> ✔ **#21 The twenty-first sign of the "*last days*" is "they which creep into houses, and lead captive silly women" (2 Timothy 3:6).**

I believe this gives us a picture of prostitutes and the men who go after these "*silly women.*"

The Greek word for "*creep*" is ENDUNO. It has various meanings: "*to put on, to envelop in, to hide in; literally: to put on, clothe with a garment; metaph. put on armour; to creep into, insinuate one's self into, to enter.*"

Creeping Into Houses For Sin

The word implies men who insinuate themselves into houses to search for wicked women for pursuit of sexual immorality of all sorts. These men are creeping in like you slip on a coat. That's what they are doing. There are many warnings in the Bible concerning these "*strange women.*" There might also be a danger from women who are friends and acquaintances.

- Proverbs 2:16
  To deliver thee from the strange woman, *even* from the stranger *which* flattereth with her words;
- Proverbs 5:3, 6
  For **the lips of a strange woman** drop *as* an honeycomb, and her mouth *is* smoother than oil: . . .
  Lest thou shouldest ponder the path of life, **her ways are moveable**, *that* thou canst not know *them*.

- Proverbs 5:20
  And **why wilt thou, my son, be ravished with a strange woman, and embrace the bosom of a stranger**?
- Proverbs 6:23-29
  For the commandment *is* a lamp; and the law *is* light; and reproofs of instruction *are* the way of life: **·To keep thee from the evil woman, from the flattery of the tongue of a strange woman. ·Lust not after her beauty in thine heart**; neither let her take thee with her eyelids. **·For by means of a** whorish woman *a man is brought* to a piece of bread: and the adulteress will hunt for the precious life. **Can a man take fire in his bosom, and his clothes not be burned? Can one go upon hot coals, and his feet not be burned? ·So he that goeth in to his neighbour's wife; whosoever toucheth her shall not be innocent.**

  When I was a Navy Chaplain on active duty, there were many of our marines and navy men going off with prostitutes and other immoral women..
- Proverbs 6:32-33
  But **whoso committeth adultery with a woman lacketh understanding: he** *that* **doeth it destroyeth his own soul. A wound and dishonour shall he get; and his reproach shall not be wiped away.**

  Several years ago, there was an adulterous situation in a church where we were members. The one with whom this "*silly woman*" had committed adultery was the pastor of her church. After this all came to light, the pastor thought he should still be the pastor. This is unthinkable. Fortunately, he was dismissed as pastor of the church, but unfortunately there was a margin of only a few votes.

  I wrote to the church that ordained this man and I told the committee who ordained him the entire situation. I had talked at length with the adulteress woman and found out many details the pastor was hiding. Because of these facts, fortunately, the ordaining church removed his ordination certificate from him. I felt that I should do this. As far as I know now, this man is no longer a pastor.
- Proverbs 7:5
  That they may **keep thee from the strange woman**, from the stranger *which* flattereth with her words.
- Proverbs 22:14
  The mouth of strange women *is* **a deep pit**: he that is abhorred of the LORD shall fall therein.

- Proverbs 23:27
  For **a whore** *is* **a deep ditch; and a strange woman** *is* **a narrow pit.**
- Proverbs 23:33
  Thine eyes shall behold strange women, and thine heart shall utter perverse things.

Randall Swift wrote a recent article entitled *"The Oldest Profession-- Shocking Facts and Statistics About Prostitution."* In that article, he estimated that *"Over 1 million people in the US have worked as prostitutes."* That is only an estimate. There are probably many more *"silly women"* than this who are *"laden with sins,"* and *"led away with divers lusts."* There are untold numbers of additional women who willingly sin by fornication or adultery without charging the men. These are equally *"silly women."*

2 Timothy 3:7

"Ever learning and never able to come to the knowledge of the truth."

✔ **#22 The twenty-second sign of the *"last days"* is *"ever learning"* (2 Timothy 3:7).**

According to statistics for college graduates, *"learning"* is widespread today and is increasing each year. According to the U. S. Census Bureau News as of March 21, 2003,

"According to new tables released on the Internet, titled Educational Attainment in the United States: March 2001 and March 2002, more than one-quarter (27 percent) of adults age 25 and older had at least a bachelor's degree in 2002, about 1 percentage point higher than the previous year. The jump in the percentage of college graduates resulted from significant increases for women, non-Hispanic whites and African-Americans. About 3-in-10 young adults, ages 25 to 29 in 2002, had completed a bachelor's degree, matching the 2000 record high. (See attached table.)"

The Error of Wrong "Learning"

There is nothing wrong with learning per se, but the wrong kind of learning is harmful to the learners. Teachers are teaching evolution in the classrooms all over our country. In this regard, these teachers are teaching lies and hoaxes. They are telling our children and young people about evolution as though it is true.

- Proverbs 1:5
  A wise *man* **will hear, and will increase learning**; and a man of understanding shall attain unto wise counsels:
- Proverbs 9:9
  Give *instruction* to a wise *man*, and he will be yet wiser: **teach a just** *man*, **and he will increase in learning.**
- Acts 26:24
  And as he thus spake for himself, Festus said with a loud voice, Paul, thou art beside thyself; **much learning doth make thee mad.**
- Romans 15:4
  For **whatsoever things were written aforetime were written for our learning**, that we through patience and comfort of the scriptures might have hope.

Whatever *"learning"* we do, we must ask God to give us wisdom and discernment in this process to make sure it conforms to Bible truth.

✔ **#23 The twenty-third sign of the *"last days"* is *"never able to come to the knowledge of the truth"* (2 Timothy 3:7).**

The Purpose of "Learning"

That is the same thing as wrong *"learning."* All learning should end in the *"knowledge of the truth."* This includes, among other things, the truth about creation, the truth about salvation through faith in Christ, the truth of Heaven, the truth about hell, and the truth about all the other doctrines of the Christian faith. It is indeed sad that those *"learning"* are not able to come to God's *"truth."* The reason, often times, is that they are searching for it in the wrong place.

- **John 14:6**
  Jesus saith unto him, **I am the way, the truth**, and the life: no man cometh unto the Father, but by me.
  The Lord Jesus Christ is the real *"Truth."* In these *"last days,"* people must come to the Lord Jesus Christ who is the *"Truth."*
- **John 17:17**
  Sanctify them through thy truth: **thy word is truth**.
  That's why I urge every born-again Christian to be reading 85 Bible verses a day in order to complete the whole Bible each year so that they might know the *"truth."*
- **Ephesians 6:14**
  Stand therefore, **having your loins girt about with truth**, and having on the breastplate of righteousness;
- **1 Timothy 2:4**
  Who will have all men to be saved, and **to come unto the knowledge of the truth.**
  This verse reveals the heart of God.
- **1 Timothy 6:5**
  Perverse disputings of men of corrupt minds, and **destitute of the truth**, supposing that gain is godliness: from such withdraw thyself.
- **2 Timothy 2:15**
  Study to shew thyself approved unto God, a workman that needeth not to be ashamed, **rightly dividing the word of truth.**

Get The Right "Word" To Divide

First, we must have the right *"Word"* or Bible. In English, this is the King James Bible. In Hebrew, Aramaic, and Greek, it is the traditional Words which underlie the King James Bible. Once we have the right Bible, we have to have rightly divide that *"Word of truth."*

- **2 Timothy 4:4**
  And they shall **turn away *their* ears from the truth**, and shall be turned unto fables.

Gnostic Bible Versions Are "Fables"

I believe the new Gnostic Bible versions are *"fables,"* to a greater or lesser degree. They are filled with *"dynamic equivalency."*

In using this translation technique, these versions either add to the Words of God, subtract from the Words of God, or change the Words of God in some other way. They have the wrong Hebrew and Aramaic Words and the wrong Greek Words. If you want to make somebody angry, just talk to them about your Bible. We have to expound the truth of the Words of God.

2 Timothy 3:8

"Now as Jannes and Jambres withstood Moses, so do those also resist the truth men of corrupt minds, reprobate concerning the faith."

Though the Old Testament does not name them, I believe Jannes and Jambres were the magicians that Moses met up with in Exodus 7 and 8.

- **Exodus 7:10-12**
And Moses and Aaron went in unto Pharaoh, and they did so as the LORD had commanded: and Aaron cast down his rod before Pharaoh, and before his servants, and it became a serpent. **Then Pharaoh also called the wise men and the sorcerers: now the magicians of Egypt, they also did in like manner with their enchantments.** For they cast down every man his rod, and they became serpents: but Aaron's rod swallowed up their rods.

The first miracle by *"Jannes and Jambres"* was made possible by the power of Satan.

- **Exodus 7:20-22**
And Moses and Aaron did so, as the LORD commanded; and he lifted up the rod, and smote the waters that *were* in the river, in the sight of Pharaoh, and in the sight of his servants; and all the waters that *were* in the river were turned to blood. And the fish that *was* in the river died; and the river stank, and the Egyptians could not drink of the water of the river; and there was blood throughout all the land of Egypt. **And the magicians of Egypt did so with their enchantments:** and Pharaoh's heart was hardened, neither did he hearken unto them; as the LORD had said.

The magicians imitated the second miracle as well. Satan imitates God's miracles in many cases. Don't believe when you see people being healed in God's Name that God is necessarily behind the healing. It might be Satan at work. He is still imitating God's miracles.

- **Exodus 8:6**
  And Aaron stretched out his hand over the waters of Egypt; and the frogs came up, and covered the land of Egypt.

The sorcerers and magicians, Jannes and Jambres also imitated this miracle.

- **Exodus 8:16**
  And the LORD said unto Moses, Say unto Aaron, Stretch out thy rod, and smite the dust of the land, that it may become lice throughout all the land of Egypt.

- **Exodus 9:10**
  And they took ashes of the furnace, and stood before Pharaoh; and Moses sprinkled it up toward Heaven; and it became a boil breaking forth *with* blains upon man, and upon beast.

The boils got on the magicians as well. Their Satanic powers did not guard them from the hand of God in this miracle.

- **Zechariah 3:1**
  And he shewed me Joshua the high priest standing before the angel of the LORD, and **Satan standing at his right hand to resist him**.

Satan resists the truth, and these men resisted the truth in the days of Moses as well.

- **Acts 7:51**
  Ye stiffnecked and uncircumcised in heart and ears, **ye do always resist the Holy Ghost: as your fathers** *did*, **so do ye.**

- **James 4:7**
  Submit yourselves therefore to God. **Resist the devil**, and he will flee from you.

Satan Cannot Indwell Christians

One of the men asked me a question after the morning service last Sunday. He asked me if Satan can possess Christians. My answer was "No." If you are a born-again Christian, you have God the Holy Spirit of God inside of you. If this is true, Satan can not indwell you. However, he is certainly able to resist you and influence you as he did Peter.

- 1 Peter 5:9
  Whom resist stedfast in the faith, knowing that the same afflictions are accomplished in your brethren that are in the world.

In the *"last days,"* people will *"resist the truth"* even more than before.

> ✔ **#24   The twenty-fourth sign of the *"last days"* is *"men of corrupt minds"* (2 Timothy 3:8).**

The Greek Word for *"corrupt"* is KATPHTHEIRO, It means: *"to corrupt, deprave; corrupted in mind; to destroy; to be destroyed, to perish."* The minds of these men and those who follow them are *"depraved and corrupted."* They are like those before the flood of Noah.

- **Genesis 6:11-13**
  The earth also was corrupt before God, and the earth was filled with violence. And God looked upon the earth, and, behold, it was corrupt; for **all flesh had corrupted his way upon the earth.** And God said unto Noah, The end of all flesh is come before me; for the earth is filled with violence through them; and, behold, I will destroy them with the earth.

  Some people, who call themselves creationists, believe there was only a local flood. If that were the case, Noah could have moved to dry ground. It was a universal flood. That universal flood is what changed the mountains, made the strata, and all of the other changes in our earth.

- **2 Corinthians 2:17**
  For **we are not as many, which corrupt the word of God** : but as of sincerity, but as of God, in the sight of God speak we in Christ.

- **Ephesians 4:22-23**
  That ye put off concerning the former conversation **the old man, which is corrupt according to the deceitful lusts**; And be renewed in the spirit of your mind;

- **1 Timothy 6:5**
  Perverse disputings of men of corrupt minds, and destitute of the truth, supposing that gain is godliness: from such withdraw thyself.

> ✔ **#25 The twenty-fifth sign of the "last days" is "reprobate concerning the faith" (2 Timothy 3:8).**

Another characteristic of these "*reprobate*" men is that they are "*reprobate concerning the faith.*" The Greek word for "*faith*" has the definite article in front of it. Whenever this occurs, it stands for "*the faith*" which means the body of Christian doctrine and truth found in the Bible (including its original Words). The word for "*reprobate*" is ADOKIMOS. It means:

> "*not standing the test, not approved; properly used of metals and coins; that which does not prove itself such as it ought; unfit for, unproved, spurious, reprobate.*"

There is no genuineness concerning their Christian and Biblical doctrine.

2 Timothy 3:9

"But they shall proceed no further for their folly shall be manifest unto all men as theirs also was."

God tells about this in
- 1 Corinthians 3:13

Every man's work shall be made manifest: for the day shall declare it, because it shall be revealed by fire; and the fire shall try every man's work of what sort it is.

Those of us who are born-again Christians will one day stand before the Judgment Seat of Christ. All of our works will be made manifest. You cannot hide from God. The unbelievers will be judged at the Great White Throne Judgment (Revelation 20:11).
- 1 Corinthians 4:5

Therefore judge nothing before the time, until the Lord come, who both **will bring to light the hidden things of darkness, and will make manifest the counsels of the hearts**: and then shall every man have praise of God.

All of our heart attitudes will be brought out into the open, I believe in the following verse:
- 1 John 1:9

If we confess our sins, he is faithful and just to forgive us *our* sins, and to cleanse us from all unrighteousness.

Christians--"Confess" Your Sins

If you know the Lord Jesus Christ as your Saviour, and you sin, be sure to confess your sins and agree with God that you have sinned in thought, word, or deed. He has promised to forgive you. I believe that, if we are redeemed, our genuinely confessed sins will no longer be remembered. They will not be brought up against us at the Judgment Seat of Christ. It is the unconfessed sins that will be brought up against us at that time.

Some of the unsaved people say that they want to be cremated because they think that they will not have to stand up before the Lord Jesus Christ at the Great White Throne (Revelation 20:11) because they do not believe that the Lord will be able to put them back together, give them a permanent body which will have to undergo the pain of an eternal and literal lake of fire. They think that cremation will allow them to escape the literal fires of Hell. They should not be so sure. God who made this earth from nothing, is fully able to put that cremated dust back together in a split second. God made man from the dust (APHAR) of the ground. Our God Who can do that can also put together people who were cremated. Those unbelievers who think they will get away from God's righteous judgment because they have been cremated will be very surprised indeed.

- Hebrews 4:13
   Neither is there any creature that is not manifest in his sight: but all things *are* naked and opened unto the eyes of him with whom we have to do.

Our Omniscient God

We have a God who is Omniscient. He knows everything. Our God is also Omnipotent. He is all-powerful. Our God is Omnipresent. He is present in every place at the same time. Our God is able and will see into every one of our hearts. We can't hide from God. God knows that these twenty-five signs of the "*last days*" will take place.

I am not setting dates because the next prophetic event that will take place is the rapture of the "*Church which is His body*" (Ephesians 1:22-23). The rapture could take place at any moment. After the rapture comes the

Tribulation which is called Daniel's 70th week is found in Daniel Chapter 9:24. This verse mentions: "Seventy weeks are determined upon thy people and upon thy holy city." The 70th week of Daniel (the Tribulation) is a judgment on the Jews, God's chosen people. No born-again Christian will be in any part of this seven-year Tribulation. This is the hope of the church. The saved ones are going to face the Lord at the Judgment Seat of Christ (2 Corinthians 5:10).

Those lost and unsaved people who are still here on the earth will go through the Tribulation. Can those people be saved? I believe if they have heard the gospel before the believers are snatched away, and have rejected the Lord Jesus Christ while the Holy Spirit is still here, then I do not believe they will have the opportunity to accept Christ as their Saviour. I believe that those who have never heard the gospel can be saved during the Tribulation if they genuinely receive the Lord Jesus Christ as their Saviour. That is why God will seal 144,000 Jews (twelve thousand from every Jewish tribe). These people will preach the gospel, and men and women will be saved during the Tribulation. The ones who have already heard the gospel will be confused because the Antichrist is going to be slick. God has given to us a road map with twenty-five signs of the *"last days."*

25 Signs Of The Last Days

1. Men will be lovers of their own selves
2. Covetous
3. Boasters
4. Proud
5. Blasphemers
6. Disobedient to parents
7. Unthankful
8. Unholy
9. Without natural affection
10. Trucebreakers
11. False accusers
12. Incontinent
13. Fierce
14. Despisers of those who are good
15. Traitors
16. Heady
17. High minded
18. Lovers of pleasures more than lovers of God
19. Having a form of godliness
20. Denying the power thereof
21. Those who creep into houses and lead silly woman captive
22. Ever learning
23. Never able to come to the knowledge of the truth
24. Men of corrupt minds
25. Reprobate concerning the faith.

God gave to Paul the revelation of these twenty-five signs of the last days. Paul told Timothy and Timothy was to tell his people as a pastor at the church of Ephesus.

Be Ready For Christ's Coming

May we who are saved be ready for the coming of Christ! If you do not know Christ as your Saviour and Redeemer, may you genuinely trust Him today and be born-again. Otherwise you are facing serious consequences. Those of us who are saved, may we live for him each day.

2 Timothy 3:10

"But thou hast fully known my doctrine, manner of life, purpose, faith, long suffering, charity, patience."

Timothy had *"fully known"* Paul. He had observed him as he went with him on many of his missionary journeys. Notice the things that Timothy knew about him.

There are at least nine things that Timothy knew about the apostle Paul. Timothy traveled with Paul as recorded in the book of Acts from Chapter 16 and beyond.

✔ #1 Timothy knew Paul's *"doctrine."*

In the Bible, doctrine is important. That means the faithful teaching of the Words of God.
- Matthew 7:28
 And it came to pass, when Jesus had ended these sayings, **the people were astonished at his doctrine**:
- John 7:17
 If any man will do his will, he shall know of the doctrine, whether it be of God, or *whether* I speak of myself.
- Acts 2:42
 And **they continued stedfastly in the apostles' doctrine** and fellowship, and in breaking of bread, and in prayers.

I Preach "Doctrine" In Our Church

The Apostle's *"doctrine"* was a part of the early church. That's why we preach *"doctrine"* as found in the Words of God in the 𝔅ible 𝔉or 𝔗oday 𝔅aptist 𝔗hurch. It's Biblical to do so.

- Romans 16:17
  Now I beseech you, brethren, **mark them which cause divisions and offences contrary to the doctrine** which ye have learned; and avoid them.
  We have to stay away from those who teach false doctrines, claiming to be true to the Bible.
- Ephesians 4:14
  That we *henceforth* be no more children, tossed to and fro, and **carried about with every wind of doctrine**, by the sleight of men, *and* cunning craftiness, whereby they lie in wait to deceive;

Stay Firm On Bible "Doctrines"
We must stay firm on the doctrines which are taught in the Bible. Don't be *"tossed to and fro."*

- 1 Timothy 4:13
  Till I come, give attendance to reading, to exhortation, to doctrine.
- 2 Timothy 4:2-3
  Preach the word; be instant in season, out of season; reprove, rebuke, **exhort with all longsuffering and doctrine**. For the time will come when they will not endure sound doctrine; but after their own lusts shall they heap to themselves teachers, having itching ears;

Preach The Words of God
Pastors are urged, as Paul charged Timothy, to preach the Words of God with sound doctrine so that when the time comes and people are heralding false doctrine, Christians will be informed and be able to stay away from those false teachers.

- 2 John 10
  If there come any unto you, and **bring not this doctrine**, receive him not into *your* house, neither bid him God speed:
  Paul and Timothy were on the same wavelength in their doctrine.

✔ #2 Timothy knew Paul's *"manner of life."*

Timothy Knew Paul Well

Timothy had observed Paul closely. He had traveled with him ever since Acts Chapter 16. I am sure that Paul's *"manner of life"* was a godly influence on young Timothy.

✔ #3 Timothy knew Paul's *"purpose."*

It is good to have a godly *"purpose"* in our lives. Do you have a godly *"purpose"*? Paul had a godly *"purpose."* Daniel had a godly *"purpose."*
- **Daniel 1:8**
  But **Daniel purposed in his heart** that he would not defile himself with the portion of the king's meat, nor with the wine which he drank: therefore he requested of the prince of the eunuchs that he might not defile himself.
- **Acts 26:16**
  But rise, and stand upon thy feet: for I have appeared unto thee for this purpose, to make thee a minister and a witness both of these things which thou hast seen, and of those things in the which I will appear unto thee;

What is your *"purpose"*? What did God save you for if you are saved? Paul had a godly *"purpose,"* and if we are saved, we must have a godly *"purpose"* too.
- **Romans 8:28**
  And we know that all things work together for good to them that love God, to **them who are the called according to** *his* **purpose**.

Timothy knew that Paul's purpose was to please the Lord Jesus Christ.

✔ #4 Timothy knew Paul's *"faith."*

Paul was a man of *"faith."* Remember when Paul was in the storm and the guards were going to kill the prisoners because the ship was going to be capsized. In Acts 27:25, Paul said the following:

"Wherefore, sirs, be of good cheer: for **I believe God**, that it shall be even as it was told me."

God told Paul that there would be no loss of life in that furious storm. Paul had strong *"faith"* and believed God's Words to him.

✔ **#5 Timothy knew Paul's *"longsuffering."***

The Meaning Of "Longsuffering"

That is a word that refers to putting up with people for a long time. It comes from two words, MACRO (*"large* or *long"*), and THUMOS (*"burning"* or *"heat"*). Longsuffering literally means that our *"burning"* or *"anger"* is still a *"long way off"* and we do not *"burn up"* or get angry quickly.

- Exodus 34:6
  And the LORD passed by before him, and proclaimed, The LORD, **The LORD God, merciful and gracious, longsuffering**, and abundant in goodness and truth,
- Numbers 14:18
  The LORD *is* longsuffering, and of great mercy, forgiving iniquity and transgression, and by no means clearing *the guilty*, visiting the iniquity of the fathers upon the children unto the third and fourth *generation*.
- Psalm 86:15
  But **thou, O Lord, *art* a God full of compassion, and gracious, longsuffering**, and plenteous in mercy and truth.
- Galatians 5:22
  But **the fruit of the Spirit is** love, joy, peace, **longsuffering**, gentleness, goodness, faith,

"Longsuffering" As "Fruit of the Spirit"

Longsuffering is one of the parts of the *"fruit of the Spirit."* It is manifested when a born-again Christian is led, filled, or controlled by God the Holy Spirit.

- Ephesians 4:2
  With all lowliness and meekness, with longsuffering, forbearing one another in love;
- Colossians 1:10-11
  That ye might walk worthy of the Lord unto all pleasing, being fruitful in every good work, and increasing in the knowledge of God; Strengthened with all might, according to his glorious power, **unto all patience and longsuffering** with joyfulness;
  All born-again Christian must have *"longsuffering."*
- Colossians 3:12-13
  Put on therefore, as the elect of God, holy and beloved, bowels of mercies, kindness, humbleness of mind, meekness, **longsuffering;** Forbearing one another, and forgiving one another, if any man have a quarrel against any: even as Christ forgave you, so also *do* ye.

Forgive And Forbear

We must forgive and forbear one another.

- 2 Timothy 4:2
  Preach the word; be instant in season, out of season; reprove, rebuke, exhort **with all longsuffering** and doctrine.
  A preacher must have *"longsuffering"* and be able to put up with his people no matter what might happen in his church.
- 2 Peter 3:9
  The Lord is not slack concerning his promise, as some men count slackness; but **is longsuffering to us-ward**, not willing that any should perish, but that all should come to repentance.
  God does not want a lost sinner to die and go to Hell and yet He does not force people to accept His Son, the Lord Jesus Christ. He wants all people to have an opportunity to genuinely trust the Lord Jesus Christ as their Saviour.

✔ **#6 Timothy knew Paul's *"charity."***

This is evidence of Paul's love. Paul was strong in conviction and defense of the faith, yet he had an emotional love for Christ and God's people. It is possible for a pastor to *"preach the Word"* and be *"instant in season,"* and lack the *"charity"* he must have. Timothy saw *"charity"* in the life of Paul the apostle.

I hope that people can see this quality in you and in me. Do we have love first for the Lord Jesus and second for the brethren?

✔ **#7 Timothy knew Paul's *"patience."***

"Longsuffering" Versus *"Patience"*

From the study by Archbishop Trench of the Greek synonyms involved, *"longsuffering"* is putting up with difficult people. *"Patience"* is putting up with difficult circumstances. Which of the two is harder to put up with? You can often take care of circumstances, but handling problem people takes a great deal of *"longsuffering."* People are watching us today, just as people were watching Paul.

- Romans 5:3
And not only so, but we glory in tribulations also: knowing that **tribulation worketh patience**;
- Romans 15:4
For whatsoever things were written aforetime were written for our learning, that we **through patience and comfort of the scriptures might have hope**.
We can find in the Bible the *"patience"* that we need on a daily basis.

- Romans 15:5
Now **the God of patience** and consolation grant you to be likeminded one toward another according to Christ Jesus:
- 2 Thessalonians 1:4
So that we ourselves glory in you in the churches of God **for your patience** and faith in all your persecutions and tribulations that ye endure:
The church at Thessalonica was noted for its *"patience."*
- Titus 2:2
That **the aged men** be sober, grave, temperate, sound in faith, in charity, **in patience**.
Whether we are young or old, we must be *"patient."*

- Hebrews 10:36
For **ye have need of patience**, that, after ye have done the will of God, ye might receive the promise.
God promises things, but we must patiently wait for his promises to be fulfilled.
- Hebrews 12:1
Wherefore seeing we also are compassed about with so great a cloud of witnesses, let us lay aside every weight, and the sin which doth so easily beset us, and **let us run with patience the race that is set before us,**

Run Our Own Race With "Patience"

We must be *"patient,"* regardless of the circumstances. Our race is not somebody else's race. We must run with *"patience"* our own personal race which is set before us day by day.

- James 5:11
Behold, we count them happy which endure. Ye have heard of **the patience of Job**, and have seen the end of the Lord; that the Lord is very pitiful, and of tender mercy.
Job is the epitome of *"patience."* He lost his servants, family, his possessions, and his health, yet he still gave us an example of *"patience."*

2 Timothy 3:11

"Persecutions, afflictions, which came unto me at Antioch at Iconium at Lystra, what persecutions I endured, but out of them all the Lord delivered me."

✔ **#8 Timothy knew Paul's *"persecutions."***

These *"persecutions"* came to him especially when he was at Antioch, Iconium, and at Lystra.

- Mark 10:29-30
  And Jesus answered and said, Verily I say unto you, There is no man that hath left house, or brethren, or sisters, or father, or mother, or wife, or children, or lands, for my sake, and the gospel's, But he shall receive an hundredfold now in this time, houses, and brethren, and sisters, and mothers, and children, and lands, **with persecutions**; and in the world to come eternal life.
- 2 Corinthians 12:10
  Therefore I take pleasure in infirmities, in reproaches, in necessities, **in persecutions**, in distresses for Christ's sake: for when I am weak, then am I strong.
- 2 Thessalonians 1:4
  So that we ourselves glory in you in the churches of God for your patience and faith **in all your persecutions** and tribulations that ye endure:
  The churches have been persecuted in the New Testament, and they are being persecuted now as well.

✔ **#9 Timothy knew Paul's "afflictions."**

- An "*affliction*" [PATHEMA] is something that brings suffering.
- Psalm 34:19
  Many *are* the afflictions of the righteous: but the LORD delivereth him out of them all.

The Righteous Are "Afflicted"
If you are righteous, you are going to be "*afflicted.*"

- Acts 7:10
  And **delivered him out of all his afflictions**, and gave him favour and wisdom in the sight of Pharaoh king of Egypt; and he made him governor over Egypt and all his house.
  God delivered Joseph out of all his "*afflictions.*"
- 1 Thessalonians 3:3
  That no man should be **moved by these afflictions**: for yourselves know that we are appointed thereunto.

Don't Be "Moved" By "Afflictions"

When *"afflictions"* hit you, don't be moved or swept away. Don't leave your faith.

'TIS HIS WILL

I do not know what lies ahead,
I only know
I need not dread.

I do not know of joy or pain
Or if may be a loss or gain
If 'tis His will for me.

I do not know how it can be
That trials hard are best for me,
Yet 'tis His way for me.

I do not know how I can sing
Except that God's in everything,
And He will strengthen me.

I do not need to fret o cry
Or need to ever wonder why
If 'tis His will for me.
(By Gertrude Grace Sanborn
From *With Tears in My Heart*
Composed 1977)

- **2 Timothy 1:8**
  Be not thou therefore ashamed of the testimony of our Lord, nor of me his prisoner: but **be thou partaker of the afflictions of the gospel** according to the power of God;
  If you are a preacher of the gospel, you also have to accept the "*afflictions*" that go with it.
- **2 Timothy 4:5**
  But watch thou in all things, **endure afflictions**, do the work of an evangelist, make full proof of thy ministry.
  "*Antioch*" was the city where believers were first called "*Christians*" (Acts 11:26)
- **Acts 13:14**
  But when they departed from Perga, **they came to Antioch** in Pisidia, and went into the synagogue on the sabbath day, and sat down.
- **Acts 13:50**
  [At Antioch] But **the Jews stirred up the devout and honourable women**, and the chief men of the city, and raised persecution against Paul and Barnabas, and expelled them out of their coasts.

"Stirring Up" Kind Of Women

Have you ever had any women "*stirred up*" at you? Some devout women can be more bitter than the worldly women.

- **Acts 14:1-3**
  And it came to pass **in Iconium**, that they went both together into the synagogue of the Jews, and so spake, that a great multitude both of the Jews and also of the Greeks believed. But **the unbelieving Jews stirred up the Gentiles, and made their minds evil affected against the brethren**. Long time therefore abode they speaking boldly in the Lord, which gave testimony unto the word of his grace, and granted signs and wonders to be done by their hands.

Have you ever had anyone made their "*minds evil affected*" against you? We had an incident just this last week of someone who used to be very loving and all of the sudden this person called up someone and that someone just poured out poison against our church. This person is furious. Sometimes people's minds can be *"stirred up."* When the mind gets stirred up then the heart gets stirred up. Am I right?

The third city where Paul found all these afflictions was Lystra.

- **Acts 14:19-22**

    And there came thither certain Jews from Antioch and Iconium, who persuaded the people, and, **having stoned Paul, drew him out of the city, supposing he had been dead**. Howbeit, as the disciples stood round about him, he rose up, and came into the city: and the next day he departed with Barnabas to Derbe. And when they had preached the gospel to that city, and had taught many, **they returned again to Lystra**, and to Iconium, and Antioch, Confirming the souls of the disciples, and exhorting them to continue in the faith, and that we must through much tribulation enter into the kingdom of God.

I believe that, when he was stoned, Paul died and was taken up into the *"third Heaven"* where *"paradise"* is now (2 Corinthians Chapter 12:2, 4).

Paul was clear on giving glory to the Lord for His *"deliverance"* from all of his *"persecutions"* and *"afflictions"* which he *"endured."* There are many verses that show that God many times *"delivers"* his people when it is His will to do so.

- **2 Corinthians 1:10**

    Who delivered us from so great a death, and **doth deliver**: in whom we trust that **he will yet deliver us;**

- **Galatians 1:4**

    Who gave himself for our sins, **that he might deliver us** from this present evil world, according to the will of God and our Father:

God doesn't want us to get corrupted by this evil world. On the contrary, He wants to *"deliver"* us from this *"present evil world."*

- **Colossians 1:13**

    Who hath delivered us from the power of darkness, and hath translated us into the kingdom of his dear Son:

- **1 Thessalonians 1:10**

    And to wait for his Son from Heaven, whom he raised from the dead, even Jesus, **which delivered us from the wrath to come.**

The Pre-Tribulation Rapture

If you are saved, you are *"delivered"* from the *"wrath"* of Hell's *"lake of fire"* and the *"wrath"* of every part of the seven-year Tribulation period after the rapture of the church.

- 2 Timothy 4:18
  And **the Lord shall deliver me from every evil work**, and will preserve *me* unto his Heavenly kingdom: to whom *be* glory for ever and ever. Amen.

The Meaning of "Endure"

Paul wanted to mention that he *"endured"* all of these difficulties that came upon him. He said, *"what persecutions I endured."* The word for *"endure"* is HYPOPHERO. Some of the meanings for this are as follows:

"to bear by being under, bear up (a thing placed on one's shoulders); to bear patiently, to endure"

This is truly a descriptive word picture. It meant that when heavy weights were placed upon Paul's shoulders, he was still able to remain standing up despite such a load.

2 Timothy 3:12

"Yea, and all that will live godly in Christ Jesus shall suffer persecution."

The word *"will"* (THELEO) is not the simple indicator of the future tense. On the other hand here are some of the various meanings:

"to will, have in mind, intend; to be resolved or determined, to purpose; to desire, to wish; to love; to like to do a thing, be fond of doing; to take delight in, have pleasure" It means those who are actually *"willing"* to *"live godly in Christ Jesus."*

Willing to Live "Godly"= "Persecution"

Are you willing to *"live godly in Christ Jesus"*? If so, you *"shall suffer persecution."* The verb, *"live"* (ZAO), is a present tense and implies *"continuous living godly"* rather than *"living godly"* just once in a while.

- Titus 2:12
  Teaching us that, denying ungodliness and worldly lusts, we should live soberly, righteously, and godly, in this present world;

- 2 Peter 2:9
  The Lord knoweth how to deliver the godly out of temptations, and to reserve the unjust unto the day of judgment to be punished:
  We should want to *"live godly"* even though *"persecution"* will come as a result of this godly living.

"Persecution" and Being A Christian

"Persecution" is something that has come to pass many times in the Bible. It is part of being a born-again Christian.

- Matthew 13:20-22
  But he that received the seed into stony places, the same is he that heareth the word, and anon with joy receiveth it; Yet hath he not root in himself, but dureth for a while: for **when tribulation or persecution ariseth because of the word**, by and by he is offended. He also that received seed among the thorns is he that heareth the word; and the care of this world, and the deceitfulness of riches, choke the word, and he becometh unfruitful.
- Romans 8:35
  Who shall separate us from the love of Christ? *shall tribulation*, or distress, or persecution, or famine, or nakedness, or peril, or sword?

2 Timothy 3:13

"**But evil men and seducers shall wax worse and worse, deceiving, and being deceived.**"

From this verse, it is made crystal clear that there will not be a large revival in the "last days." Some Bible-believing pastors, teachers, and others are teaching that we are going to see a huge revival before the coming of the Lord. On the contrary, Paul said that "*evil men and seducers shall wax worse and worse, deceiving and being deceived.*" Here are some verses on "*evil*" people

.Proverbs 4:14
Enter not into the path of the wicked, and **go not in the way of evil men**.
God doesn't want us to even travel on the path of "*evil*" people.

- Proverbs 24:1
Be not thou envious against evil men, neither desire to be with them.

Some people love to be with others who are "*evil.*" God says that Christians are not to be with them.

"*Seducers*" (GOES) are also going to "*wax worse and worse.*" That word means:

"*a wailer, a howler; a juggler, enchanter (because incantations used to be uttered in a kind of howl); a deceiver, imposter*"

There Are Many "Imposters"

There are many such "*imposters*" in churches, in colleges, in seminaries, on the radio, on television, on the web, in books, magazines, and all around the world today. These "*evil men and seducers*" are both "*deceiving and being deceived.*"

"*Deceiving*" (PLANAO) has various meanings:
"*to cause to stray, to lead astray, lead aside from the right way; to go astray, wander, roam about; metaph.; to lead away from the truth, to lead into error, to deceive; to be led into error; to be led aside from the path of virtue, to go astray, sin; to sever or fall away from the truth; of heretics; to be led away into error and sin*"

The structure of this phrase means that these false teachers "*deceive*" others by their heresies and yet they themselves are "*deceived*" as well.

False Teachers Reproduce

I believe that false teachers beget false teachers. False teachers spew out their false teachings, and the people who listen to them become false themselves, and these teach others to become false teachers, and so on and on. This is what is happening in the day in which we live.

2 Timothy 3:14

"But continue thou in the things which thou hast learned and hast been assured of, knowing of whom thou has learned them."

Paul is telling Timothy to "*continue*" (MENO) ceaselessly and without interruption (Greek present tense) to follow exactly what he has "*learned and been assured of.*" This includes all of the doctrines and teachings of Paul as found in the New Testament. Timothy was "*assured*" of the truth and value of these teachings. This is what pastors should do in their pulpits today, but very, very few are doing it.

Here are seven other things found in Scripture that we are to continue in.

✔ **#1 We are to "*continue*" in Christ's "*Words.*"**

- John 8:31
  Then said Jesus to those Jews which believed on him, **If ye continue in my word**, *then* are ye my disciples indeed;
  Every Christian should read the Words of God and continue to do it from Genesis through Revelation at least once per year.

✔ **#2 We are to "*continue*" in "*Christ's love.*"**

- John 15:9
  As the Father hath loved me, so have I loved you: **continue ye in my love.**

✔ **#3 We are to "*continue*" in "*the grace of God.*"**

- Acts 13:43
  Now when the congregation was broken up, many of the Jews and religious proselytes followed Paul and Barnabas: who, speaking to them, **persuaded them to continue in the grace of God.**

> ✔ **#4 We are to "*continue*" in "*faith.*"**

- Acts 14:22
  Confirming the souls of the disciples, *and* **exhorting them to continue in the faith**, and that we must through much tribulation enter into the kingdom of God.

> ✔ **#5 We are to "*continue*" in God's "*goodness.*"**

- Romans 11:22
  Behold therefore the goodness and severity of God: on them which fell, severity; but toward thee, goodness, if thou **continue in *his* goodness**: otherwise thou also shalt be cut off.

> ✔ **#6 We are to "*continue*" in "*prayer.*"**

- Colossians 4:2
  Continue in prayer, and watch in the same with thanksgiving;

> ✔ **#7 We are to "*continue*" in "*brotherly love.*"**

- Hebrews 13:1
  Let brotherly love continue.
  Paul told Timothy to "*continue*" in the things he had learned from Paul. What did Paul teach concerning various things? Here are a few.
- Romans 16:17
  Now I beseech you, brethren, **mark them which cause divisions and offences contrary to the doctrine which ye have learned; and avoid them.**

- Philippians 4:8
  Finally, brethren, **whatsoever things are true, whatsoever things** are **honest, whatsoever things** are **just, whatsoever things** are **pure**, whatsoever things are lovely, whatsoever things are of good report; if *there be* any virtue, and if *there be* any praise, **think on these things**.
  You might say that you were taught the truth when you were younger. When I went to college, I was taught things that were against what I was taught in my youth.
  Paul is telling Pastor Timothy (and it applies to all of us as well) that he should follow the truth he was taught by Paul and not to vary from it, no matter what others might teach. Timothy was *"assured"* (PISTOO) of these truths, and we should be also. This word means *"to make firm, establish, to be firmly persuaded of, to be assured of."*
- Isaiah 32:17
  And the work of righteousness shall be peace; and the effect of righteousness quietness and **assurance for ever**.

"Assurance" Is Needed

If we don't have *"assurance"* of our salvation, we are in a pitiful condition indeed. If we don't have *"assurance"* we are going to Heaven we have an eternal problem. Do you have *"assurance"*? Are you sure you are saved?

- Colossians 2:2
  That their hearts might be comforted, being knit together in love, and **unto all riches of the full assurance of understanding**, to the acknowledgement of the mystery of God, and of the Father, and of Christ;
- 1 Thessalonians 1:5
  For **our gospel came** not unto you in word only, but also in power, and in the Holy Ghost, and **in much assurance**; as ye know what manner of men we were among you for your sake.

Elements Of The "Gospel" Message

The gospel message says that, in our natural condition, everyone in the world is lost and bound for the everlasting fires of Hell. The Lord Jesus Christ came to save every person in the world who will genuinely accept and receive Him as their Saviour. He died for the sins of the world. This genuine faith in that Saviour is what saves us and gives us the *"assurance"* we need to have. If you don't have that *"assurance,"* ask the Lord to give it to you. If you are not saved and born-again, you can't have any *"assurance"* of eternal life because you are not saved in the first place.

2 Timothy 3:15

"And that from a child thou hast known the holy scriptures, which are able to make thee wise unto salvation through faith which is in Christ Jesus."

Now we come to the seven purposes of the Scripture.

✔ **The 1st Purpose of the Bible–It is *"able to make us wise unto salvation."***

God has given us His Words found in the Old and the New Testaments. In this verse He tells us that in the *"holy Scriptures"* we can find *"salvation through faith which is in Christ Jesus."*

Salvation's Source–The Bible

Nowhere but in the *"Scriptures"* can anyone find out about God's plan of salvation through genuine faith in His beloved Son. For this reason, we must protect and preserve the Hebrew, Aramaic, and Greek Words underlying our King James Bible and the King James Bible itself which is the only accurate English translation of those preserved Words.

- Matthew 21:42
  Jesus saith unto them, **Did ye never read in the scriptures,** The stone which the builders rejected, the same is become the head of the corner: this is the Lord's doing, and it is marvellous in our eyes?
- Matthew 22:29
  Jesus answered and said unto them, **Ye do err, not knowing the scriptures,** nor the power of God.

The Yearly Bible Reading Schedule

We must know the *"Scriptures."* That is why I encourage everyone to read through the Bible at least once per year. This can be done at the rate of 85 verses per day as found in my YEARLY BIBLE READING SCHEDULE. My reading of the entire Bible on one MP-3 disk can be ordered at this URL, http://www.biblefortoday.org/idx_bible_reading.htm if you wish to order it.

- Matthew 26:54
  But how then shall **the scriptures be fulfilled,** that thus it must be?
  This is talking about Calvary's cross which was predicted in the Old Testament *"Scriptures."*
- Matthew 26:56
  But all this was done, **that the scriptures of the prophets might be fulfilled.** Then all the disciples forsook him, and fled.
- Luke 24:27
  And beginning at Moses and all the prophets, **he expounded unto them in all the scriptures the things concerning himself.**
  The Old Testament is replete with things concerning the Lord Jesus Christ.
- Luke 24:45
  Then opened he their understanding, **that they might understand the scriptures,**

No Old Testament "Corrections"

The Lord Jesus Christ never made a correction in the Old Testament *"Scriptures"* that He had in His day. The Hebrew *"Scriptures"* were the same when the Lord Jesus Christ was on earth as when Moses wrote them. The Lord Jesus Christ was the source of the Words found in both the Old and the New Testaments.

- John 5:39
  Search the scriptures; for in them ye think ye have eternal life: and they are they which testify of me.

  We must obey the command of our Saviour and search the Scriptures daily.
- Acts 17:2
  And Paul, as his manner was, went in unto them, and three sabbath days **reasoned with them out of the scriptures**,

  Paul reasoned with these people out of the *"Scriptures."* All he had was the Old Testament. Paul knew the *"Scriptures."*

Knowing The Bible

Do you know the Bible?

- Acts 17:11
  These were more noble than those in Thessalonica, in that **they received the word with all readiness of mind, and searched the scriptures daily**, whether those things were so.

  My wife and I went to high school in Berea, Ohio, graduating in 1945. I try to be like the *"Bereans"* of the Bible and *"receive the Word with all readiness of mind"* and *"search the Scriptures daily."* I hope you are also like those *"Bereans."*
- Acts 18:24
  And a certain Jew named Apollos, born at Alexandria, an eloquent man, and **mighty in the scriptures**, came to Ephesus.

Be "Mighty In The Scriptures"

Every Christian should be "*mighty in the Scriptures.*"

- Acts 18:28
  For he mightily convinced the Jews, *and that* publickly, **shewing by the scriptures that Jesus was Christ**.
  Can you take the Old Testament and prove to the Jews of our day that Jesus is the Messiah?
- Romans 1:2
  (Which he had promised afore **by his prophets in the holy scriptures**,)
- Romans 15:4
  For whatsoever things were written aforetime were written for our learning, that we **through patience and comfort of the scriptures might have hope**.

The Bible Gives "Comfort"

"*Scriptures*" really give us "*comfort.*"

- 1 Corinthians 15:3
  For I delivered unto you first of all that which I also received, how that **Christ died for our sins according to the scriptures**;

Christ Died For the Sins of Everyone

According to the "Scriptures" of the Old Testament, the Lord Jesus Christ "*died for our sins.*"

- 1 Corinthians 15:4
  And that he was buried, and that **he rose again the third day according to the scriptures**:
  The Old Testament teaches the resurrection of the Lord Jesus Christ on the "*third day.*" Paul preached that.

- **2 Peter 3:16**
  As also in all *his* epistles, speaking in them of these things; in which are some things hard to be understood, which they that are **unlearned and unstable wrest, as *they do* also the other scriptures**, unto their own destruction.

Peter referred to Paul's letters as *"the other Scriptures."* Here is a stamp of approval from Peter on Paul's letters.

Paul reminds Timothy that he knew of the *"Scriptures"* at an early age (*"from a child."*) He learned these from his mother, no doubt. She was a Jewess (Acts 16:1).

Teach Children God's Words

Children can learn the Words of God at an early age, just as Timothy. You and I can teach them and read to them, and they will understand.

---

2 Timothy 3:16

"All scripture is given by inspiration of God, and is profitable for doctrine, for reproof, for correction, for instruction in righteousness."

This is the chief verse in the Bible for the doctrine of God's verbal, plenary, inspiration (VPI) of the Bible. God's purposes are given to us.

✔ **The 1st purpose of the Bible involves its "inspiration."**

. Paul is speaking about the *"Scripture"* which refers to the **process** used by God for the original composition of the Hebrew and Aramaic Old Testament Words. I believe, by extension, that the same **process** was used by God for the original composition of the Greek Words of the New Testament.

Only Original Words "God-Breathed"

The words, *"given by inspiration of God"* are the translation of just one Greek Word (THEOPNEUSTOS). This is a compound Word composed of THEOS (*"God"*) and PNEUSTOS which comes from PNEO (*"to breathe"*). It means literally *"breathed out by God"* or *"God-breathed."*

This "God-breathed" process is plenary or full. It refers to "*all*" (PASA) of the original Hebrew, Aramaic, and Greek Words in all the books of the Bible from Genesis through Revelation. Not a single Bible book is excepted.

Inspiration--"Words" Versus "Word"

By the term, "*Scripture*," this "*God-breathed*" process refers to the original Bible Words (GRAPHE) of Hebrew and Aramaic of the Old Testament at the time. By extension, this would also refer to the New Testament Words that have already been written and are continuing to be written in Paul's day. This is "*verbal*" inspiration. It does not refer to only the "*thoughts, message, concepts, or ideas*." It refers to the Words.

Though this process has never been repeated, the product of that process is "*inspired Words*." Therefore exact copies of those Hebrew, Aramaic and Greek Words can be called "*inspired Words*" even though they were not made by the process of God's inspiration. I believe those original Hebrew, Aramaic, and Greek Words of the Bible have been verbally and plenarily preserved (VPP) in the Traditional Hebrew, Aramaic, and Greek Words underlying the King James Bible.

Translations Are Not "Inspired Of God"

One further thing regarding God's inspiration of the Bible. I believe that neither the process nor the product of inspiration refer to Bible translations in any way. God did not breathe out any other Words in any other languages except Hebrew, Aramaic, and Greek. No translations should be referred to "*inspired of God*" or "*inspired*" because God did not "*breathe them out*." They were translated by men, they were not "breathed out by God."

This view differs strongly both with the followers of Peter Ruckman and also with others who use and defend the King James Bible (or any other translation) and yet wrongfully refer to it as being "*inspired.*"

✔ **The 2nd Purpose of the Bible–It is "*profitable for doctrine."***

Before we look at the purpose of *"doctrine,"* let us look at a few verses that show some *"profitable"* things in the Bible.
- **Acts 20:20**
  And how **I kept back nothing that was profitable *unto you*,** but have shewed you, and have taught you publickly, and from house to house,
- **2 Timothy 4:11**
  Only Luke is with me. **Take Mark, and bring him with thee: for he is profitable to me for the ministry**.
- **Titus 3:8**
  This is a faithful saying, and these things I will that thou affirm constantly, that they which have believed in God might be careful to maintain good works. **These things are good and profitable unto men.**
- **Philemon 11**
  Which in time past was to thee unprofitable, **but now profitable to thee and to me:**

The Bible Is For "Doctrine"

This second purpose of the Bible is for *"doctrine"* or teaching. Our Bible should be the very source of every *"doctrine"* that we believe and teach. That's why it is so important that we have the right Bible. The King James Bible in English is the right Bible with the right underlying and plenarily and verbally preserved original Hebrew, Aramaic, and Greek Words.

Some preachers say they don't like *"doctrine."* They just want to preach about life, and philosophy with the use of many stories and illustrations. No, as Paul told Pastor Timothy, preachers today must faithfully use the Bible to teach its "doctrines."

✔ **The 3rd Purpose of the Bible—It is *"profitable for reproof."***

The word for *"reproof"* is ELEGCHOS. It refers to exposing or shedding light on something. If you shed the light on cockroaches what do they do? They run away. That's what God wants us to do. The Bible sheds the light on

the sins in our life so that we might put them away.
- Proverbs 10:17
  He *is in* the way of life that keepeth instruction: but **he that refuseth reproof erreth**.
- Proverbs 15:5
  A fool despiseth his father's instruction: but **he that regardeth reproof is prudent.**
- Proverbs 15:32
  He that refuseth instruction despiseth his own soul: but **he that heareth reproof getteth understanding**.
- Proverbs 17:10
  A reproof entereth more into a wise man than an hundred stripes into a fool.
- Proverbs 29:15
  The rod and reproof give wisdom: but a child left *to himself* bringeth his mother to shame.

  The *Scripture* points out our sins as we read it.

> ✔ **The 4th Purpose of the Bible–It is *"profitable for correction."***

The Word for *"correction"* is EPANORTHOSIS. It is made up of three Greek words: EPI (*"upon"*), ANA (*"again,"*) and ORTHOSIS (*"straight."*) The root *"ortho"* is taken from the Greek language and means *"straight." "Orthodoxy"* means *"straight praise." "Orthography"* means *"straight writing or spelling."* Many other illustrations could be mentioned. The resultant meaning in this Word, EPANORTHOSIS, is *"to straighten again."* One source says the meaning of this is:

"restoration to an upright or right state; correction, improvement of life or character"

When the Words of God show us our sins with reproof, God wants us then to take the *"correction"* found in His Words and be *"straightened out"* once again and restored to the place of God's blessing.
- Proverbs 3:11
  My son, despise not the chastening of the LORD; **neither be weary of his correction:**
  The Lord wants to *"straighten us out."*
- Proverbs 15:10
  Correction *is* grievous unto him that forsaketh the way: *and* **he that hateth reproof shall die.**

2 Timothy 3:16

- Proverbs 22:15
  Foolishness *is* bound in the heart of a child; *but* **the rod of correction shall drive it far from him.**
- Proverbs 23:13
  Withhold not correction from the child: for *if* thou beatest him with the rod, he shall not die.

I was a teacher in the School District of Philadelphia for 19 years. I know exactly how a child turns out who has not been *"corrected"* by his parents.

✔ **The 5th Purpose of the Bible—It is *"profitable for instruction in righteousness."***

Except for the Bible, there is no other place in all the world where the born-again Christian, or anyone else, can find '*instruction in righteousness.*" God's *"instruction"* is invaluable for the believer.

- Proverbs 1:3
  To receive the instruction of wisdom, justice, and judgment, and equity;
- Proverbs 19:20
  Hear counsel, and **receive instruction**, that thou mayest be wise in thy latter end.

The word for *"instruction"* is PAIDEIA. It has various meanings, depending on the context.

"the whole training and education of children (which relates to the cultivation of mind and morals, and employs for this purpose now commands and admonitions, now reproof and punishment) It also includes the training and care of the body; whatever in adults also cultivates the soul, esp. by correcting mistakes and curbing passions; instruction which aims at increasing virtue; chastisement, chastening, (of the evils with which God visits men for their amendment)."

"Instruction in Righteousness" Needed

It almost seems like God is telling us we are babes and need some training and *"instruction in righteousness."* This is true of every born-again Christian. We are indeed like babes and need the *"instruction in righteousness"* that can come only from God's Words. This is one more reason why we must use and defend the King James Bible and its underlying plenarily and verbally preserved Hebrew, Aramaic and Greek Words that underlie it. Because there is no other English Bible translation that contains an accurate translation of ALL of the Words of God in English. We need ALL of these Words for *"instruction in righteousness."*

2 Timothy 3:17

"That the man of God may be perfect throughly furnished unto all good works."

> ✔ **The 6th Purpose of the Bible–It is so that** *"the man of God may be perfect."*

The word for *"perfect"* is ARTIOS. It means: *"fitted; complete, perfect; having reference apparently to 'special aptitude for given uses'"* This does not mean sinless perfection. It signifies a maturity and full growth which is so vital and necessary in this world of spiritual babies.

- Romans 12:2
  And be not conformed to this world: but be ye transformed by the renewing of your mind, that ye may prove what *is* that good, and acceptable, and **perfect, will of God.**
- 2 Corinthians 13:11
  Finally, brethren, farewell. **Be perfect**, be of good comfort, be of one mind, live in peace; and the God of love and peace shall be with you.
- Colossians 1:28
  Whom we preach, warning every man, and teaching every man in all wisdom; **that we may present every man perfect in Christ Jesus:**

- Colossians 4:12
  Epaphras, who is *one* of you, a servant of Christ, saluteth you, always labouring fervently for you in prayers, **that ye may stand perfect and complete in all the will of God**.
- Hebrews 13:21
  Make you perfect in every good work to do his will, working in you that which is wellpleasing in his sight, through Jesus Christ; to whom *be* glory for ever and ever. Amen.
- James 1:4
  But **let patience have** *her* **perfect work, that ye may be perfect and entire, wanting nothing**.
- 1 Peter 5:10
  But the God of all grace, who hath called us unto his eternal glory by Christ Jesus, **after that ye have suffered a while, make you perfect,** stablish, strengthen, settle *you*.

> ✔ **The 7th Purpose of the Bible–It is to be *"throughly furnished unto all good works."***

In the Bible, we see repeatedly that our God reproves bad works, but approves *"good works."*

> ### Furnished to "Good Works"
> What unregenerate man considers to be *"good works"* are not necessarily those that God calls *"good works."* The Bible is the only standard from Heaven where the *"man of God"* and all born-again Christians can be *"throughly furnished unto all good works."* We cannot be saved by *"good works,"* but after we are saved, God expects *"good works"* to follow.

- Matthew 5:16
  Let your light so shine before men, **that they may see your good works**, and glorify your Father which is in Heaven.

"Good Works" Found In The Bible

The Bible is *"throughly"* (an old variation of *"thoroughly"*) furnishing us with a vast number of *"good works."* If we don't know what to do, the Bible has the answer. Read the Bible and see the *"good works"* we are to do.

- Ephesians 2:8-10
  For by grace are ye saved through faith; and that not of yourselves: it is the gift of God: **Not of works**, lest any man should boast. ⁹For we are his workmanship, created in Christ Jesus unto good works, which God hath before ordained that we should walk in them.

Not Saved By "Good Works"

We are not saved by good works, but we are created unto good works.

- 1 Timothy 2:10
  But (which becometh women professing godliness) with good works.

"Good Works" As An "Adornment"

"Good works" are looked at in this verse as an adornment.

- 1 Timothy 6:18
  That they do good, **that they be rich in good works**, ready to distribute, willing to communicate;
- Titus 2:7
  In all things shewing thyself a pattern of good works: in doctrine *shewing* uncorruptness, gravity, sincerity,

- Titus 2:14
  Who gave himself for us, that he might redeem us from all iniquity, and purify unto himself a peculiar people, **zealous of good works**.
- Titus 3:8
  This is a faithful saying, and these things I will that thou affirm constantly, that **they which have believed in God might be careful to maintain good works**. These things are good and profitable unto men.

How are saved people going to maintain *"good works"* if we don't know what they are? Where do we find them? Every *"good work"* that we need to do is right here in the Scriptures. Every born-again Christian should read his Bible closely. When he follows its precepts, he is doing a *"good work."*

- Titus 3:14
  And **let ours also learn to maintain good works** for necessary uses, that they be not unfruitful.

When the maintenance light comes on in your car or your computer it reminds you to maintain service. That is what we must do in our Christian walk. We must maintain good works. We aren't supposed to do good works for just a little while, but for our whole life.

- Hebrews 10:24
  And let us consider one another to provoke unto love and to good works:
- 1 Peter 2:12
  Having your conversation honest among the Gentiles: that, whereas they speak against you as evildoers, they may by *your* good works, which they shall behold, glorify God in the day of visitation.

The World Observes Christians

The whole world is looking at the believers. These are the principles and purposes for the Words of God. That's why we need to read daily and know thoroughly God's Words.

DEEP IN GOD'S WORD

Deep in God's Word there are hidden
Such wonders, I gasp to behold
The purpose of God and the mysteries
The Spirit of Truth doth unfold.

Hidden behind words so common,
Yet plain to the heart that will look,
Are the treasures of Truth and His glory;
They are here in my wonderful Book.

Over and over and over again,
I read--and the pages are new,
I sing in my heart and I praise Him
And behold what the reading will do.

Old, tho the same old story
The Gospel, the good news from God
It warms all my soul with its kindness,
Seeing now the dark road I once trod.

Chosen in Him and elected
predestined, conformed to His Son
Placed in position as brethren,
With God it is already done.

My mind is so eager to study;
My heart is so slow to believe.
But here on the page it is written;
And the Spirit leads me to receive.

2 Timothy 3:17

How can I ever stop seeking?
The profit is greater each day;
And I find it is Christ I discover
As I meditate, study, and pray.

I find the fullness of the Spirit
Is the fruit that God wants me to bear;
The "much fruit" which pleaseth the Father
Is Christ manifest everywhere.
His virtue, His Person, His Glory,
The Blue and the Red and the Gold,
The wonder that I am beloved--
All that in my BOOK, I behold.
(By Gertrude Grace Sanborn
From *With Tears in My Heart* (written in 1945)

Second Timothy
Chapter Four

2 Timothy 4:1

"I charge thee therefore before God, and the Lord Jesus Christ, who shall judge the quick and the dead at his appearing and his kingdom."

Here's a very solemn charge that Paul is giving to Pastor Timothy. This charge is before God and before the Lord Jesus Christ, His Son. It shows the equality and unity of God the Father and God the Son. Notice that it is the Lord Jesus Christ Who will *"judge the quick and the dead at his appearing and his kingdom."* This refers to the living and the dead, the saved and the lost.

- Acts 10:42
  And he commanded us to preach unto the people, and to testify that **it is he** [the Lord Jesus Christ] **which was ordained of God** *to be* **the Judge of quick and dead**.
- Hebrews 4:12
  For **the word of God** *is* **quick**, and powerful, and sharper than any twoedged sword, piercing even to the dividing asunder of soul and spirit, and of the joints and marrow, and *is* a discerner of the thoughts and intents of the heart.
- 1 Peter 4:5
  Who shall give account to him that is ready to judge the quick and the dead.

- 1 Corinthians 3:10-15
  According to the grace of God which is given unto me, as a wise masterbuilder, I have laid the foundation, and another buildeth thereon. But let every man take heed how he buildeth thereupon. ¹For other foundation can no man lay than that is laid, which is Jesus Christ. ²Now if any man build upon this foundation gold, silver, precious stones, wood, hay, stubble; ³Every man's work shall be made manifest: for the day shall declare it, because it shall be revealed by fire; and **the fire shall try every man's work of what sort it is.** ⁴**If any man's work abide which he hath built thereupon, he shall receive a reward.** ⁵If any man's work shall be burned, he shall suffer loss: but he himself shall be saved; yet so as by fire.

The Judgment Seat Of Christ

The Lord Jesus Christ is talking to Christians in this verse. He is going to be the Judge for the saved ones (the quick) at the Judgment Seat of Christ. He is also going to be the Judge of the lost (the *"dead in trespasses and sins"* (Ephesians 2:1) at the Great White Throne Judgment.

- Revelation 20:11-15
  And **I saw a great white throne**, and him that sat on it, from whose face the earth and the Heaven fled away; and there was found no place for them. ²And I saw the dead, small and great, stand before God; and the books were opened: and another book was opened, which is *the book* of life: and **the dead were judged out of those things which were written in the books**, according to their works. ³And **the sea gave up the dead which were in it; and death and hell delivered up the dead which were in them:** and they were judged every man according to their works. ⁴And death and hell were cast into the lake of fire. This is the second death. ⁵And whosoever was not found written in the book of life was cast into the lake of fire.

The Great White Throne Judgment

These are the lost ones (the dead ones). You can't take a body and throw it into the sea and hope that that body will never be judged because the body will be lost in the sea. No, the sea is going to *"give up the dead."* "Death and Hell" will also *"deliver up the dead which are in them."* *"Hell"* in this place is the word "Hades," or the unseen world.

I believe that the phrase *"at his appearing"* refers to the rapture of the saved ones. That is when the saved will be judged at the Judgment Seat of Christ.

- 1 Timothy 6:14
  That thou keep *this* commandment without spot, unrebukeable, **until the appearing of our Lord Jesus Christ**:
- 1 Peter 1:7
  That the trial of your faith, being much more precious than of gold that perisheth, though it be tried with fire, might be found unto praise and honour and glory **at the appearing of Jesus Christ:**

The Lord Jesus Christ The Judge

The Lord Jesus Christ is the Judge of the entire world. He's the Judge of the saved at the Judgment Seat of Christ. He's the Judge of the lost at the Great White Throne Judgment.

2 Timothy 4:2

"Preach the word, be instant, in season, out of season, reprove, rebuke, exhort with all longsuffering and doctrine."

Our church repeats this verse at every Lord's Day morning service. We call it *"The Preacher's Purpose."* We say this each Lord's Day because this is what I believe to be the Biblical purpose of the pastor of every local church–to *"preach the Word"* of God.

The Command To "Preach" The Words

The word for *"preach"* here is KERUSSO. It is in the Greek imperative mood. It is not merely a suggestion, but it is a command by the Apostle Paul to Pastor Timothy. I believe it should be a command as well for pastors today.

It means:
"to be a herald, to officiate as a herald; to proclaim after the manner of a herald; always with the suggestion of formality, gravity and an authority which must be listened to and obeyed; to publish, proclaim openly: something which has been done; used of the public proclamation of the gospel and matters pertaining to it, made by John the Baptist, by Jesus, by the apostles and other Christian teachers"

A *"herald"* does not change the message when he is given a message by the king. He is the king's emissary. His mission is simply to proclaim the message that the king has written.

Be A Herald Of All God's Words

That is what a preacher is to do as a *"herald"* of God's Divine Words. First of all, the preacher cannot *"preach the Word"* unless he knows where that *"Word"* is and holds to it without deviation. This is why I stand for the King James Bible in English and the Hebrew, Aramaic, and Greek Words that underlie it. That's why I want the Bible to be translated accurately from the proper Hebrew and Greek texts into all the languages of the world. I believe that the most systematic and thorough way to *"preach the Word"* (which implies all of the Words of God) is to preach on a verse-by-verse basis through Bible books. In this way every Word of God will be *"heralded."*

As to when this *"preaching the Word"* is to be done by Timothy, it is to be *"in season"* or *"out of season."* This means that Timothy was to perform this sort of *"preaching"* whether it was convenient or inconvenient, whether it was seasonable or unseasonable, whether it was well received or ill received. He was not to cease from this practice. Because this has not been done in local churches through the centuries, modernism, apostasy, post modernism, and the emerging church have entered and now control many denominations.

Preaching is found in many verses of the Bible.
- Matthew 10:27
  What I tell you in darkness, *that* speak ye in light: and what ye hear in the ear, *that* **preach ye upon the housetops**.
- Mark 1:38
  And he said unto them, Let us go into the next towns, **that I may preach there also:** for therefore came I forth.
- Acts 5:42
  And daily in the temple, and in every house, **they ceased not to teach and preach Jesus Christ**.
- Acts 10:42
  And **he commanded us to preach unto the people**, and to testify that it is he which was ordained of God *to be* the Judge of quick and dead.
- Romans 1:15
  So, as much as in me is, **I am ready to preach the gospel** to you that are at Rome also.
- Romans 10:15
  And how shall they preach, except they be sent? as it is written, **How beautiful are the feet of them that preach the gospel of peace**, and bring glad tidings of good things!

Preachers should not decide for themselves that they want to be a preacher. They must be sent and called by the Lord.
- 1 Corinthians 9:16
  For **though I preach the gospel**, I have nothing to glory of: for necessity is laid upon me; yea, **woe is unto me, if I preach not the gospel!**
- Galatians 1:15-16
  But when it pleased God, who separated me from my mother's womb, and called *me* by his grace, to reveal his Son in me, **that I might preach him among the heathen**; immediately I conferred not with flesh and blood:
- Ephesians 3:8
  Unto me, who am less than the least of all saints, is this grace given, that I should preach among the Gentiles the unsearchable riches of Christ;

In "*preaching the Word*," Paul commanded Timothy to do three things along with two other things. He said: *"reprove, rebuke, exhort with all longsuffering and doctrine."*

Pastors Should "Reprove"

In the first place, as pastors today should, Timothy was to *"reprove."*

The Greek word is ELEGCHO, It has various meanings.
"to convict, refute, confute; generally with a suggestion of shame of the person convicted; by conviction <u>to bring to the light, to expose</u>; to find fault with, correct; by word; to reprehend severely, chide, admonish, reprove; to call to account, show one his fault, demand an explanation; by deed; to chasten, to punish"
- Ephesians 5:11
  And have no fellowship with the unfruitful works of darkness, but rather **reprove** *them*.

Pastors Should "Rebuke"

In the second place, as pastors today should, Timothy was to *"rebuke."*

This is one valid reason why pastors are to be *"elders"* both in physical maturity and maturity in the Christian faith, but also in age. This will enable them to do a wiser job in *"rebuke"* from the Words of God.
The Greek word is EPITIMAO. It has various meanings.
"to show honour to, to honour; to raise the price of; to adjudge, award, in the sense of merited penalty; to tax with fault, rate, <u>chide, rebuke, reprove, censure severely; to admonish or charge sharply</u>."
- Luke 17:3
  Take heed to yourselves: If thy brother trespass against thee, **rebuke him**; and if he repent, forgive him.
- Philippians 2:15
  That ye may be blameless and harmless, the sons of God, **without rebuke**, in the midst of a crooked and perverse nation, among whom ye shine as lights in the world;

- 1 Timothy 5:1
  Rebuke not an elder, but intreat *him* as a father; *and* the younger men as brethren;
- 1 Timothy 5:20-21
  Them that sin rebuke before all, that others also may fear.
  ²¹ I charge *thee* before God, and the Lord Jesus Christ, and the elect angels, that thou observe these things without preferring one before another, doing nothing by partiality.
- Titus 1:13
  This witness is true. Wherefore **rebuke them sharply**, that they may be sound in the faith;
- Revelation 3:19
  As many as I love, **I rebuke** and chasten: be zealous therefore, and repent.

Pastors Should "Exhort"
In the third place, as pastors today should, Timothy was to *"exhort."*

The Greek word is PARAKALEO. It has many varied meanings.
"to call to one's side, call for, summon; to address, speak to, (call to, call upon), which may be done in the way of exhortation, entreaty, comfort, instruction, etc.; to admonish, exhort; to beg, entreat, beseech; to strive to appease by entreaty; to console, to encourage and strengthen by consolation, to comfort; to receive consolation, be comforted; to encourage, strengthen; exhorting and comforting and encouraging; to instruct, teach"
- Titus 2:6
  Young men likewise exhort to be sober minded.
- Titus 2:15
  These things speak, and exhort, and rebuke with all authority. Let no man despise thee.
- Hebrews 3:13
  But **exhort one another daily**, while it is called To day; lest any of you be hardened through the deceitfulness of sin.

- 1 Peter 5:1
  The elders which are among you I exhort, who am also an elder, and a witness of the sufferings of Christ, and also a partaker of the glory that shall be revealed:
- Jude 3
  Beloved, when I gave all diligence to write unto you of the common salvation, **it was needful for me to write unto you, and exhort *you*** that ye should earnestly contend for the faith which was once delivered unto the saints.

All of the *"preaching the Word"* by *"reproving, rebuking, and exhorting"* was to be done with *"longsuffering and doctrine."* The *"longsuffering"* must be present in order to *"put up with"* the people to whom the pastor preaches. It will help him because he will need it because of the resistance on the part of carnal believers that comes when the Words of God *"reprove,"* and *"rebuke."*

Pastors Should Preach Sound Doctrine

With the faithful *"preaching the Word,"* there must be *"doctrine."* This must be sound and true *"doctrine."* It must correct any false *"doctrine"* that is all around us. It must also encourage born-again Christians to seek daily the profound teachings of the Words of God as they read their Bibles.

2 Timothy 4:3

"For the time will come when they will not endure sound doctrine, but after their own lusts, shall they heap to themselves teachers having itching ears."

No Endurance Of "Sound Doctrine"

When Paul wrote *"the time will come,"* it was still future to him. I believe firmly that *"the time"* has already come. The people in most churches do not want to *"endure sound doctrine."* Instead they want light sermons, book reviews, or one story after another with little, if any, reference to the Bible or its *"doctrine."*

"*Sound doctrine*" is mentioned in Scripture in other places as well.
- 1 Timothy 1:10
  For whoremongers, for them that defile themselves with mankind, for menstealers, for liars, for perjured persons, and if there be **any other thing that is contrary to sound doctrine**;
- Titus 1:9
  Holding fast the faithful word as he hath been taught, that he may be able **by sound doctrine both to exhort and to convince the gainsayers**.
- Titus 2:1
  But **speak thou the things which become sound doctrine**:

Once people will not "*endure sound doctrine*," they will do the next thing mentioned in this verse. They will follow "*their own lusts.*" These "*lusts*" will cause them to "*heap to themselves teachers.*" These "*teachers*" will be false in their teaching. The Greek word for "*heap*" is EPISOREUO. Among other things, it means "*to accumulate in piles.*" This would seem to indicate that these false teachers are more numerous than any would imagine.

The reason people will "*heap up*" these false teachers is that they have "*itching ears.*" It is clear from the Greek structure that it is the people rather than the "*teachers*" who have the "*itching ears.*" The Greek word for "*itching*" is KNETHO. It comes from a primary word (KNAO) which means "*to scrape.*"—The resultant meanings are:
"*to scratch, tickle, make to itch; to itch; desirous of hearing something pleasant*"

"Itching Ears" Need Scratching

From this figure of speech, it means that these people who had no interest in "*sound doctrine*," could not get their "*itch*" scratched with truth. They had to hear something "*pleasant*" to their ears so their ears would stop "*itching.*"

Sad to say, that is the state of our churches today. They have people with continual "*itching ears*" that need scratching. They want to be made comfortable. They don't want any preaching about sin, about Hell, about eternal death, about the Lake of Fire, about what people do. The churches just want happy, smiling, "doctrineless" sermons. Our churches today are *"piling up"* teachers to scratch their *"ears."* That is why liberalism, *"post-modernism,"* and the *"emerging church"* heresies have come into our mainline churches.

2 Timothy 4:4
"And they shall turn away their ears from the truth, and shall be turned unto fables."

Once anyone's *"ears"* are *"turned away from the truth,"* what's left? They turn to *"fables"*! The Greek word for this is MUTHOS. Though it sometimes means *"a narrative or a story,"* yet the word also means, as in this context, *"a fiction, an invention, and a falsehood."* They are fairy stories.

Accuracy of the King James Bible

We must stick to the *"truth."* God's *"truth"* is found in an accurate Bible. I believe that the original Words of Hebrew, Aramaic, and Greek have been preserved in those Hebrew, Aramaic, and Greek Words underlying our King James Bible. The King James Bible is the only accurate English translation of those original preserved Words. As such, God's *"truth"* is found therein.

Gnostic Versions Turn Away Ears

As many have departed from the King James Bible and its underlying Words, this verse is being fulfilled. This includes those who follow the Revised Standard Version, the New Revised Standard Version, the New American Standard Version, the New International Version, the English Standard Version, and others. All of these English versions are based on the Gnostic Greek words which have 8,000 differences compared to the Traditional Greek New Testament underlying the King James Bible. Because of this, there are over 356 doctrinal passages where they have *"turned away their ears from the truth."*

- John 4:24
  God *is* a Spirit: and they that worship him **must worship *him* in spirit and in truth**.
- John 8:32
  And **ye shall know the truth, and the truth shall make you free**.
- John 14:6
  Jesus saith unto him, **I am the way, the truth**, and the life: no man cometh unto the Father, but by me.
- John 16:13
  Howbeit when he, **the Spirit of truth**, is come, he will guide you into all truth: for he shall not speak of himself; but whatsoever he shall hear, *that* shall he speak: and he will shew you things to come.
- John 17:17
  Sanctify them through thy truth: thy word is truth.

What if you have the wrong "*Word*"? If you have a translation that doesn't have all the Words of "*truth*," how can you be "*sanctified*" or set apart? In English, you have true confidence only in the King James Bible for the accurate Words of "*truth*."

- Romans 1:25
  Who changed the truth of God into a lie, and worshipped and served the creature more than the Creator, who is blessed for ever. Amen.

This is exactly what our false Bible versions and perversions have been doing ever since the 1881 English Revised Version (ERV). This includes the ASV (1901), the RSV, the ERSV, the NASV, the NIV, the ESV, the Message, the Broadman/Holman Version, and many more. Because these versions are based on a New Testament that have 8,000 differences with the Traditional Received Greek text and 356 differences in doctrinal passages, they have to this extent "*changed the truth of God into a lie*."

- Galatians 4:16
  Am I therefore become your enemy, because I tell you the truth?

Many people get upset when they are told the "*truth*." "*Truth*," even if it hurts us, should be welcomed, accepted, and embraced.

- **Ephesians 6:14**
  Stand therefore, **having your loins girt about with truth**, and having on the breastplate of righteousness;

  If you are a battle warrior for the Lord Jesus Christ, God has given you many weapons. One of them is *"truth"* around the loins. Someone has pointed out that the *"loins"* include the sexual organs that millions of boys, girls, men, and women are abusing by fornication, adultery, lesbianism, male homosexuality, bestiality, and other sexual perversions. Only by following the *"truths"* of the Bible, which speaks out against these sins, can this kind of iniquity be corrected. The only proper Bible in English is the King James Bible. It has the *"truth"* by which to *"stand"* in these evil days.

- **2 Timothy 2:15**
  Study to shew thyself approved unto God, a workman that needeth not to be ashamed, **rightly dividing the word of truth**.

  We must *"rightly divide"* the *"truth"* God has given us in the Bible. That's why we teach the dispensational position of our Scriptures.

  The result of turning from the "truth" of the Words of God is the turning to *"fables."*

- **1 Timothy 1:4**
  Neither give heed to fables and endless genealogies, which minister questions, rather than godly edifying which is in faith: so do.

- **1 Timothy 4:7**
  But **refuse profane and old wives' fables**, and exercise thyself *rather* unto godliness.

- **Titus 1:14**
  Not giving heed to Jewish fables, and commandments of men, that turn from the truth.

- **2 Peter 1:16**
  For **we have not followed cunningly devised fables**, when we made known unto you the power and coming of our Lord Jesus Christ, but were eyewitnesses of his majesty.

Preaching Gnostic "Fables"

I believe that we have all too many preachers and teachers today who teach *"fables"* by using versions based on Gnostic Greek Texts. We must be careful. Keep your ears and your eyes on the *"truth"* of God found fully in English in the King James Bible and its underlying Hebrew, Aramaic, and Greek Words.

2 Timothy 4:5

"But watch thou in all things, endure afflictions, do the work of an evangelist, make full proof of thy ministry."

In this verse, Paul is commanding Pastor Timothy to do four things: He is (1) to *watch,* (2) to *endure afflictions,* (3) to *do the work of an evangelist,* and (4) to *make full proof of his ministry.*

✔ **1. Pastor Timothy was to *"watch."***

The word used for *"watch"* is NEPHO. That word and the adjective that goes with it (NEPHALIOS) have a root meaning of abstinence from wine or any alcohol. They should be *"sober"* so they would be able to *"watch"* and observe things for the Lord.

Watch Out for Doctrinal Drifts

The Pastor must be alert to all of the movements and drifts around him. He must know what is happening to him in whatever land he might be and to warn his people concerning the evil around them.

- Matthew 24:42
  Watch therefore: for ye know not what hour your Lord doth come.
  We today also must be *"watching"* in all areas

- Matthew 26:41
  Watch and pray, that ye enter not into temptation: the spirit indeed *is* willing, but the flesh *is* weak.
- 1 Corinthians 16:13
  Watch ye, stand fast in the faith, quit you like men, be strong.
- Colossians 4:2
  Continue in prayer, and watch in the same with thanksgiving;
- 1 Thessalonians 5:6
  Therefore let us not sleep, as *do* others; but **let us watch and be sober.**
- 1 Peter 4:7
  But the end of all things is at hand: **be ye therefore sober, and watch unto prayer.**

No Alcohol In Order to "Watch"

Pastor Timothy was to watch. He was not to be drunk or to have any alcoholic beverages so he would be able to *"watch"* carefully as to what was happening that would affect the Christians.

✔ 2. Pastor Timothy was to *"endure afflictions."*

Paul (who was in prison for his faith in the Lord Jesus Christ) knew that *"afflictions"* would be coming to all of the born-again Christians in his day. They are coming. Preachers must be able to *"endure"* and put up with any of the *"afflictions"* that might come, no matter what they might be.

✔ 3. Pastor Timothy was to *"do the work of an evangelist."*

An evangelist is one who proclaims the true and Biblical gospel of the Lord Jesus Christ. This is good news but there is also some bad news that goes along with it. The bad news precedes the good news. The bad news is that all are sinners who are destined for Hell, the Lake of Fire. The only thing that will stop their burning in Hell for all eternity is for the person to repent or change his mind concerning two things: (1) that he or she is a sinner and is therefore lost, and (2) that the Lord Jesus Christ is able to be their Saviour. Then he or she must genuinely believe on the Lord Jesus Christ and receive him as their Saviour from sin and sin's penalty. That's what is meant by *"doing the work of an evangelist."*

> ✔ **4. Pastor Timothy was to "make full proof of his ministry."**

The Greek word for *"full proof"* is PLEROPHOREO.
"to bear or bring full, to make full; to cause a thing to be shown to the full; <u>to fulfil the ministry in every part; to carry through to the end</u>, accomplish; things that have been accomplished; to fill one with any thought, conviction, or inclination; to make one certain, to persuade, convince one; to be persuaded, fully convinced or assured; to render inclined or bent on"

Pastor Timothy was not to stop his ministry for the Lord Jesus Christ until it had been completed. This does not pertain to unscriptural ministries that liberals, neo-evangelicals, modernists, or other compromisers are performing all around the world. However, all faithful, godly pastors have various Biblical ministries that the Lord has burdened them to fulfill. They should bring them to a conclusion in a satisfactory manner.

> ## What Is Your Biblical Ministry?
> What is the Biblical ministry that God has given you? Whatever it is, God wants you to complete it. I certainly want to fulfill the Biblical ministries God has given to me through these many years.

2 Timothy 4:6

"For I am now ready to be offered and the time of my departure is at hand."

Paul knew that his death was imminent. He said to Pastor Timothy that he was *"was ready to be offered."* The Greek word for *"offered"* is SPENDO, It means:

"to pour out as a drink offering, make a libation; in the NT to be offered as a libation; fig. used of one whose blood is poured out in a violent death for the cause of God"

Are you ready to be offered up in death because of your stand for the Lord Jesus Christ as Paul was? He said that *"the time of my departure is at hand."* This means that the time of his death was near. The word for *"departure"* is ANALUSIS. It means:

"an unloosing (as of things woven); a dissolving (into separate parts); departure; a metaphor drawn from loosing from moorings preparatory to setting sail"

This is a graphic picture of death.

Paul Was Ready To Depart Earth

Paul was ready to cast off all the lines that held him to this earth and go Home to Heaven to be with the Lord Jesus Christ in that Home that He was preparing for him (John 14:1-3). He knew that the time was near and he was ready. Are you ready for this *"departure"*?

Paul's Death Was an "Offering"

Paul talked about his death for the Lord Jesus Christ as an "offering." He was *"ready"* and willing to be *"offered"* for this reason. There are many times in the Bible that speak of *"offerings"* or being *"offered."*

- Judges 5:2
 Praise ye the LORD for the avenging of Israel, when **the people willingly offered themselves.**
- Judges 5:9
 My heart *is* toward the governors of Israel, that **offered themselves willingly among the people.** Bless ye the LORD.
- 1 Chronicles 29:9
 Then the people rejoiced, for that **they offered willingly,** because **with perfect heart they offered willingly to the LORD**: and David the king also rejoiced with great joy.

Our Church Has "Willing" Offerings

Our church is like that. We have a box in the back of our church, and every offering that comes into our church, whether from those present or those attending by the Internet, is a *"willing"* offering. There is no pressure or hype to give, yet the Lord supplies our needs for His glory.

- 1 Chronicles 29:17
 I know also, my God, that thou triest the heart, and hast pleasure in uprightness. As for me, in the uprightness of mine heart I **have willingly offered all these things**: and now have I seen with joy thy people, which are present here, to offer willingly unto thee.
- 2 Chronicles 17:16
 And next him *was* Amasiah the son of Zichri, who **willingly offered himself unto the LORD**; and with him two hundred thousand mighty men of valour.
- Romans 12:1
 I beseech you therefore, brethren, by the mercies of God, that ye **present your bodies a living sacrifice**, holy, acceptable unto God, *which is* your reasonable service.
- Philippians 2:17
 Yea, and **if I be offered** upon the sacrifice and service of your faith, I joy, and rejoice with you all.

- Hebrews 7:27
 Who needeth not daily, as those high priests, to offer up sacrifice, first for his own sins, and then for the people's: for **this he did once, when he offered up himself**.
- Hebrews 9:14
 How much more shall the blood of Christ, **who through the eternal Spirit offered himself without spot to God**, purge your conscience from dead works to serve the living God?
- Hebrews 9:28
 So **Christ was once offered to bear the sins of many**; and unto them that look for him shall he appear the second time without sin unto salvation.
- Hebrews 10:12
 But this man, after **he had offered one sacrifice for sins** for ever, sat down on the right hand of God;

2 Timothy 4:7

"I have fought a good fight, I have finished my course, I have kept the faith."

In this one verse, Paul gives a threefold autobiography of his life. My wife's mother, Mom Sanborn, wrote a chorus when her pastor preached on this verse. The song is entitled, *"Faithful to the Fight."* We sing it in our church each Sunday morning.

You will notice that Paul did not say anything like the following: *"I have built many church buildings, I have had huge attendances at each service, I have had a huge bus (or camel) ministry bringing in hundreds of people, and I have baptized hundreds each Sunday."* No, though Paul did minister to many people, he summed up his life to Pastor Timothy in just three short sentences.

✔ **#1 The first part of Paul's life's summary was: *"I have fought a good fight."* Paul was a good warrior for the Lord Jesus Christ.**

The Greek word for *"fought"* is AGONIZOMAI. It means: *"to enter a contest: contend in the gymnastic games; to contend with adversaries, fight; metaph. to contend, struggle, with difficulties and dangers; to endeavour with strenuous zeal, strive: to obtain something."*

He realized that the Christian faith is a battle. He was not a Christian pacifist when it came to battling with the world, the flesh, and the Devil. But Paul distinguished his *"fight"* to be a *"good"* one. The Greek word for *"good"* is KALOS. It has many meanings.

"beautiful, handsome, excellent, eminent, choice, surpassing, precious, useful, suitable, commendable, admirable; beautiful to look at, shapely, magnificent; good, excellent in its nature and characteristics, and therefore well adapted to its ends; genuine, approved; precious; joined to names of men designated by their office, competent, able, such as one ought to be; praiseworthy, noble; beautiful by reason of purity of heart and life, and hence praiseworthy; morally good, noble; honourable, conferring honour; affecting the mind agreeably, comforting and confirming"

Our "Fight" Must Be A Good One

With the use of *"fight"* in the Bible, it should always be a *"good fight,"* as Paul's was.

- Psalm 144:1
Blessed *be* the LORD my strength, **which teacheth my hands to war, *and* my fingers to fight**:
My mother-in-law used to always say that this could be applied to a Christian's use of the typewriter or the computer. She said that our *"fingers"* could *"fight"* in a solid, Christ-honoring written ministry. I agree with her in this. It makes good sense.
- 1 Corinthians 9:26
I therefore so run, not as uncertainly; **so fight I**, not as one that beateth the air:
- 1 Timothy 6:12
Fight the good fight of faith, lay hold on eternal life, whereunto thou art also called, and hast professed a good profession before many witnesses.

- Hebrews 11:34
  Quenched the violence of fire, escaped the edge of the sword, out of weakness were made strong, **waxed valiant in fight**, turned to flight the armies of the aliens.

Paul did not *"fight"* in an underhanded manner. His was a *"good"* and noble *"fight."* He fought fairly, yet determinedly. Like David of old, Paul did not flee from the unbelieving Goliaths.

#2 The second part of Paul's life's summary was: "I have finished my course."

A *"course"* might be defined as a planned goal with a specific way to accomplish it.

What Is Your Christian "Course"?
Though each of us should have a *"course"* or plan to pursue during our lifetime, many don't seem to have one. If this be the situation, they are certainly not going to *"finish"* that *"course."*

Paul knew what his *"course"* was ever since his conversion to the Lord Jesus Christ. When he came to the end of his life in a Roman prison, he said he had *"finish*ed*"* that *"course."*

The Greek word for *"finished"* is TELEO. This word has various meanings.

"to bring to a close, to finish, to end; passed, finished; to perform, execute, complete, fulfil, (so that the thing done corresponds to what has been said, the order, command etc.); with special reference to the subject matter, to carry out the contents of a command; with reference also to the form, to do just as commanded, and generally involving the notion of time, to perform the last act which completes a process, to accomplish, fulfil; to pay; of tribute"

- Acts 20:24
  But none of these things move me, neither count I my life dear unto myself, **so that I might finish my course with joy**, and the ministry, which I have received of the Lord Jesus, to testify the gospel of the grace of God.

✔ **#3 The third part of Paul's life's summary was:**
"I have kept the faith."

"The Faith" Means Bible Doctrine

It is important to note that *"the faith"* is the Greek HE PISTIS. It is not the simple PISTIS, but has HE which is the Greek article. With the article, *"the faith"* refers to the entire body of Christian doctrine including the original Bible Words. This is what Paul has "*kept.*"

The Greek word for "*kept*" is TEREO. It means:
"*to attend to carefully, take care of; to guard; metaph. to keep, one in the state in which he is; to observe; to reserve: to undergo something*"

The following chorus is sung at our 𝕭ible 𝔉or 𝕿oday 𝕭aptist 𝕮hurch each Sunday morning. It sums up Paul's threefold remembrance of his life.

FAITHFUL TO THE FIGHT

(From 2 Timothy 4:7)
Faithful to the fight
Faithful to the Faith
Faithful to the finish for God
Faithful to the right,
Faithful in His might
Faithful to the Word of God.
Faithful in the fray,
Faithful every day,
Faithful in the fight for the Faith.
Faithful to the fight,
Faithful to the Faith,
Faithful to the finish for God.
(By Gertrude Grace Sanborn--Dedicated to her son-in-law)

Part of that "*keeping*" of "*the faith*" or Bible doctrine involves the preservation of God's original Words of the Hebrew and Aramaic Old Testament and the Greek of the New Testament. This is why our Bible For Today ministry and the Dean Burgon Society have gone to such lengths to "*keep*" and "*guard*" these Words. I believe they are the original, verbally, plenarily, preserved Hebrew, Aramaic, and Greek Words underlying the King James Bible. The reader is urged to request a copy of BFT Brochure #1 which gives a list of over eighty-five of the over 1,000 items defending the King James Bible and the underlying Hebrew, Aramaic, and Greek Words.

"*The faith,*" as Christian doctrine which Paul "*kept*" and defended is emphasized throughout the New Testament.

- Acts 6:7
  And the word of God increased; and the number of the disciples multiplied in Jerusalem greatly; and **a great company of the priests were obedient to the faith**.
- Acts 14:22
  Confirming the souls of the disciples, *and* **exhorting them to continue in the faith**, and that we must through much tribulation enter into the kingdom of God.

That's the body of doctrine and teaching of the Old and New Testaments.
- Acts 16:5
And **so were the churches established in the faith**, and increased in number daily.
- 1 Corinthians 16:13
Watch ye, **stand fast in the faith**, quit you like men, be strong.

Are we in the doctrinal position that we ought to be in? Every born-again Christian should "*stand fast in the faith.*"
- Philippians 1:27
Only let your conversation be as it becometh the gospel of Christ: that whether I come and see you, or else be absent, I may hear of your affairs, that ye stand fast in one spirit, with one mind **striving together for the faith of the gospel**;
- Colossians 1:23
If ye continue in the faith grounded and settled, and *be* not moved away from the hope of the gospel, which ye have heard, *and* which was preached to every creature which is under Heaven; whereof I Paul am made a minister;
- Colossians 2:7
Rooted and built up in him, and **stablished in the faith, as ye have been taught**, abounding therein with thanksgiving.

Do we know our Bibles as we should? Do we know our Bible doctrines as we should?
- 1 Timothy 4:1
Now the Spirit speaketh expressly, that in the latter times **some shall depart from the faith**, giving heed to seducing spirits, and doctrines of devils;

That is exactly what has happened in our day and it is getting worse, not better.
- 1 Timothy 6:10
For the love of money is the root of all evil: which while some coveted after, **they have erred from the faith**, and pierced themselves through with many sorrows.

- 1 Timothy 6:21
  Which **some professing have erred concerning the faith**. Grace be with thee. Amen. (*The first to Timothy was written from Laodicea, which is the chiefest city of Phrygia Pacatiana*).
- 2 Timothy 3:8
  Now as Jannes and Jambres withstood Moses, so do these also resist the truth: men of corrupt minds, **reprobate concerning the faith.**
- Titus 1:13
  This witness is true. Wherefore rebuke them sharply, **that they may be sound in the faith**;
- 1 Peter 5:9
  Whom resist **stedfast in the faith**, knowing that the same afflictions are accomplished in your brethren that are in the world.
- Jude 1:3
  Beloved, when I gave all diligence to write unto you of the common salvation, it was needful for me to write unto you, and exhort *you* that ye should earnestly contend for the faith which was once delivered unto the saints.

Paul made an autobiography in these three goals and purposes of his life:
  (1) he fought a "*good fight*,"
  (2) he "*finished his course*," and
  (3) he "*kept the faith*." The "*faith*" is worth guarding.

"The Faith" Means Bible Doctrine

"*The faith*" is based on the Words of God. If we have the wrong copies of the Hebrew, Aramaic, and Greek Words, as I have said repeatedly, we cannot "*keep the faith*." We must have proper translations from those Hebrew, Aramaic, and Greek Words. That is what we have in our English King James Bible. We are trying to get good translations in all of the languages of the world. That is one thing both our Bible For Today ministry and the Dean Burgon Society seek to assist in doing.

The Summary Of Paul's Life

Paul fought a good fight.
Paul finished his course.
Paul kept the faith.
(2 Timothy 4:7)

2 Timothy 4:8

"**Henceforth there is laid up for me a crown of righteousness, which the Lord, the righteous judge, shall give me at that day: and not to me only, but unto all them also that love his appearing.**"

When Paul dies and goes to Heaven, he said he would receive a "*crown of righteousness,*" which the Lord Jesus Christ would give him and also to all the Christians who "*love His appearing.*" This "*crown*" is one of five that are mentioned in the New Testament.

The Five Crowns

My memory hint to remember all five "*crowns*" is **R-GIRL**.

R--the "*crown of rejoicing*"

- 1 Thessalonians 2:19

For what *is* our hope, or joy, or crown of rejoicing? *Are* not even ye in the presence of our Lord Jesus Christ at his coming?

G--the "*crown of glory*"

- 1 Peter 5:4

And when the chief Shepherd shall appear, ye shall receive a crown of glory that fadeth not away.

I--the "*incorruptible*" crown

- 1 Corinthians 9:25

And every man that striveth for the mastery is temperate in all things. Now they *do it* to obtain a corruptible crown; but we an incorruptible.

R--the "*crown of righteousness*"

- 2 Timothy 4:8

Henceforth there is laid up for me a crown of righteousness, which the Lord, the righteous judge, shall give me at that day: and not to me only, but unto all them also that love his appearing.

L--the "*crown of life*"

- James 1:12

Blessed *is* the man that endureth temptation: for when he is tried, he shall receive the crown of life, which the Lord hath promised to them that love him.

- Revelation 2:10

Fear none of those things which thou shalt suffer: behold, the devil shall cast *some* of you into prison, that ye may be tried; and ye shall have tribulation ten days: be thou faithful unto death, and I will give thee a crown of life.

The "Crown Of Righteousness"

Notice that this *"crown of righteousness"* will not only be given to the Apostle Paul, *"but unto all them also that love His appearing."* We believe that the occasion of the awarding of this *"crown"* to these people will be at the rapture of the *"Church which is His Body"* (Ephesians 1:22-23), the born-again Christians. The Lord Jesus Christ alone will decide who is to receive this *"crown."*

Those to whom God will give these *"crowns"* (represented by the *"four and twenty elders"*) will cast them before the throne of God in Heaven.
- Revelation 4:10
The four and twenty elders fall down before him that sat on the throne, and worship him that liveth for ever and ever, and **cast their crowns before the throne**, saying,

Notice that Paul mentions Who it is Who will *"give"* him a crown at *"that day"* when rewards will be distributed.

Lord Jesus Christ–Righteous Judge

It will be the Lord Jesus Christ Who is called *"the righteous Judge."* He is totally *"righteous"* in all of His judgment.

- John 5:22
For the Father judgeth no man, but **hath committed all judgment unto the Son:**
- Genesis 18:25
That be far from thee to do after this manner, to slay the righteous with the wicked: and that the righteous should be as the wicked, that be far from thee: **Shall not the Judge of all the earth do right?**

God is always *"right"* in His judgment whether it be for Christians or for the unsaved.

- Exodus 18:13
  And it came to pass on the morrow, that **Moses sat to judge the people:** and the people stood by Moses from the morning unto the evening.
- Deuteronomy 32:36
  For **the LORD shall judge his people**, and repent himself for his servants, when he seeth that *their* power is gone, and *there is* none shut up, or left.
- Psalm 9:8
  And **he shall judge the world in righteousness, he shall minister judgment to the people in uprightness**.

All Deserve The Lake Of Fire

If we had our just desserts all of us would go to Hell, but the Lord Jesus Christ has borne the *"judgment"* and died for the sins of the world so that those who genuinely trust Him might escape Hell and go to be with Him in Heaven for all eternity to come.

- Psalm 67:4
  O let the nations be glad and sing for joy: for **thou shalt judge the people righteously**, and govern the nations upon earth. Selah.
- Psalm 72:2
  He shall judge thy people with righteousness, and thy poor with judgment.
- Psalm 96:10
  Say among the heathen *that* the LORD reigneth: the world also shall be established that it shall not be moved: **he shall judge the people righteously**.
- Psalm 96:13
  Before the LORD: for he cometh, **for he cometh to judge the earth: he shall judge the world with righteousness**, and the people with his truth.

- Ecclesiastes 3:17
  I said in mine heart, **God shall judge the righteous and the wicked:** for *there is* a time there for every purpose and for every work.
- John 5:30
  I can of mine own self do nothing: as I hear, **I judge: and my judgment is just**; because I seek not mine own will, but the will of the Father which hath sent me.

Christ Makes No Mistakes
The Lord Jesus Christ will never make a mistake because He is Omniscient.

- John 7:24
  Judge not according to the appearance, but judge righteous judgment.
- John 8:16
  And yet **if I judge, my judgment is true**: for I am not alone, but I and the Father that sent me.
- John 12:47
  And if any man hear my words, and believe not, I judge him not: for **I came not to judge the world, but to save the world**.

When the Lord Jesus Christ came to earth in His incarnation at His first coming, His purpose was not to judge the world, but to offer salvation to whosoever would genuinely trust in Him. But when He comes at His second coming, it will be to judge the saved at the Judgment Seat of Christ and the lost at the Great White Throne Judgment.

- Acts 10:42
  And he commanded us to preach unto the people, and to testify that it is **he which was ordained of God** *to be* **the Judge of quick and dead**.

- Acts 17:31
  Because **he hath appointed a day, in the which he will judge the world in righteousness** by *that* man whom he hath ordained; *whereof* he hath given assurance unto all *men*, in that he hath raised him from the dead.
- Romans 2:16
  In the day when **God shall judge the secrets of men by Jesus Christ according to my gospel.**

2 Timothy 4:9

"Do thy diligence to come shortly unto me."

Paul wants Timothy to visit him in the Roman prison *"shortly."* This means as soon as possible. Among other reasons for this is to bring the *"cloak"* (v. 13) *"before winter"* sets in to keep Paul warm.

- 2 Timothy 4:21
  Do thy diligence to come before winter.

I'm sure that Timothy made every effort to visit Paul and bring his *"cloak"* to him before the *"winter."*

2 Timothy 4:10

"For Demas hath forsaken me, having loved this present world, and is departed unto Thessalonica, Crescens to Galatia, Titus unto Dalmatia."

Another reason why Paul wanted his close friend, Timothy, to visit him as soon as possible was that *"Demas hath forsaken me."* In other places, *"Demas"* was a close follower of Paul.

- Colossians 4:14
  Luke, the beloved physician, and **Demas, greet you.**
- Philemon 24
  Marcus, Aristarchus, **Demas, Lucas, my fellowlabourers.**

In these verses, *"Demas"* greeted the saints in Colosse and was called one of Paul's *"fellowlabourers."* What happened between the writing of Colossians, Philemon, and 2 Timothy? *"Demas"* was formerly a friend of Paul and of the Lord. Suddenly (or perhaps gradually) he turned his back on Paul and possibly on the Lord as well.

Perhaps *"Demas"* was ashamed of Paul and his bonds, but his real motivation for leaving Paul was that he *"loved this present world."*

Beware Of Loving This Present World"

There is nothing wrong with loving life, but our desire towards this wicked *"world"* should never take the place of our strong love for God's people and the things of the Lord Jesus Christ.

John cautions us on *"loving the world."*
* 1 John 2:15-17
    Love not the world, neither the things *that are* **in the world. If any man love the world,** the love of the Father is not in him. For all that *is* in the world, the lust of the flesh, and the lust of the eyes, and the pride of life, is not of the Father, but is of the world. **And the world passeth away,** and the lust thereof: but he that doeth the will of God abideth for ever.

This verse speaks of the *"world"* of sin and wickedness, not the things that God has created and placed upon the earth. *"Demas"* had it all wrong. He *"forsook"* Paul and *"loved the world."* He should have *"loved Paul"* and *"forsaken the world."* Are there so-called *"worldly"* Christians today? Yes, I believe that there are multitudes of them. You might ask, "What is the mark of a *"worldly"* Christian?"

Definition Of "The World"

Pastor Earl V. Willetts who married Mrs. Waite and me in August of 1948 gave the following definition of what was *"of the world"* as follows: *"Anything is of the world that lessens my love for the Lord Jesus Christ."* Sad to say, we have many worldly Christians today.

2 Timothy 4:11

"Only Luke is with me. Take Mark and bring him with thee: for he is profitable to me for the ministry."

Just think of it. Paul is in a dark, cold, dirty Roman prison and the only one with him is Dr. Luke. This is sad indeed. Luke is called a *"physician"* in Scripture.

- **Colossians 4:14**
  Luke, the beloved physician, and Demas, greet you.

  I believe that Luke is the author of the Gospel of Luke that bears his name as well as the book of Acts, though he is not named in that book. Luke joined Paul in the middle of the book of Acts. Wherever you see the word, *"we,"* in the book of Acts, it includes Luke, the writer of the book.

  When Paul said, *"Take Mark and bring him with thee: for he is profitable to me,"* he revealed for us an example of Christian forgiveness. Paul didn't want Timothy to come to visit him by himself. Here are a few references to Mark in the New Testament.

- **Acts 12:12**
  And when he had considered *the thing*, **he came to the house of Mary the mother of John, whose surname was Mark**; where many were gathered together praying.

- **Acts 12:25**
  And Barnabas and Saul returned from Jerusalem, when they had fulfilled *their* ministry, and **took with them John, whose surname was Mark**.

- **Acts 15:36-38**
  And some days after Paul said unto Barnabas, Let us go again and visit our brethren in every city where we have preached the word of the Lord, *and see* how they do. And **Barnabas determined to take with them John, whose surname was Mark. But Paul thought not good to take him with them, who departed from them from Pamphylia, and went not with them to the work**.

  Paul was not going to take Mark with him on this missionary journey because he thought that Mark was not faithful to the ministry. He thought Mark would leave them again in the middle of their missionary journey. He did not want that. It is most difficult to count on a person to help you and have that person let you down!

- **Acts 15:39**
  And the contention was so sharp between them, that **they departed asunder one from the other: and so Barnabas took Mark, and sailed unto Cyprus;**

  Paul and Barnabus were good friends, but they separated from each other on the subject of the fitness of Mark for the ministry. How did Mark, who forsook Paul and his ministry in Acts, become *"profitable"* to Paul *"for the ministry*" here in the book of 2 Timothy? It is the same way that you and I can become *"profitable"* for the Lord.

If there is anything in a born-again Christian that is *"profitable"* it has to come from the Lord. It cannot come from his flesh. The Word of God can speak to our heart and convict us of sin. The Word of God can make us understand that we serve a Saviour. One of the missions of the Word of God is to make us *"profitable"* in teaching, doctrine, reproof, and correction.

Apparently Mark had made some changes in his life and had become *"profitable"* to the Lord and to Paul. Does that mean there is hope for us who are saved? Yes there is. Was there hope for Jonah who disobeyed God and didn't go where God told him to go? Yes.

A Second Chance For Jonah

Jonah straightened himself out after he first fled from the will of the Lord. Jonah repented for his unbelief and error and came back to where he ought to the will of God. The only way to get on the right road is to come back to the place where you got off. You have to come back to the very juncture where you got off, and Mark did that.

Mark Had a Second Chance

In commending Mark, Paul was giving every Christian from then to now an example of the important area of forgiveness. When born-again Christians fight and battle one another (and they do more often than we would want to think about), they should be able to reconcile and get back into fellowship one with the other. This does not mean that they have to agree with each other in every area of doctrine or practice, but they should practice what the Lord Jesus Christ called for when he said:

- John 13:35
By this shall all *men* know that ye are my disciples, **if ye have love one to another.**

2 Timothy 4:12

"And Tychicus have I sent to Ephesus"

Paul spoke of having sent *"Tychicus"* to Ephesus. There are several other places in the New Testament where he is mentioned.

- Acts 20:4
  And **there accompanied him into Asia** Sopater of Berea; and of the Thessalonians, Aristarchus and Secundus; and Gaius of Derbe, and Timotheus; and of Asia, **Tychicus** and Trophimus.

  "Asia" refers to Asia Minor which is now called Turkey.

- Ephesians 6:21
  But that ye also may know my affairs, *and* how I do, **Tychicus, a beloved brother and faithful minister in the Lord**, shall make known to you all things:

- Colossians 4:7
  All my state shall Tychicus declare unto you, *who is* **a beloved brother, and a faithful minister and fellowservant in the Lord:**

  Paul's *"state"* was that he was in prison.

- Titus 3:12
  When I shall send Artemas unto thee, or Tychicus, be diligent to come unto me to Nicopolis: for I have determined there to winter.

Paul didn't undertake his entire ministry by himself. He often lists the many names of people who helped him.

2 Timothy 4:13

"The cloke that I left at Troas with Carpus, when thou comest bring with thee, and the books but especially the parchments."

Paul asked Timothy to bring his *"cloak"* with him when he came to Paul's prison cell in Rome. The word for *"cloak"* is PHELONES. It means: *"a travelling cloke, used for protection against stormy weather."* It is like an overcoat. Paul was cold in his prison cell. Apparently, Carpus was cold so Paul left the cloak *"at Troas with Carpus."* Now, Paul has need of this *"cloak"* and asked Timothy to bring it to Rome for Paul's use.

- Matthew 5:40
  And if any man will sue thee at the law, and take away thy coat, let him have *thy* **cloak** also.

Notice something else that Paul asked Timothy to bring. He requested "*the books, but especially the parchments.*" Paul was "*ready to be offered*" for the Lord. The "*time of his departure was at hand.*" This was his last journey on this earth. Why was he interested in books? These "*books*" were probably commentaries on the Scripture.

The "Parchments"–The Words of God

When he said "*especially the parchments,*" he was referring to the skins which contained the Scriptures of the Old Testament. These were scrolls. He still loved the Scriptures. Paul, in his last hours wanted the Words of God with him so he could read and study.

How special is your Bible to you? If fire came to your house and everything was about to be burned up, and you could only bring out one item, what would you bring out with you? Would it be your clothes, your pictures, your jewelry, your money? Or would it be your Bible? What if you were on a desert island alone, nobody else around? What would you want to comfort you? Would it be your clothes, your pictures, your jewelry, your money? Or would it be your Bible? Paul wanted his Bible. Even in a cold prison Paul wanted the "*parchments.*" Our mind, heart, and soul should never stop growing more and more in God's grace and in the knowledge of the Lord Jesus Christ.
- 2 Peter 3:18
  But **grow in grace, and *in* the knowledge of our Lord and Saviour Jesus Christ**. To him *be* glory both now and for ever. Amen.

2 Timothy 4:14

"Alexander the coppersmith did me much evil: the Lord reward him according to his works."

There are at least four "*Alexanders*" mentioned in the New Testament.
- Mark 15:21
  And they compel one Simon a Cyrenian, who passed by, coming out of the country, **the father of Alexander** and Rufus, to bear his cross.

As mentioned in this verse, this "*Alexander*" was the father of "*Simon*" who carried the Lord Jesus Christ's cross.

- **Acts 4:6**
  And Annas the high priest, and Caiaphas, and John, and **Alexander**, and as many as were of the kindred of the high priest, were gathered together at Jerusalem. .

  This "*Alexander,*" as we learn in this verse, was a relative of "*Annas the high priest.*"

- **Acts 19:33**
  And **they drew Alexander out of the multitude**, the Jews putting him forward. And **Alexander beckoned with the hand**, and would have made his defence unto the people.

  This "*Alexander*" was apparently a friend of the Jews who selected him from the "*multitude*" who were present at Ephesus.

- **1 Timothy 1:20**
  Of whom is Hymenaeus and **Alexander**; whom I have delivered unto Satan, that they may learn not to blaspheme.

  This is the "*Alexander*" who is here identified as "*the coppersmith*" who "*did* [Paul] *much evil.*" The word for "*did*" is ENDEIKNUMI. It is not the usual word for "*did.*" It means:

  "*to point out; to show, demonstrate, prove, whether by arguments or by acts; to manifest, display, put forth*"

  This would indicate that "*Alexander*" did not do his "*much evil*" in a secret way. Rather, he "*manifested, demonstrated, and displayed*" that "*evil*" in a public way for all to see. "*Alexander*" did not oppose Paul in his heart, but he showed it in a public way. His opposition and probable hatred for Paul was well known. How sad!

How To Handle "Evil"

I'm sure there are people who "*do evil*" unto you and to me. How do we handle it? Paul is no different from the rest of us. Do people always do good unto us? No. Some (or many) are bitter and angry against us. This could be either among the saved or the lost. They may either curse us to our face, behind our backs, or both. It reminds me of Psalm 55:21.

- **Psalm 55:21**
  The words of his mouth were smoother than butter, but **war was in his heart**: his words were softer than oil, **yet were they drawn swords**.

  "*Alexander,*" being a "*coppersmith,*" was probably a well-to-do man according to the standards of his day. He most likely was a good businessman.

Paul probably *"got on his nerves"* as we say, because of his bold preaching of the Words of God. If this were the case, in order to *"get even,"* he did him *"much evil."* I hope you and I don't do *"evil"* to people, even if they strongly disagree with us. We need to do good even to those who do us *"evil."*

Paul Named Names Again

Another thing that I should mention here is that Paul was not afraid to *"name names"* of those who were against the Words of God and godly men. Some pastors and other church leaders oppose any mention of those who teach false doctrines. Paul was not one of those people. He named *"Alexander,"* as he did many others in his letters, in order to warn others of their false teachings.

I Warn Against Many Things

For this reason, I have had no problem with warning against certain specific false teachings of some people. Here is a partial list of my warnings where I *"name names."*

✔ 1. **I warn against Harold Camping** for his allegorizing of the Bible, for his saying we're in the Tribulation, for his amillennialism, for his saying that there are no more churches today, that the Lord Jesus Christ came back in spirit in 1984, that He will come back physically in 2011, and many other things.

✔ 2. **I warn against John MacArthur** for his heresy on the Blood of the Lord Jesus Christ, for his teaching that Christians have only one nature rather than two, for his *"Lordship salvation"* teaching, for his false *"gospel according to Jesus"* and for many other things.

✔ 3. **I warn against the false teachings** of Rick Warren, Bill Hybels, Joel Osteen, Robert Schuller, Billy and Franklin Graham, and others.

✔ 4. **I warn against atheism, agnosticism, the ecumenical movement, and apostasy** as found in the World Council and National Council of Churches, the Roman Catholic Church and in other groups,

✔ 5. **I warn against all of the false doctrines of various religions and cults in America**, and around the world, such as Muhammadanism, Taoism, Buddhism, Confucianism, Judaism, Christian Science, Jehovah's Witnesses, Seventh Day Adventism, Unitarianism, Oprah Winfrey's cults, the New Age Movement, the Emerging Church, Post-Modernism, and others.

✔ 6. **I warn against all new evangelicalism** such as is found in the National Association of Evangelicals, the World Evangelical Fellowship, Evangelicals and Catholics Together, and others.

✔ 7. **I warn against all of the false doctrines** of the Pentecostal and Charismatic Movement, Benny Hinn, and others.

✔ 8. **I warn against the Fundamentalist schools and teachers who stand against the Traditional Hebrew, Aramaic, and Greek Words underlying the King James Bible.** This includes Bob Jones University, Detroit Baptist Seminary, Central Baptist Seminary, Calvary Baptist Seminary, Northland Baptist College, International Baptist College, and other sister-schools.

✔ 9. **I warn against the erroneous words and translation techniques** that underlie the perverted versions such as the RSV, NRSV, NASV, NIV, ESV, NKJV and others.

2 Timothy 4:15

"Of whom be thou ware also; for he hath greatly withstood our words."

Here Paul warns Pastor Timothy about the evils of *"Alexander the coppersmith."* The word for *"be thou ware"* is PHULASSO. Among other meanings, it means to *"avoid, shun, flee from; to guard for one's self; (i.e. for one's safety's sake)."*

Avoid These "Alexanders"

Timothy was to steer clear of men like *"Alexander."* Timothy was a pastor of the church at Ephesus. No doubt he had *"Alexanders"* in his church also. Every church seems to have an *"Alexander."*

If he is not in the church, then certainly there are many outside the church. Paul is telling Timothy to *"be ware,"* take heed, observe, and maybe flee from that fellow. There are lots of bewares in Scripture.

- **Matthew 7:15**
  Beware of false prophets, which come to you in sheep's clothing, but inwardly they are ravening wolves.
- **Matthew 10:17**
  But **beware of men**: for they will deliver you up to the councils, and they will scourge you in their synagogues;
  This verse refers to unsaved men.
- **Matthew 16:6**
  Then Jesus said unto them, Take heed and **beware of the leaven of the Pharisees and of the Sadducees** .
- **Mark 12:38**
  And he said unto them in his doctrine, **Beware of the scribes**, which love to go in long clothing, and *love* salutations in the marketplaces,
  These *"scribes"* were the *"clergy"* of their day.
- **Luke 12:15**
  And he said unto them, Take heed, and **beware of covetousness**: for a man's life consisteth not in the abundance of the things which he possesseth.

- Colossians 2:8
  Beware lest any man spoil you through philosophy and vain deceit, after the tradition of men, after the rudiments of the world, and not after Christ.

Beware Of False "Wisdom"

"Philosophy" is what is taught in secular colleges (and even in so-called *"Christian"* schools). Sometimes you can be *"spoiled"* by *"philosophy"* which is the love of wisdom.

- 2 Peter 3:17
  Ye therefore, beloved, seeing ye know *these things* before, **beware lest ye also, being led away with the error of the wicked**, fall from your own stedfastness.

  Timothy was to watch out for this man, *"Alexander."* Paul told Timothy that *"Alexander"* would continue to do him evil as he had done Paul evil. This gives us an understanding of why pastors are to warn the flock of those who are false teachers wherever they may be. This is done best by faithfully *"preaching the Words"* of God verse by verse and book by book.

Withstanding God's Words

Paul mentioned that *"Alexander"* *"greatly withstood our Words."* These Words were given by the Lord Jesus Christ, and communicated to Paul by God the Holy Spirit. To *"withstand"* Paul's *"words"* is to *"withstand"* the Words of the Lord Jesus Christ. This is a serious sin. There are others as well who have *"withstood"* the truth of our God.

- Acts 13:8
  But **Elymas the sorcerer** (for so is his name by interpretation) **withstood them**, seeking to turn away the deputy from the faith.
- Galatians 2:11
  But when Peter was come to Antioch, **I withstood him to the face**, because he was to be blamed.

  Paul spoke out against even his fellow apostle, Peter. He *"withstood"* and opposed him in this instance.

- 2 Timothy 3:8
  Now as **Jannes and Jambres withstood Moses**, so do these also resist the truth: men of corrupt minds, reprobate concerning the faith.
  These two men were likely the magicians that resisted Moses.
  This man, *"Alexander,"* was to be marked out, looked after, and warned lest he do further evil to Timothy and others.

Don't "Withstand" God's Words

We should not *"withstand"* God's Words. We should absorb and receive every one of them. This is why I stand for the original, preserved Hebrew, Aramaic, and Greek Words underlying the King James Bible and the King James Bible which accurately translates them into English.

---

2 Timothy 4:16

"At my first answer no man stood with me, but all men forsook me. I pray God that it may not be laid to their charge."

The Greek word for *"answer"* is APOLOGIA. It is a *"reasoned statement or argument"* that Paul made by himself to save his life. An *"apology"* in the Greek sense is a defense. Maybe this was the first time Paul stood before the Roman court. Paul was all by himself, because *"no man stood with him."* He was, as we say, *"pro se."* Paul said *"all men forsook me."* The Greek word for *"forsook"* is EGKATALEIPO. It means:

"abandon, desert; leave in straits, leave helpless; totally abandoned, utterly forsaken; to leave behind among, to leave surviving."

Apparently, Paul's former friends didn't want to be anywhere near him while he was standing for his life before a heathen Roman judge.

Two Kinds Of "Forsaking"

There are two kinds of *"forsaking,"* the bad kind and the good kind. We should not *"forsake"* the Lord and His ways. We should *"forsake"* sin and evil.

- **Matthew 26:56**
  But all this was done, that the scriptures of the prophets might be fulfilled. Then **all the disciples forsook him, and fled**.
- **Mark 1:18**
  And straightway **they forsook their nets, and followed him**.
  That's a good *"forsaking."* They *"forsook"* their old lives and their old trade.
- **Luke 5:11**
  And when they had brought their ships to land, **they forsook all, and followed him**.
- **Hebrews 11:27**
  By faith **he forsook Egypt**, not fearing the wrath of the king: for he endured, as seeing him who is invisible.

That was a good *"forsaking."* But in Paul's case, it was different. Have you ever been forsaken? Have you ever felt forsaken? Have you ever been all alone and it seemed like you were all by yourself? Paul prayed that the Lord would not lay this *"forsaking"* to their *"charge."*

2 Timothy 4:17

"Notwithstanding the Lord stood with me, and strengthened me that by me the preaching might be fully known and that all the Gentiles might hear, and I was delivered out of the mouth of the lion."

Though *"all men forsook"* him, Paul said *"the Lord stood with me, and strengthened me."* The Greek word for *"stood"* is PARISTEMI. This a compound Word, made up of PARA (*"along side"*), and HISTEMI (*"to stand"*). It has various meanings:

"to place beside or near; to set at hand; to present; to proffer; to provide; to place a person or thing at one's disposal; to present a person for another to see and question; to present or show; to bring to, bring near; metaph. i.e to bring into one's fellowship or intimacy; to present (show) by argument, to prove; <u>to stand beside, stand by or near, to be at hand, be present; to stand by; to stand beside one</u>, a bystander; to appear; to be at hand, stand ready; to stand by to help, to succour; to be present; to have come; of time"

2 Timothy 4:17

God "Strengthened" Paul

With the Lord Jesus Christ *"strengthening"* him, Paul was in strong hands. That is the greatest *"strength"* anyone could have, with the Saviour right by your side. We should be thankful for God's strength.

- Ephesians 3:16
  That he would grant you, according to the riches of his glory, to be **strengthened with might by his Spirit in the inner man**;
  God wants to strengthen every saved person. Paul prayed for that.

Gnostic MSS Remove "Christ" Here

- Philippians 4:13
  I can do all things through Christ which strengtheneth me.

  The sad thing is that, in the modern versions, the word *"Christ"* has been removed from this verse because the Gnostic critical Greek Texts (Westcott and Hort, United Bible Societies, Nestle/Aland), following the Gnostic manuscripts, Vatican ("B") and Sinai (Aleph) have removed it. The Gnostics did not believe in the Deity of the Lord Jesus Christ, but believed He was just a *"sinful man"* who needed to be *"saved"* and therefore could not *"strengthen"* anyone.

- Colossians 1:11
  Strengthened with all might, according to his glorious power, unto all patience and longsuffering with joyfulness;
  We may be weak in our bodies, but, if we are saved, the Lord Jesus Christ can *"strengthen"* us, and that's what He did to Paul.

  Paul said that the reason that *"the Lord stood with me, and strengthened me"* was in order *"that by me the preaching might be fully known"* and *"that all the Gentiles might hear."* Though in prison, Paul wanted to minister the gospel to everyone possible before his death.

  He then said *"I was delivered out of the mouth of the lion."* Whether that refers to deliverance from the arena where Christians were thrown to the lions, or whether this refers to Satan as a *"roaring lion"* (1 Peter 5:8), we can't be sure. Either way, the Lord *"delivered"* Paul from *"the lion."* God has *"delivered"* in the past and is able to deliver in the present and future as well.

- Acts 7:34

    I have seen, I have seen the affliction of my people which is in Egypt, and **I have heard their groaning, and am come down to deliver them**. And now come, I will send thee into Egypt.

    The Lord was the only One Who could *"deliver"* His people from Egypt and all of their terrible suffering.

- Galatians 1:4

    Who gave himself for our sins, **that he might deliver us** from this present evil world, according to the will of God and our Father:

- 2 Timothy 4:18

    And **the Lord shall deliver me from every evil work**, and will preserve *me* unto his heavenly kingdom: to whom *be* glory for ever and ever. Amen.

- Hebrews 2:15

    And **deliver them who through fear of death** were all their lifetime subject to bondage.

Delivered From "Fear of Death"

The Lord Jesus Christ delivered us who are saved from the *"fear of death."* We have no *"fear of death."* Though we may have, in some cases, a fear of the process of dying, death is for us, the door to Heaven and being with the Lord Jesus Christ for all eternity to come.

- 2 Peter 2:9

    The Lord knoweth how to deliver the godly out of temptations, and to reserve the unjust unto the day of judgment to be punished:

    He is a *"delivering"* God. There is a poem that my mother-in-law wrote back in 1949 called *"My Times are in Thy Hands."* I used that poem and also the verse on which it is based (Psalm 31:15) when I had cancer of the lymph glands in 1986. The Lord spared my life at that time and *"delivered"* me from death, though I was prepared and ready to die and go Home to be with Him. My times are still *"in His Hand."*

- Psalm 31:15

    My times *are* in thy hand: deliver me from the hand of mine enemies, and from them that persecute me.

MY TIMES ARE IN THY HANDS

Such hands as Thine
Can never fail nor falter;
My times, my goings, and my comings
Thou dost know.
So strong – such hands,
So wise in all their moving,
Directing worlds and all the teeming
Nations here below!

Thy hands, my God,
Are holding me!
My times so small they seem
As I compare
Thy hands, which wrote the Law
And shook the Mountain
Those hands, deal tenderly with me in care!

My times, Thy hands!
Sweet peace I find in this, O Lord
And grace to meet the problems of each day.
So, I put my hand in Thine,
O God my Father;
And holding thus will walk my brief
And earthly way!
(By Gertrude Grace Sanborn from *With Tears In My Heart*)

Paul had his times in God's Hands. It was time for him to set sail for Glory. He put his hands in the powerful Hands of his Saviour, the Lord Jesus Christ. All of us should do this as well.

2 Timothy 4:18

"And the Lord shall deliver me from every evil work, and will preserve me unto his heavenly kingdom to whom be glory for ever and ever. Amen"

In verse 17, Paul said that the Lord *"strengthened"* him, and that he was *"delivered out of the mouth of the lion."* In this verse, he says, *"And the Lord shall deliver me from every evil work, and will preserve me unto his heavenly kingdom."* This is eternal security.

Christians Have Eternal Security
Everyone who is saved has eternal security.

Both of these things were true for Paul and can be true for every born-again Christian as well. He is able to *"deliver"* them from *"every evil work"* and also to *"preserve"* them *" unto His heavenly kingdom."* God is able to *"preserve"* in many ways.

- Psalm 12:7
  Thou shalt keep them, O LORD, **thou shalt preserve them from this generation for ever.**
  This is talking about the Words of God.

God's Promise Of Preserving Words
God has promised to *"preserve"* those Hebrew and Aramaic (and by extension Greek) Words *"for ever."* He is a *"preserving"* God.

- Psalm 31:23
  O love the LORD, all ye his saints: *for* **the LORD preserveth the faithful,** and plentifully rewardeth the proud doer.
- Psalm 32:7
  Thou *art* my hiding place; **thou shalt preserve me from trouble**; thou shalt compass me about with songs of deliverance. Selah.

- Psalm 37:28
  For the LORD loveth judgment, and forsaketh not **his saints; they are preserved for ever**: but the seed of the wicked shall be cut off.

Saved People Cannot Be Lost

I don't go along with those who teach that a person can be saved today and if you sin, you are lost tomorrow. All of us are sinners and we have a sinful nature. If we are not controlled by the Spirit of God, we will sin. The Lord still *"preserves"* us if we are His children.

- Psalm 97:10
  Ye that love the LORD, hate evil: **he preserveth the souls of his saints**; he delivereth them out of the hand of the wicked.
- John 10:27-30
  My sheep hear my voice, and I know them, and they follow me: ²⁸And **I give unto them eternal life; and they shall never perish**, neither shall any *man* pluck them out of my hand. ²⁹My Father, which gave *them* me, is greater than all; and no *man* is able to pluck *them* out of my Father's hand. ³⁰I and *my* Father are one.
  That is preservation of the souls of those who are saved.
- 1 Thessalonians 5:23
  And the very God of peace sanctify you wholly; and *I pray God* **your whole spirit and soul and body be preserved blameless** unto the coming of our Lord Jesus Christ.
- Jude 1
  Jude, the servant of Jesus Christ, and brother of James, to them that are sanctified by God the Father, and **preserved in Jesus Christ**, *and* called:

  The Lord Jesus Christ was going to save and deliver Paul from many more hardships and sufferings of this earthly life and take him Home to Heaven. He is going to be safe *"unto His Heavenly kingdom."* Paul's *"times"* were in God's *"Hand."*

The Meanings of "Amen"

Paul said *"Amen"* to that. The Greek word *"Amen"* has been described as follows:

"The word 'amen' is a most remarkable word. It was transliterated directly from the Hebrew into the Greek of the New Testament, then into Latin and into English and many other languages, so that it is practically a universal word. It has been called the best known word in human speech. The word is directly related -- in fact, almost identical -- to the Hebrew word for 'believe' (amam), or faithful. Thus, it came to mean 'sure' or 'truly', an expression of absolute trust and confidence."

Paul says he is sure that God is going to *"preserve him into his heavenly kingdom"* so he said *"Amen"* to it. Paul did not have a single doubt that he was saved and safe in the *"Hand"* of his Heavenly Father. If you and I are saved, we should have no doubt either.

2 Timothy 4:19

"Salute Prisca and Aquila, and the household of Onesiphorus."

Paul is greeting both *"Prisca and Aquila." "Prisca"* is *"Priscilla."* They are found various places in the New Testament.

- Acts 18:2
  And found a certain **Jew named Aquila, born in Pontus, lately come from Italy, with his wife Priscilla**; (because that Claudius had commanded all Jews to depart from Rome:) and came unto them.
- Acts 18:18
  And Paul *after this* tarried *there* yet a good while, and then took his leave of the brethren, and sailed thence into Syria, and **with him Priscilla and Aquila**; having shorn *his* head in Cenchrea: for he had a vow.

"Priscilla and Aquila" were partners with Paul. They must have been at Ephesus where Timothy was the pastor.

- Acts 18:26
And he began to speak boldly in the synagogue: whom **when Aquila and Priscilla had heard**, they took him unto *them*, and expounded unto him the way of God more perfectly.

"*Priscilla and Aquila*" had been taught the Words of God by Paul. "*Priscilla and Aquila*" were husband and wife. They worked as a team in the things of the Lord.

- Romans 16:3
Greet Priscilla and Aquila my helpers in Christ Jesus:
- 1 Corinthians 16:19
The churches of Asia salute you. **Aquila and Priscilla salute you** much in the Lord, with the church that is in their house.

House Churches Are Biblical

"*Priscilla and Aquila*" had a church "*in their house.*" They decided they would put their furniture somewhere else and put a space in their house for a "*church.*" That's exactly what we have in our 𝕭ible 𝔉or 𝕿oday 𝕭aptist 𝕮hurch, a "*church in our house.*"

Paul also greeted the "*household of Onesiphorus.*"
- 2 Timothy 1:16
The Lord give mercy unto the house of Onesiphorus; for he oft refreshed me, and was not ashamed of my chain:

2 Timothy 4:20

"**Erastus abode at Corinth; but Trophimus have I left at Miletum sick.**"

Now Paul mentions "*Erastus*" and "*Trophimus.*" "*Erastus*" was at "*Corinth*" at this point in time.
- Acts 19:22
So he sent into Macedonia **two of them that ministered unto him, Timotheus and Erastus**; but he himself stayed in Asia for a season.

"*Erastus*" was one of the men who "*ministered*" to Paul. As an apostle, Paul still needed someone to help him.

Preachers Need Ministers Also
Preachers today also need some people to "*minister*" unto them.

- **Romans 16:23**
  Gaius mine host, and of the whole church, saluteth you. **Erastus the chamberlain of the city saluteth you**, and Quartus a brother.

  "*Trophimus*" is mentioned by Paul as well. He was left on the island of "*Miletum sick.*" "*Miletum*" is an island now called "*Malta.*" It is right off the coast of Sicily. That's where Paul was shipwrecked in Acts Chapter 27
- **Acts 20:4**
  And **there accompanied him into Asia** Sopater of Berea; and of the Thessalonians, Aristarchus and Secundus; and Gaius of Derbe, and Timotheus; and of Asia, Tychicus and **Trophimus**.

  "*Trophimus*" was one of Paul's traveling companions.

Don't Forget Your Friends
Paul didn't forget his friends. Do you forget your friends?

In his last letter before he went Home to be with the Lord Jesus Christ, he mentions name after name because they were fellowhelpers.
- **Acts 21:29**
  (For **they had seen before with him in the city Trophimus an Ephesian**, whom they supposed that Paul had brought into the temple.)

  "*Trophimus*" was most likely a Gentile. They thought that Paul brought him into the temple and desecrated the temple so they were after Paul and wanted to imprison him.

2 Timothy 4:21

"Do thy diligence to come before winter. Eubulus greeteth thee, and Pudens and Linus and Claudia, and all the brethren."

I mentioned before why Paul wanted Timothy to bring his *"cloak"* (4:13) and *"come before winter"* so he wouldn't be cold in the Roman dungeon.

Here are some more men whom Paul listed. This is the only place in Scripture that they are mentioned. If we didn't have them here we wouldn't have them anywhere. *"Eubulus, Pudens, Linus and Claudia"* are some of Paul's friends. It seems as though Paul led these individuals to Christ possibly right there in the prison.

2 Timothy 4:22

"The Lord Jesus Christ be with thy spirit. Grace be with you. Amen."

There are many verses about the Lord Jesus Christ being with the born-again Christian.

- Matthew 28:20
  Teaching them to observe all things whatsoever I have commanded you: and, **lo, I am with you alway,** *even* **unto the end of the world**. Amen.

When Will The World End?

When is the end of the world or "age" coming? We don't know. How long is the Lord Jesus Christ going to be with those whom He has saved by genuine faith in Him?

The Lord Jesus Christ is going to be with the saved ones until *"the end of the world"* and throughout eternity.

- John 14:20
  At that day ye shall know that I *am* in my Father, and **ye in me, and I in you.**

This speaks of the Lord Jesus Christ being in the saved people as well as God the Holy Spirit.

- John 14:23
  Jesus answered and said unto him, **If a man love me, he will keep my words: and my Father will love him, and we will come unto him, and make our abode with him**.

The Trinity Indwells The Saved

According to the New Testament, born-again Christians have God the Father, God the Son, and God the Holy Spirit of God indwelling them.

- Colossians 1:27
  To whom God would make known what *is* the riches of the glory of this mystery among the Gentiles; which is **Christ in you, the hope of glory**:
  Though it is true, we normally speak of the saved being indwelt by God the Holy Spirit of God, we must never forget that the Lord Jesus Christ is in the Christian as well.
- Hebrews 13:5
  Let *your* conversation *be* without covetousness; *and be* content with such things as ye have: for he hath said, **I will never leave thee, nor forsake thee.**
  That's why the Lord Jesus Christ stood with Paul.

We Need God's "Grace"

Paul's final wish to Timothy was that *"Grace be with you."* "Grace" has been defined as *"getting something we do not deserve."* There are many verses that deal with God's *"grace."*

- Acts 15:11
  But we believe that **through the grace of the Lord Jesus Christ we shall be saved**, even as they.
  Whether you are a Jew or a Gentile we all must be saved by God's matchless *"grace,"* getting something we don't deserve.
- Acts 20:24
  But none of these things move me, neither count I my life dear unto myself, so that I might finish my course with joy, and the ministry, which I have received of the Lord Jesus, **to testify the gospel of the grace of God**.

The Gospel of God's "Grace"

The *"gospel"* is called *"the gospel of the grace of God."* Not a single one of us deserves to go to Heaven and to be forgiven of our sins. It's all of God's grace.

- Romans 3:24
  Being justified freely by his grace through the redemption that is in Christ Jesus:
  It is God's "grace" that justifies.
- 1 Corinthians 15:10
  But **by the grace of God I am what I am**: and his grace which *was bestowed* upon me was not in vain; but I laboured more abundantly than they all: yet not I, but **the grace of God which was with me.**
  Paul was a murderer. He was on the road to Damascus to kill and imprison Christians. The Lord Jesus Christ met him and turned him around 180 degrees.

No Other Means But God's "Grace"

If anyone thinks he is saved by any other means than by God's *"grace,"* he is wrong. That's false. If you are saved, it is by God's *"grace."* God has given you something you do not deserve.

- 2 Corinthians 8:9
  For **ye know the grace of our Lord Jesus Christ**, that, though he was rich, yet for your sakes he became poor, **that ye through his poverty might be rich.**
  This is a precious verse on the clearest definition of the *"grace of our Lord Jesus Christ."*
- 2 Corinthians 12:9
  And he said unto me, **My grace is sufficient for thee**: for my strength is made perfect in weakness. Most gladly therefore will I rather glory in my infirmities, that the power of Christ may rest upon me.

God's "Grace" In Sickness And Pain

God's *"grace"* was with Paul in sickness and pain.

- Ephesians 3:8
  Unto me, who am less than the least of all saints, is this grace given, that I should preach among the Gentiles the unsearchable riches of Christ;
- Ephesians 4:29
  Let no corrupt communication proceed out of your mouth, but that which is good to the use of edifying, **that it may minister grace unto the hearers.**

Our Mouths Must "Minister Grace"

Many times our mouths get us into trouble. We need to use our mouths to *"minister grace unto the hearers."*

- Colossians 4:6
  Let your speech *be* alway with grace, seasoned with salt, that ye may know how ye ought to answer every man.

Seasoned With "Salt"

Sometimes *"salt"* stings, if you have an open wound. We need to season our speech. If our brothers and sisters are off base, we need to speak with grace and straighten that thing out.

- 2 Timothy 2:1
  Thou therefore, my son, **be strong in the grace that is in Christ Jesus.**

Be "Strong" In God's "Grace"

Paul could have told Timothy to be strong in *"faith,"* or the *"knowledge"* of the Words of God, but he wanted him to be strong in *"grace."* If we have *"grace"* we are going to give something to people that they don't deserve and they are not expecting.

- Titus 2:11
  For the grace of God that bringeth salvation hath appeared to all men,

  How do we get *"salvation"*? We get *"salvation"* by the grace of God. No person deserves *"salvation."* It is only by God's "grace" that we can be saved. It is a free gift.

- Hebrews 2:9
  But we see Jesus, who was made a little lower than the angels for the suffering of death, crowned with glory and honour; that **he by the grace of God should taste death for every man**.
- Hebrews 4:16
  Let us therefore come boldly unto the **throne of grace**, that we may obtain mercy, and find grace to help in time of need.

God's "Throne of Grace"

God has a throne in Heaven called *"the throne of grace."* God still wants to give us more. We need more of God's abundant *"grace"* when we come to His throne in prayer.

- 1 Peter 5:10
  But **the God of all grace**, who hath called us unto his eternal glory by Christ Jesus, after that ye have suffered a while, make you perfect, stablish, strengthen, settle *you*.

  God certainly is *"the God of all grace."* He is a giving God, and we should be giving as well.
- 2 Peter 3:18
  But **grow in grace**, and *in* the knowledge of our Lord and Saviour Jesus Christ. To him *be* glory both now and for ever. Amen.

Christians Need to "Grow in Grace"

There is some "*growing*" that has to be done in gracious living. Paul ends his last letter of his life with the words, "*Grace be with you.*" "*We must grow in grace and in the knowledge of our Lord and Saviour Jesus Christ.*"

GRACE

Hard is the pathway of training,
Stern is the way He may use
To take our dim eyes from the earth things,
To make us His own will to choose.

How often our hands seem to cling to
The baubles and toys of this sphere,
But a wonderful wise Overseer
Will give us of things far more dear.

He seats us in Heavenly places,
Enfolds us around with His care,
Bestows on us gifts for His glory
That we may be used everywhere.

He lets us see failure in others,
Permits us to weep over loss,
And does all this while He is turning
Our eyes from this world to His cross.

(By Gertrude Grace Sanborn (April, 1953)
From *With Tears In My Heart*

Index of Words and Phrases

1 Timothy .. 1, 4, 5, 11, 15, 27, 39, 56, 59, 84, 86, 93, 95, 101, 103-105, 109, 111, 112, 118, 121, 127, 154, 161, 165, 167, 170, 177, 181, 194
1300 to 1769 81
1945 graduation 55
2 Timothy ... iv, 1, 2, 4, 6, 8, 11, 14, 15, 20, 22-24, 27, 28, 31, 32, 34-36, 40, 43-46, 48, 51, 53, 55, 57, 58, 60-63, 65, 70, 72-76, 78-80, 84-87, 89-93, 95, 96, 99-114, 116-119, 121, 122, 126, 127, 130, 132, 135, 137, 139, 140, 143, 147, 149, 152, 159, 161, 166, 168, 170, 171, 174, 176, 180, 182-184, 188, 189, 191-193, 197, 199, 200, 202, 204, 206, 207, 209, 212
2 Timothy Chapter Four iv
2 Timothy Chapter One iv
2 Timothy Chapter Three iv
2 Timothy Chapter Two iv
25 Signs Of The Last Days 125
356 .... 168, 169
356 doctrinal passages 168
8,000 .... 39, 73, 168, 169
8,000 differences 39, 168, 169
85 verses per day 45, 82, 144
856-854-2464 iii
856-854-4452 iii
856-854-4747 iii
A Second Chance For Jonah 191
About the Author iv
ABOVE THE DIN 8
Accuracy Of The King James Bible 168
Acknowledgments .... ii, iv
adultery 89, 115, 116, 170
afflictions .. 2, 20, 21, 23, 24, 45, 57, 121, 132, 133, 135, 136, 171, 172, 182
Africa 33
agnosticism 196
alcoholic beverages 172
Alexander 14, 193, 194
All Deserve The Lake Of Fire 186
Alzheimer's disease 20
Ann Arbor, Michigan 44
aorist 20, 21, 37
apostle 2-4, 10, 31, 32, 47, 64, 76, 126, 131, 162, 185, 198, 207

appearing 27, 28, 61, 159, 161, 183-185
Approved By The Lord Jesus Christ 83
Aquila 206, 207
Archbishop Trench 131
Are You Willing to Live Godly? 34
ashamed 2, 17, 18, 20-23, 32, 33, 44-47, 80, 82, 97, 113, 118, 135, 170, 188, 207
ASHAMED OF JESUS 23
Asia Minor 1, 43, 192
atheism 196
audience iii
Audrey Sanborn's Favorite Verse 47
Author .... iv, 38, 55, 107, 190
Author of every Word of the Bible 38
Avoid These "Alexanders" 197
Barbara Egan ii
battle 40, 57, 59, 60, 73, 93, 170, 177, 191
Be A Herald Of All God's Words 162
Be Faithful In "Least" And "Much" 55
Be Ready For Christ's Coming 126
Be "Mighty In The Scriptures" 146
Be "Strong" In God's "Grace" 213
Believers Identified With Christ 74
beloved physician 188, 190
Bennett, Dr. David 13
Benny Hinn 196
Berea High School 55
Berea, Ohio 55, 145
bestiality 106, 170
Beware Of False "Wisdom" 198
BFT #3105VC1-2 iii
BFT 3105 BK iii
bft@BibleForToday.org iii
Bible For Today Baptist Church .... ii, iii, 53, 126, 179, 207
Bible For Today Press iii
Bill Hybels 195
Billy and Franklin Graham 195
blood 6, 15, 16, 25, 31, 52, 119, 163, 174, 176, 195
Bob Jones University 36, 196
born-again .. 21, 29, 34, 41, 42, 53, 56, 59, 60, 62, 65, 69, 70, 73, 77, 89, 90, 102, 118, 120, 122, 124, 126, 129, 130, 138, 143, 151-153, 155, 166, 172, 181, 185, 191, 204, 209, 210

Index of Words and Phrases 217

Buddhism	196
buried with Him	74
By The Waters Of Galilee	55
Calvary Baptist Seminary	36, 196
captive silly women	114
Census Bureau News	116
Central Baptist Seminary	36, 196
chain	2, 22, 44, 207
chaplaincy	5, 101
Chapter Four	iv, 159
Chapter One	iv, 1
Chapter Three	iv, 99
Chapter Two	iv, 51
Charismatic movement	196
charity	11, 23, 91, 92, 109, 126, 131
chemical engineer	20
China	33
chosen as a corporate body	60
Chosen To Be A Soldier	60
Christ Bare All People's Sins	76
Christ Died For The Sins Of Everyone	146
Christ Makes No Mistakes	187
Christ Rose Bodily	67
Christ The Only True Foundation	88
Christian pacifists	59
Christian Science	196
Christians Have Eternal Security	204
Christians Need To "Grow In Grace"	214
Christ's Bodily Resurrection	69
church that is in their house	207
cloke	192
Collingswood, New Jersey	iii, iii
Coming To Seek & Save Sinners	47
Commander-in-Chief	59
Confucianism	196
congregation	ii, 72, 79, 141
conscience	6, 7, 11, 86, 176
consider	63, 64, 155
Contending For God's Words	40
corporate body	60
correction	ii, 145, 147, 150, 151, 191
Cosby, Dianne	ii

covetous 93, 100, 101, 125
creep into houses 114, 125
Creeping Into Houses For Sin 114
Critical Greek Text 17
crown of glory 61, 184
crown of life 61, 184
crown of rejoicing 61, 184
crown of righteousness 28, 61, 183, 184
crucified with Christ 74, 76
Current USA Murder Statistics 108
Daniel S. Waite ii
Daniel's 70th week 124
David Bennett 13
DEEP IN GOD'S WORD 156
Defined King James Bible Orders iv
Definition Of "The World" 189
deliver 15, 21, 54, 114, 136-138, 197, 201, 202, 204, 205
deliverance 47, 201, 204
delivered .. ii, 8, 23, 39, 47, 75, 110, 132, 133, 136, 146, 160, 166, 182, 194, 200-202
Delivered From "Fear Of Death" 202
Demas 188, 190
Demas hath forsaken me 188
dementia 20
Denying Preservation Of Words 38
depart 87, 88, 174, 181, 206
departure 174, 193
Derbe 2, 4, 136, 192, 208
Detroit Baptist Seminary 36, 196
Devil 15, 19, 37, 59-61, 91, 92, 96, 97, 107, 120, 177, 184
Dianne W. Cosby ii
did me much evil 14, 193
died for the sins of the world 143, 186
Differing Gifts 12
diligence 12, 39, 80, 166, 182, 188, 209
dispensational 170
Do You Have "Fear Of Death"? 16
doctrine .. 23, 53, 86, 122, 126, 127, 130, 141, 147, 148, 154, 161, 164, 166, 167, 179-182, 191, 197
Don't Be Ashamed Of The Lord 21
Don't Be "Moved" By "Afflictions" 134
Don't Forget Your Friends 208

Index of Words and Phrases

Don't "Withstand" God's Words 199
dot (a tittle or hiriq) 38
Dr. H. A. Ironside iii
Dr. H. D. Williams ii
Dr. Jack Moorman 39
Dr. Thomas Strouse 38
drunk 172
earnestly contend for the Faith 39, 166, 182
earthen vessels 42
ecumenical movement 196
edifying 14, 170, 212
Egan, Barbara ii
election 73
Elements Of The "Gospel" Message 143
Elymas 198
Emerging Church 163, 168, 196
ENDURE HARDNESS 57, 58
Enduring "Hardness" Of Persecution 57
English Standard Version 168
entangled 59, 97
Ephesians 1:22-23 .... 73, 105, 123, 185
Ephesians, Philippians, Colossians, and Philemon 44, 72
Ephesus 1, 4, 10, 26, 32, 48, 71, 125, 145, 192, 194, 197, 206
equal with God the Father 5
ESV (English Standard Version) 73, 169, 196
Eunice 11
Evangelicals and Catholics Together 196
every Word 37, 38, 162
faith . 4-6, 11-14, 16-18, 23-26, 28, 34, 36, 39, 41, 42, 47, 51-53, 57, 60, 62,
  63, 71-74, 76, 78, 79, 86, 87, 91, 92, 95-97, 109, 111, 117, 119,
  121, 122, 125, 126, 129-131, 133, 134, 136, 141, 143, 154, 161,
  164-166, 170, 172, 175-177, 179-182, 198-200, 209
faithful .. ii, 4, 10, 35, 53, 55, 56, 59, 61, 62, 74, 78, 79, 104, 107, 122, 126,
  149, 155, 166, 167, 173, 180, 184, 190, 192, 204, 206
FAITHFUL TO THE FIGHT 180
Faithful To The Saviour & His Words 56
false prophets 197
false teachers 86, 87, 127, 139, 140, 167, 198
False Teachers Reproduce 140
False Teachers Ruin Others 86
False Teaching Is Like Cancer 85
False Teachings Are Unsure 87

Father	. 2, 4-6, 8-10, 18, 21, 26, 41, 43, 54, 62, 74, 76, 77, 91, 109, 118, 133, 136, 140, 142, 153, 157, 159, 165, 169, 185, 187, 189, 193, 202, 203, 205, 206, 209, 210
fear	15-17, 41, 61, 95, 111, 165, 184, 202
fellowsoldiers	10
fire	21, 28, 51, 69, 70, 85, 115, 122, 123, 160, 161, 168, 172, 178, 186, 193
first Roman imprisonment	2, 44, 72
Flee Youthful Lusts	91
flesh	6, 15, 24, 25, 33, 40, 59, 67, 74-76, 83, 89, 91, 92, 121, 163, 172, 177, 189, 191
Foreword	iii, iv
Forgive And Forbear	130
fornication	89, 116, 170
forsake	210
forsaken	43, 188, 199, 200
four leading fundamentalist Critical Text institutions	36
fruit	18, 42, 62, 89, 95, 112, 129, 157
Fundamentalist schools and teachers	196
Fundamentalists and Gnostic Texts?	36
Furnished To "Good Works"	153
Genesis through Revelation each year, Bible reading	45
Gentile	2, 4, 33, 208, 210
Gertrude Grace Sanborn	8, 58, 134, 157, 180, 203, 214
Get The Right "Word" To Divide	118
gifts	12-15, 214
Giving The Gospel In Meekness	97
Gnostic	17, 30, 36, 39, 73, 119, 168, 171, 201
Gnostic Bible Versions Are "Fables"	119
Gnostic critical Greek text	30, 36, 39
Gnostic critical texts	17
Gnostic Greek Texts	171
Gnostic MSS Remove "Christ" Here	201
Gnostic Texts Leave Out "On Me"	30
Gnostic Texts Remove "Christ" Here	17
Gnostic Versions Turn Away Ears	168
Gnostics	201
God Is Faithful	78
God Knows Who Are Saved	88
God Promised Words Preservation	79
God the Father	4, 5, 26, 76, 159, 205, 210
God the Holy Spirit	89, 120, 129, 198, 209, 210
God the Son	5, 26, 65, 159, 210

Index of Words and Phrases 221

God "Strengthened" Paul 201
God's Fruit In Houses Of Clay 42
God's Grace Has Appeared 27
God's Promise Of Preserving Words 204
God's Will Is In His Words 65
God's Words ... iii, 40, 45, 65, 73, 81, 86, 87, 129, 147, 152, 155, 162, 180,
198, 199
God's "Grace" In Sickness And Pain 212
God's "Throne Of Grace" 213
Good News And Bad News 69
good soldier 57
gospel ... 2, 6, 7, 17, 20, 21, 23, 27, 29, 32, 41, 44, 45, 65, 67, 69, 70, 76, 97,
113, 124, 135, 136, 142, 143, 156, 162, 163, 172, 179, 181, 188,
190, 201, 210, 211
gospel of Christ 17, 21, 45, 97, 113, 181
grace 4-6, 8, 10, 12, 13, 15, 19, 24-27, 44, 51-53, 58, 73, 74, 77, 82, 90,
102, 134, 135, 140, 141, 153, 154, 157, 160, 163, 179-181, 193,
203, 209-214
Grace Bible Church 44
Grace, Mercy, And Peace 4, 5
Graham, Billy and Franklin 195
great house 89
great white throne 122, 123, 160, 161, 187
Greek . iii, 4, 17, 20, 21, 30, 36-40, 45, 70, 72, 73, 79, 96, 97, 100, 102, 106-
108, 110, 111, 113, 114, 118, 119, 121, 122, 131, 140, 143, 147-
150, 152, 162, 164, 165, 167-169, 171, 173, 174, 176-180, 182,
196, 199-201, 204, 206
Greek synonyms 131
Greek text 17, 30, 36, 39, 73, 169
Greek texts 162, 171, 201
grieve not the Holy Spirit 42
Heaven 2, 3, 6, 7, 37, 38, 48, 69, 76, 77, 84, 86, 113, 117, 120, 136, 142,
153, 160, 174, 181, 183, 185, 186, 202, 205, 211, 213
Hebrew consonant 38
Hebrew vowel 38
Hebrew, Aramaic, and Greek Words .. 36-40, 70, 72, 79, 143, 148, 149, 162,
168, 171, 180, 182, 196, 199
Hell 5, 16, 21, 31, 96, 117, 123, 130, 143, 160, 167, 172, 173, 186
herald 31, 162
heritage 11
Hodgkin's disease 47
Hold Fast Sound Words 36

Holy Spirit	15, 18, 24, 40-42, 89, 92, 120, 124, 129, 198, 209, 210
homosexuality	106, 110, 170
Hort, Professor F. H. A.	17, 39, 201
house	2, 16, 22, 23, 44, 47, 56, 89, 91, 100, 101, 103, 127, 133, 149, 163, 190, 193, 207
House Churches Are Biblical	207
How To Handle "Evil"	194
husbandman	62
Hybels, Bill	195
I warn against Harold Camping	195
I warn against John MacArthur	195
I Warn Against Many Things	195
I warn against the false teachings	195
Importance of Bodily Resurrection	69
Index of Words and Phrases	iv, 215
instruction	54, 115, 117, 147, 150, 151, 165
instruction in righteousness	147, 151
International Baptist College	36, 196
Introductory Remarks	1
Ironside, Dr. Harry	iii
Jambres	119, 120, 182, 199
Jannes	119, 120, 182, 199
Jehovah's Witnesses	196
Jewess	2, 4, 147
Joel Osteen	195
John MacArthur	25, 195
jot	38
joy	8, 10, 18, 46, 61, 95, 129, 134, 138, 175, 179, 184, 186, 210
Judaism	196
Judas Iscariot	24, 110
judgment	16, 19, 34, 122-124, 138, 151, 160, 161, 185-187, 202, 205
Julia Monaghan	ii
justified	24-26, 52, 211
justifies	25, 211
justifieth	25
justify	24, 25
keep	18, 21, 22, 27, 32, 33, 35, 37, 39, 40, 78, 79, 81, 84, 97, 101, 102, 111, 115, 161, 171, 179, 188, 204, 209
Keep Away From "Pride"	102
keep by the Holy Ghost	40
King James Bible	iii, iv, 36, 37, 39, 40, 65, 72, 73, 79, 94, 118, 143, 148, 149, 152, 162, 168-171, 180, 182, 196, 199

Index of Words and Phrases

Knowing The Bible 145
lake of fire 21, 70, 123, 160, 168, 172, 186
last days 99, 106, 125
lesbianism 170
libation 174
liberals 5, 70, 173
Liberia 33
Life and Immortality In The Gospel 29
loins 118, 170
Lois 11
longsuffering 18, 20, 23, 95, 96, 127, 129, 130, 161, 164, 201
Lord Jesus Christ . 1-5, 7, 11-14, 16, 19, 21, 25, 27-33, 37-39, 42, 44-48, 51-
53, 55-57, 59-62, 64-67, 69, 70, 72, 73, 76, 77, 80, 82, 83, 86-88,
91, 96, 97, 99, 108-110, 118, 123, 124, 128, 130, 143-146, 159-
161, 165, 170, 172-174, 176, 178, 183-187, 189, 191, 193, 195,
198, 201-203, 205, 208-211, 214
love .. 6, 9, 11, 15, 16, 18, 22, 28, 36, 39, 49, 60, 61, 64, 78, 81, 91, 95, 128-
131, 137-142, 152, 155, 165, 181, 183-185, 189, 191, 197, 198,
204, 205, 209
love not the world 18, 189
Love With Understanding 64
Luke ... 39, 47, 48, 55, 56, 63, 64, 66, 95, 101, 108, 109, 112, 144, 149, 164,
188-190, 197, 200
lusts of your father ye will do 91
Lystra 2, 4, 23, 132, 136
MacArthur, John 25, 195
manner of life 23, 126
map 1, 124
Maranatha Baptist Bible College 36
Mark . 8, 19, 21, 39, 54, 64, 127, 133, 141, 149, 163, 189-191, 193, 197, 200
Mark Had A Second Chance 191
marriage 106
marriages 106
Matthew 24:35 38
Matthew 5:17-18 .... 38, 39
meaning of the words iii
Mediterranean Sea 1
meekness 20, 95, 97, 130
mercy 2, 4, 5, 12, 22, 44, 48, 57, 78, 95, 129, 132, 207, 213
METANOIA (repentance) 96
Michigan, University of at Ann Arbor 16, 44, 87
mind 8, 9, 15, 18-20, 63, 81, 96, 121, 130, 136, 137, 145, 151, 152, 156,

Missionaries Are "Evangelists" 13
Missionary David Bennett 13
modernists 5, 67, 70, 173
Monaghan, Julia ii
Moorman Dr. Jack 39
Moses 24, 37, 56, 82, 119, 120, 144, 145, 182, 186, 199
moved 16, 23, 54, 121, 133, 134, 181, 186
much evil 14, 193, 194
Muhammadanism 196
murder 108
my dad 20
MY TIMES ARE IN THY HANDS 203
my Words shall not pass away 38
Naming Names Is Biblical 43
NASV (New American Standard Version) 73, 169, 196
National Association of Evangelicals 196
National Council of Churches 196
Navy chaplain 16, 44, 115
negative 5, 20, 38, 39
NEPHO (abstaining from alcohol in any form) 171
Never, Never "Pass Away" (Christ's O.T. & N.T. Words) 39
New Age Movement 196
New American Standard Version 168
new evangelicalism 196
New International Version 168
New Testament .. 37-40, 53, 73, 95, 103, 133, 140, 147, 148, 168, 169, 180,
                                         183, 190, 192, 193, 206, 210
NIV (New International Version) 73, 169, 196
NKJV (New King James Version) 196
No Alcohol In Order To "Watch" 172
No Endurance Of "Sound Doctrine" 166
No Old Testament "Corrections" 145
No Other Means But God's "Grace" 211
no scholastic degree 55
Northland Baptist Bible College 36
Northland Baptist College 196
Not Saved By "Good Works" 154
NRSV (New Revised Standard Version) 196
Old Testament 38, 40, 51, 119, 144-148, 180, 193
Onesiphorus 2, 22, 44-48, 206, 207
Only God's Grace Can Save Us 26

Index of Words and Phrases

Only Original Words "God-Breathed" 147
Oprah Winfrey's cults 196
Order Blank Pages iv
original Hebrew, Aramaic, and Greek Words ... 37-40, 70, 72, 79, 148, 149
Original Words Preserved 37
Osteen, Joel 195
other verses .... iii, 77
OU ME (the strongest Greek negative) 38, 39
Our Church Has "Willing" Offerings 175
Our Mouths Must "Minister Grace" 212
Our Omniscient God 123
Our "Fight" Must Be A Good One 177
Oxford English Dictionary 81
pacifist 59, 177
parchments 192, 193
Pastor .. 1-iii, 1, 2, 7, 11, 14, 21, 23, 25, 26, 32, 36, 39, 40, 43, 48, 52-54, 57, 60, 63, 65, 67, 71, 72, 79, 80, 84, 87, 90, 91, 93-95, 101, 104, 110, 113, 115, 125, 130, 142, 149, 159, 161, 162, 166, 171-174, 176, 189, 197, 206
Pastor D. A. Waite, Th.D., Ph.D. .... 1, iii
Pastor Earl V. Willetts 189
Pastor Timothy 1, 2, 11, 21, 23, 32, 36, 40, 43, 48, 52, 57, 63, 65, 67, 79, 80, 84, 90, 91, 93, 95, 142, 149, 159, 162, 171-174, 176, 197
Pastors Should Be "Apt To Teach" 94
Pastors Should Preach Sound Doctrine 166
Pastors Should "Exhort" 165
Pastors Should "Rebuke" 164
Pastors Should "Reprove" 164
Pastors' Children Must Behave 104
patience 23, 57, 62, 117, 126, 130-133, 146, 153, 201
Paul .. iii, 1-4, 6, 7, 9-12, 21, 23, 26-29, 31-36, 39, 43-49, 51-53, 59, 60, 62-65, 67, 69-73, 75-77, 79, 80, 83-86, 88, 90-93, 95, 99, 100, 117, 125-131, 135-137, 139-142, 145-147, 149, 159, 162, 163, 166, 171, 172, 174, 176-183, 185, 188-195, 197-201, 203-214
Paul Suffered Greatly For Christ 32
Paul Was Ready To Depart Earth 174
Paul–An Apostle And Teacher 32
Paul's Death Was An "Offering" 174
Paul's love 130
Paul's Two Imprisonments 72
Paul's "manner of life" 128
peace 4, 5, 10, 18, 25, 91, 92, 95, 104, 129, 142, 152, 163, 203, 205

Pentecostal 196
perfect .. 6, 10, 14, 16, 18, 27, 31, 37, 43, 52, 65, 67, 86, 108, 152, 153, 175, 211, 213
Perfect God And Perfect Man (the Lord Jesus Christ) 67, 108
perfecting 14
period 38, 137
persecution 18, 33, 34, 57, 135, 137, 138
persecutions 23, 51, 57, 70, 131-133, 137
Pharisees 59, 101, 108, 197
physician 188, 190
Pleasing Our Commanding Officer 59
Post-Modernism, ... 196
power . 2, 5, 15-17, 20, 21, 29, 33, 42, 45, 51, 52, 71, 75-77, 90, 95, 97, 113, 114, 119, 125, 130, 135, 136, 142, 144, 170, 186, 201, 211
practical application iii
pray 7, 8, 97, 157, 172, 199, 205
preached sermons iii
Preachers Need Ministers Also 208
Preaching Gnostic "Fables" 171
present tense (in Greek) 6, 20, 79, 84, 138, 140
preserve 37, 40, 137, 143, 202, 204
preserved 36, 37, 70, 72, 143, 148, 149, 152, 168, 180, 199, 205
Preserved Original Bible Words 72
preserving 204
pre-chosen body 60
pre-tribulation rapture 137
Priscilla 206, 207
prison . 1-4, 7, 10, 43-47, 61, 69-73, 172, 178, 184, 188, 189, 192, 193, 201, 209
prison cell 2, 192
prison ministry 44
prisoner 2, 20, 44, 45, 135
prisoners 44, 45, 128
prohibitions 20
prostitutes 114-116
prostitution 116
Publisher's data iv
purge 6, 90, 176
purpose   13, 14, 23, 24, 27, 59, 62, 82, 84, 117, 126, 128, 137, 143, 148-153, 156, 161, 187
put to death 3
quick 28, 71, 159, 160, 163, 187

Index of Words and Phrases

quiet	83
race	132
raised us up together	74
rapture	27, 28, 46, 69, 73, 105, 123, 137, 161, 185
Read God's Words Daily	45
ready	17, 19, 58, 95, 126, 154, 159, 163, 174, 200, 202
Received Greek text	73, 169
reproof	147, 149-151, 191
Revised Standard Version	168
RGIRL (the memory hint for the five crowns)	61
Rick Warren	195
righteous judgment	34, 123, 187
rightly dividing the Word of truth	22, 45, 80, 82, 118, 170
Robert Schuller	195
Roman Catholic	5, 48, 113, 196
Roman Catholic Church	113, 196
Rome	1, 2, 4, 10, 26, 43, 44, 46, 47, 71, 163, 192, 206
RSV (Revised Standard Version)	169, 196
Run Our Own Race With "Patience"	132
Russia	33
Sadducees	197
salutatorian	55
salutatory	55
Salvation's Source–The Bible	143
Sanborn, Gertrude Grace	ii, 8, 58, 134, 157, 176, 180, 203, 214
Satan Cannot Indwell Christians	120
Saved People Cannot Be Lost	205
scholastic degree	55
Schuller, Robert	195
scribes	197
Sealed For Eternity	42
seaport	1
Seasoned With "Salt"	212
second Roman imprisonment	26, 44, 72
selfish attitude	100
serve	3, 6, 7, 48, 58, 176, 191
Seventh Day Adventism	196
shut up in prison	3
Sierra Leone	33
silly women	114
Sinful "Pleasures" Only Temporary	113
sins of the world	143, 186

smallest Hebrew consonant (yodh, like a comma) 38
smallest Hebrew vowel (hiriq or a dot) 38
soldier 57-60
Some Gifts Are Temporary 12
Son . 1, 4-7, 14, 21, 26, 30, 41, 47, 51, 54, 63, 65-68, 74, 76, 78, 83, 99, 109,
         115, 130, 136, 143, 150, 156, 159, 163, 175, 180, 185, 210, 212
son in the faith 4, 5
son Timothy 5
sound mind 15, 18
spirit of fear 15
spiritual battle 59
spiritual gifts 13, 14
spiritual heritage 11
spiritual pacifist 59
Stay Clear Of Carnal Christians 90
Stay Firm On Bible "Doctrines" 127
strengthen 134, 153, 165, 201, 213
Striving About Words 79
strong ... 14, 17, 20, 34, 51, 52, 54, 109, 129, 130, 133, 172, 178, 181, 189,
                                                        201, 203, 212, 213
strongest negative in the Greek language (OU ME) 38, 39
Strouse, Dr. Thomas 38
student 16
study .... iii, 22, 45, 81-83, 118, 131, 156, 157, 170, 193
suffering 32-35, 85, 126, 133, 202, 213
Swift, Randal 116
synonyms 131
Table of Contents iv
Taoism 196
Teach Children God's Words 147
Teaching Those Who Disagree 54
tears 8-10, 58, 134, 157, 203, 214
temporary 12, 113
Textus Receptus 39, 94
thanks 6, 7, 60, 105
The 1611 Meaning Of "Study" 81
The Battle For God's Words 73
The Bible Gives "Comfort" 146
The Bible Is For "Doctrine" 149
The Christian's Three Enemies 92
The Command To "Preach" The Words 162
the Devil 15, 19, 37, 59-61, 91, 92, 96, 97, 107, 120, 177, 184

Index of Words and Phrases

The Error Of Wrong "Learning" 117
the faith .. 4, 5, 14, 24, 25, 39, 51, 71, 74, 76, 79, 86, 87, 119, 121, 122, 125, 130, 136, 141, 165, 166, 172, 176, 179-182, 198, 199
The Five Crowns 61, 184
The Five Crowns In The Bible 61
the flesh 6, 33, 40, 59, 67, 74-76, 83, 89, 91, 92, 172, 177, 189
The Goal Of False Teachers 87
The Gospel Of God's "Grace" 211
the grace of God 27, 141, 160, 179, 210, 211, 213
The Great White Throne Judgment 122, 160, 161, 187
The Incarnation Is Vital 27
The Indwelling Holy Spirit 40
The Judgment Seat Of Christ 122-124, 160, 161, 187
the last days 99, 106, 125
The Lord Jesus Christ The Judge 161
the Lord Jesus Christ, the Author 38
The Meaning Of Being "Heady" 111
The Meaning Of Being "Highminded" 111
The Meaning of "Abolish" 29
The Meaning Of "Covetousness" 100
The Meaning Of "Endure" 137
The Meaning Of "Longsuffering" 129
The Meaning Of "Ministering" 48
The Meaning Of "Refreshing" 46
The Meaning Of "Repentance" 96
The Meanings Of "Amen" 206
The Meanings Of "Commit" 53
The Meanings Of "Grace" 52
The Meanings of "Keep" 35
The Meanings Of "Shun" 84
The Meanings Of "Teach" 54
The Millennial Reign Of Christ 77
The Need Of Dispensationalism 82
The Old Nature & The New Nature 92
The People In The "Great House" 89
The Preacher As A "Herald" 31
The Pre-Tribulation Rapture 137
The Saved Must Depart From Sin 88
The Saved Should Not Live Ungodly 85
The Saviour Was "Good" But Hated 109
The Sin of Despising Good People 108
the sins of the world 143, 186

The Source of Salvation 24
the Tribulation 87, 124, 195
The Trinity Indwells The Saved 210
The Way To Salvation 25
The Will of God In Suffering 34
the world ... iii, 16, 18, 20, 24, 27, 30, 31, 33, 40, 41, 54, 59, 60, 68, 72, 73, 87, 92, 96, 109, 121, 133, 139, 143, 151, 155, 162, 164, 173, 177, 182, 186-189, 196, 198, 209
The World Observes Christians 155
The Yearly Bible Reading Schedule 144
The "Parchments"–The Words of God 193
THEOPNEUSTOS ("God-Breathed" only for Hebrew/Aramaic/Greek .. 147
Things "Without Natural Affection" 106
Three Purposes For Christ's Gifts 14
Thy Word is settled in Heaven 37
Timotheus (Timothy) 4, 49, 192, 207, 208
Timothy ... 1, iv, 1-8, 10, 11, 14, 15, 20-24, 26-28, 31, 32, 34-36, 39, 40, 43-46, 48, 51-53, 55-63, 65, 67, 70-76, 78-80, 83-96, 99-114, 116-119, 121, 122, 125-133, 135, 137, 139-143, 147, 149, 152, 154, 159, 161-168, 170-174, 176, 177, 180-184, 188-194, 197-200, 202, 204, 206, 207, 209, 210, 212, 213
Timothy Knew Paul Well 128
Timothy's mother 2, 11
Timothy's Spiritual Heritage 11
Titus ... 1, 26, 28, 32, 46, 80, 85, 92, 93, 104, 112, 131, 138, 149, 154, 155, 165, 167, 170, 182, 188, 192, 213
Translations Are Not "Inspired Of God" (only Hebrew/Aramaic/Greek) . 148
Trench, Bishop (author of an authoritative book on Greek synonyms) ... 131
Turkey 1, 26, 192
turn away 84, 113, 118, 168, 198
turned away 43
TV Blasphemy Is Common 103
twenty-five signs 123-125
twenty-five signs of the "last days" 123
two confinements 1
Two Heretics Named By Paul 86
Two Kinds Of Negative Commands 20
Two Kinds Of "Forsaking" 199
Two Phases Of The 2nd Coming 28
Two Things To "Remember" 65
Unitarianism 196
University of Michigan (where the author graduated in 1945) 16, 44

Index of Words and Phrases 231

unsaved 11, 16, 56, 89, 123, 124, 185, 197
verbal, plenary preservation (VPP) 38, 39
verbal, plenary preservation of the originals (Hebrew/Aramaic/Greek) 38, 39
VPP (verbal, plenary preservation) 148
Waite, Pastor D. A., Daniel, D. A., Jr., or Yvonne S. 1-iii, 10, 64, 87, 189
warn 9, 43, 171, 195, 196, 198
warn against 195, 196
Warren, Rick 195
Warring With Words 94
watch 9, 23, 35, 51, 57, 135, 141, 171, 172, 181, 198
Watch Out For Doctrinal Drifts 171
We Are Born Into Satan's Kingdom 96
We Are The Lord's 75
we shall also reign with Him if we are saved 75, 76
we use and defend the King James Bible at the BFT Baptist Church 72
Westcott, Bishop B. F. 17, 39, 201
Westcott and Hort (authors of the Gnostic Critical Greek N.T.) .. 17, 39, 201
What Is Your Biblical Ministry? 173
What Is Your Christian "Course" 178
When Not To "Strive" 80
When Will The World End? 209
Wild Deacons' Children? 104
will of God 2-4, 34, 35, 46, 79, 105, 132, 136, 152, 153, 189, 191, 202
Willetts, Pastor Earl V. (the author's second pastor) 189
Williams, Dr. H. D., M.D., Ph.D. ii
willing 19, 34, 59, 73, 96, 106, 130, 138, 154, 172, 174
willingly 116, 175
winter 188, 192, 209
wise unto salvation 143
withstood 119, 182, 197-199
withstood our words 197, 198
Words of God ... iii, 13, 14, 20, 32, 40, 53, 60, 71-73, 81, 82, 119, 126, 127,
          140, 147, 150, 152, 155, 162, 164, 166, 170, 182, 193, 195, 204,
                                                                207, 213
Works Won't Justify Us 24
world . iii, 5, 16, 18, 20, 24, 27, 30, 31, 33, 40, 41, 47, 54, 56, 59, 60, 68, 72,
        73, 85, 87, 92, 96, 99, 109, 111, 121, 133, 136, 138, 139, 143, 151,
           152, 155, 161, 162, 164, 173, 177, 182, 186-189, 196, 198, 202,
                                                                209, 214
World Council of Churches (WCC) 196
World Evangelical Fellowship (WEF) 196
Writing His Last Letter From Prison 2

Yearly Bible Reading Needed	82
Yvonne Sanborn Waite	ii, 10
Zacchaeus	47
"Assurance" Is Needed	142
"Bereans"	145
"boasters"	101
"church which is His Body"	73, 105, 123, 185
"Covenant Breaking" Divorce Data	106
"covetous"	100, 101
"Disobedience To Parents"	103
"ever learning"	116
"False Witness" A Popular Sin	107
"fierce"	108
"Good Works" As An "Adornment"	154
"Good Works" Found In The Bible	154
"having a form of godliness"	113
"heady"	110, 111
"highminded"	111
"hiriq" (the smallest Hebrew vowel, a "tittle" which is like a comma)	38
"incontinent"	107
"Itching Ears" Need Scratching	167
"Longsuffering" As "Fruit Of The Spirit"	129
"Longsuffering" Versus "Patience"	131
"lovers of pleasures more than lovers of God"	112
"men of corrupt minds"	121
"Pleasure" Brings No Spiritual Fruit	112
"Politically Correct" Preachers	33
"pride"	102
"raised from the dead"	65, 67
"reprobate concerning the faith"	122
"Stirring Up" Kind Of Women	135
"The Faith" Means Bible Doctrine (including every Word of God)	179, 182
'TIS HIS WILL	134
"tittle" (a "hiriq") which is the smallest Hebrew vowel, like a comma	38
"traitors"	109
"trucebreakers"	106
"Unholy"	105
"Unthankful"	104
"Without Natural Affection"	105, 106

About the Author

The author of this book, Dr. D. A. Waite, received a B.A. (Bachelor of Arts) in classical Greek and Latin from the University of Michigan in 1948, a Th.M. (Master of Theology), with high honors, in New Testament Greek Literature and Exegesis from Dallas Theological Seminary in 1952, an M.A. (Master of Arts) in Speech from Southern Methodist University in 1953, a Th.D. (Doctor of Theology), with honors, in Bible Exposition from Dallas Theological Seminary in 1955, and a Ph.D. in Speech from Purdue University in 1961. He holds both New Jersey and Pennsylvania teacher certificates in Greek and Language Arts.

He has been a teacher in the areas of Greek, Hebrew, Bible, Speech, and English for over thirty-five years in ten schools, including one junior high, one senior high, four Bible institutes, two colleges, two universities, and one seminary. He served his country as a Navy Chaplain for five years on active duty; pastored three churches; was Chairman and Director of the Radio and Audio-Film Commission of the American Council of Christian Churches; since 1969, has been Founder, President, and Director of THE BIBLE FOR TODAY; since 1978, has been President of the DEAN BURGON SOCIETY; has produced over 700 other studies, books, cassettes, VHS's, CD's, or VCR's on various topics; and is heard on a thirty-minute weekly radio program IN DEFENSE OF TRADITIONAL BIBLE TEXTS, on radio, shortwave, and streaming on the Internet at BibleForToday.org, 24/7/365.

Dr. and Mrs. Waite have been married since 1948; they have four sons, one daughter, and, at present, eight grandchildren, and six great-grandchildren. Since October 4, 1998, he has been the Pastor of the Bible For Today Baptist Church in Collngswood, New Jersey.

Order Blank (p. 1)

Name:_____

Address:_____

City & State:_____Zip:_____

Credit Card #:_____Expires:_____

Latest Books
[ ] Send 2 Timothy--Preaching Verse by Verse, by Pastor D. A. Waite, 248 pages, perfectbound ($11+$5 S&H) fully indexed.
[ ] Send *A Critical Answer to God's Word Preserved* by Pastor D. A. Waite, 192 pp. perfect bound ($11.00+$4.00 S&H)

The Most Recently Published Books
[ ] Send *8,000 Differences Between Textus Receptus & Critical Text* by Dr. J. A. Moorman, 544 pp., hd.back ($20+$5+ S&H)
[ ] *Early Manuscripts, Church Fathers, & the Authorized Version* by Dr. Jack Moorman, $18+$5 S&H. Hardback
[ ] Send *The LIE That Changed the Modern World* by Dr. H. D. Williams ($16+$5 S&H) Hardback book
[ ] Send *With Tears in My Heart* by Gertrude G. Sanborn. Hardback 414 pp. ($25+$5 S&H) 400 Christian Poems

Preaching Verse by Verse Books
[ ] Send 1 Timothy--Preaching Verse by Verse, by Pastor D. A. Waite, 288 pages, hardback ($11+$5 S&H) fully indexed.
[ ] Send *Romans--Preaching Verse by Verse* by Pastor D. A. Waite 736 pp. Hardback ($25+$5 S&H) fully indexed
[ ] Send *Colossians & Philemon--Preaching Verse by Verse* by Pastor D. A. Waite ($12+$5 S&H) hardback, 240 pages.
[ ] Send *Philippians--Preaching Verse by Verse* by Pastor D. A. Waite ($10+$5 S&H) hardback, 176 pages.
[ ] Send *Ephesians--Preaching Verse by Verse* by Pastor D. A. Waite ($12+$5 S&H) hardback, 224 pages.
[ ] Send *Galatians--Preaching Verse By Verse* by Pastor D. A. Waite ($12+$5 S&H) hardback, 216 pages.

Send or Call Orders to:
THE BIBLE FOR TODAY
900 Park Ave., Collingswood, NJ 08108
Phone: 856-854-4452; FAX:--2464; Orders: 1-800 JOHN 10:9
E-Mail Orders: BFT@BibleForToday.org; Credit Cards OK

Order Blank (p. 2)

Name:_____

Address:_____

City & State:_____Zip:_____

Credit Card #:_____Expires:_____

More Preaching Verse by Verse Books
[ ] Send *First Peter--Preaching Verse By Verse* by Pastor D. A. Waite ($10+$5 S&H) hardback, 176 pages.

Books on Bible Texts & Translations
[ ] Send *Defending the King James Bible* by DAW ($12+$5 S&H) A hardback book, indexed with study questions.
[ ] Send *BJU's Errors on Bible Preservation* by Dr. D. A. Waite, 110 pages, paperback ($8+$4 S&H) fully indexed
[ ] Send *Fundamentalist Deception on Bible Preservation* by Dr. Waite, ($8+$4 S&H), paperback, fully indexed
[ ] Send *Fundamentalist MIS-INFORMATION on Bible Versions* by Dr. Waite ($7+$4 S&H) perfect bound, 136 pages
[ ] Send *Fundamentalist Distortions on Bible Versions* by Dr. Waite ($6+$3 S&H) A perfect bound book, 80 pages
[ ] Send *Fuzzy Facts From Fundamentalists* by Dr. D. A. Waite ($8.00 + $4.00) printed booklet
[ ] Send *Foes of the King James Bible Refuted* by DAW ($10 +$4 S&H) A perfect bound book, 164 pages in length.
[ ] Send *Central Seminary Refuted on Bible Versions* by Dr. Waite ($10+$4 S&H) A perfect bound book, 184 pages
[ ] Send *The Case for the King James Bible* by DAW ($7 +$3 S&H) A perfect bound book, 112 pages in length.
[ ] Send *Theological Heresies of Westcott and Hort* by Dr. D. A. Waite, ($7+$3 S&H) A printed booklet.
[ ] Send *Westcott's Denial of Resurrection*, Dr. Waite ($4+$3)
[ ] Send *Four Reasons for Defending KJB* by DAW ($3+$3)

Send or Call Orders to:
THE BIBLE FOR TODAY
900 Park Ave., Collingswood, NJ 08108
Phone: 856-854-4452; FAX:--2464; Orders: 1-800 JOHN 10:9
E-Mail Orders: BFT@BibleForToday.org; Credit Cards OK

Order Blank (p. 3)

Name:_____

Address:_____

City & State:_____ Zip:_____

Credit Card #:_____Expires:_____

More Books on Texts & Translations
[ ] Send *Holes in the Holman Christian Standard Bible* by Dr. Waite ($3+$2 S&H) A printed booklet, 40 pages
[ ] Send *Contemporary Eng. Version Exposed*, DAW ($3+$2)
[ ] Send *NIV Inclusive Language Exposed* by DAW ($5+$3)
[ ] Send *26 Hours of KJB Seminar* (4 videos) by DAW($50.00)

Books By Dr. Jack Moorman
[ ] Send Manuscript Digest of the N.T. (721 pp.) By Dr. Jack Moorman, copy-machine bound ($50+$7 S&H)
[ ] *Early Manuscripts, Church Fathers, & the Authorized Version* by Dr. Jack Moorman, $18+$5 S&H. Hardback
[ ] Send *Forever Settled--Bible Doc*uments *& History Survey* by Dr. Jack Moorman, $20+$5 S&H. Hardback book.
[ ] Send *When the KJB Departs from the So-Called "Majority Text"* by Dr. Jack Moorman, $16+$5 S&H
[ ] Send *Missing in Modern Bibles--Nestle-Aland/NIV Errors* by Dr. Jack Moorman, $8+$4 S&H
[ ] Send *The Doctrinal Heart of the Bible--Removed from Modern Versions* by Dr. Jack Moorman, VCR, $15 +$4 S&H
[ ] Send *Modern Bibles--The Dark Secret* by Dr. Jack Moorman, $5+$3 S&H
[ ] Send *Samuel P. Tregelles--The Man Who Made the Critical Text Acceptable to Bible Believers* by Dr. Moorman ($2+$1)
[ ] Send *8,000 Differences Between TR & CT* by Dr. Jack Moorman [$65 + $7.50 S&H] Over 500-large-pages of data
[ ] Send *356 Doctrinal Erors in the NIV & Other Modern Versions*, 100-large-pages, $10.00+$6 S&H.

Send or Call Orders to:
THE BIBLE FOR TODAY
900 Park Ave., Collingswood, NJ 08108
Phone: 856-854-4452; FAX:--2464; Orders: 1-800 JOHN 10:9
E-Mail Orders: BFT@BibleForToday.org; Credit Cards OK

Order Blank (p. 4)

Name:_____

Address:_____

City & State:_____Zip:_____

Credit Card #:_____Expires:_____

Books By or About Dean Burgon

[ ] Send *The Revision Revised* by Dean Burgon ($25 + $5 S&H) A hardback book, 640 pages in length.
[ ] Send *The Last 12 verses of Mark* by Dean Burgon ($15+$5 S&H) A hardback book 400 pages.
[ ] Send *The Traditional Text* hardback by Burgon ($16+$5 S&H) A hardback book, 384 pages in length.
[ ] Send *Causes of Corruption* by Burgon ($15+$5 S&H) A hardback book, 360 pages in length.
[ ] Send *Inspiration and Interpretation*, Dean Burgon ($25+$5 S&H) A hardback book, 610 pages in length.
[ ] Send *Burgon's Warnings on Revision* by DAW ($7+$4 S&H) A perfect bound book, 120 pages in length.
] Send *Westcott & Hort's Greek Text & Theory Refuted by Burgon's Revision Revised--Summarized* by Dr. D. A. Waite ($7.00+$4 S&H), 120 pages, perfect bound.
[ ] Send *Dean Burgon's Confidence in KJB* by DAW ($3+$3)
[ ] Send *Vindicating Mark 16:9-20* by Dr. Waite ($3+$3S&H)
[ ] Send *Summary of Traditional Text* by Dr. Waite ($3 +$3)
[ ] Send *Summary of Causes of Corruption*, DAW ($3+$3)
[ ] Send *Summary of Inspiration* by Dr. Waite ($3+$3 S&H)

More Books by Dr. D. A. Waite

[ ] Send *Making Marriage Melodious* by Pastor D. A. Waite ($7+$4 S&H), perfect bound, 112 pages.

Send or Call Orders to:
THE BIBLE FOR TODAY
900 Park Ave., Collingswood, NJ 08108
Phone: 856-854-4452; FAX:--2464; Orders: 1-800 JOHN 10:9
E-Mail Orders: BFT@BibleForToday.org; Credit Cards OK

Order Blank (p. 5)

Name:_____

Address:_____

City & State:_____Zip:_____

Credit Card #:_____Expires:_____

Books by D. A. Waite, Jr.
[ ] Send *Readability of A.V. (KJB)* by D. A. Waite, Jr. ($6+$3)
[ ] Send *4,114 Definitions from the Defined King James Bible* by D. A. Waite, Jr. ($7.00+$4.00 S&H)
[ ] Send *The Doctored New Testament* by D. A. Waite, Jr. ($25+$5 S&H) Greek MSS differences shown, hardback
[ ] Send *Defined King James Bible* lg. prt. leather ($40+$7.50)
[ ] Send *Defined King James Bible* med. prt. leather ($35+$6)

Miscellaneous Authors
[ ] Send *The Pure Words of God* by Dr. H. D. Williams, perfect bound ($15.00 + $5 S&H)
[ ] Send *Hearing the Voice of God* by Dr. H. D. William, perfect bound ($18.00 + $5.00 S&H)
[ ] Send *The Attack on the Bible's Canon* by Dr. H. D. Williams, perfect bound ($15.00 + S&H)
[ ] Send *Word-For-Word Translating of The Received Texts* by Dr. H. D. Williams, 288 pages, paperback ($10+$5 S&H).
[ ] Send *Guide to Textual Criticism* by Edward Miller ($7+$4) Hardback book
[ ] Send *Scrivener's Greek New Testament Underlying the King James Bible*, hardback, ($14+$5 S&H)
[ ] Send *Scrivener's <u>Annotated</u> Greek New Testament*, by Dr. Frederick Scrivener: Hardback--($35+$5 S&H); Genuine Leather--($45+$5 S&H)
[ ] Send *Why Not the King James Bible?--An Answer to James White's KJVO Book* by Dr. K. D. DiVietro, $10+$5 S&H
[ ] Send Brochure #1: *"1000 Titles Defending the KJB/TR"* No Charge

Send or Call Orders to:
THE BIBLE FOR TODAY
900 Park Ave., Collingswood, NJ 08108
Phone: 856-854-4452; FAX:--2464; Orders: 1-800 JOHN 10:9
E-Mail Orders: BFT@BibleForToday.org; Credit Cards OK

The Defined King James Bible

UNCOMMON WORDS DEFINED ACCURATELY

I. Deluxe Genuine Leather

✦Large Print--Black or Burgundy✦
1 for $40.00+$7.50 S&H
✦Case of 12 for✦
$30.00 each+$30 S&H

✦Medium Print--Black or Burgundy✦
1 for $35.00+$6 S&H
✦Case of 12 for✦
$25.00 each+$24 S&H

II. Deluxe Hardback Editions

1 for $20.00+$7.50 S&H (Large Print)
✦Case of 12 for✦
$15.00 each+$30 S&H (Large Print)

1 for $15.00+$6 S&H (Medium Print)
✦Case of 12 for✦
$10.00 each+$24 S&H (Medium Print)

Order Phone: 1-800-JOHN 10:9

Pastor D. A. Waite, Th.D., Ph.D.

The Apostle Paul's Last Words

"I Have Fought A Good Fight." As the Apostle Paul wrote his last letter before going Home to Glory, he summed up his autobiography in three short clauses. First, he said *"I have fought a good fight."* He did not deny that his faithful service for the Lord and Saviour, Jesus Christ, was a *"fight."* But he hastened to add that his *"fight"* for the Saviour and His Words was a *"good fight."* He did not cut corners. He did not lie. He did not play favorites. He did not cower before his many enemies.

"I Have Finished My Course." Very few born-again Christians know when their *"course"* has come to an end. The Lord let Paul know that it was his time to go Home to Heaven. His *"course"* as a follower of His Saviour was rigorous. It entailed much suffering, pain, and sorrow. Paul did not compromise his service to comply with the morals and opinions of his day. His challenge from the Lord Jesus Christ upon his conversion was clear. He was to carry the Gospel of the grace of God to all who would listen. The Lord set before him his difficult *"course."* Now, at the end of his life Paul declared it to be *"finished."*

"I Have Kept The Faith." *"The Faith"* refers to the body of doctrine. It includes every Word found in the pages of the Old and New Testaments. Paul *"kept"* these Words in two senses. He *"kept"* them by following these Words faithfully. He also *"kept"* them by guarding them and preserving them from all of the many enemies of his day. The Gnostic-tainted New Testament manuscripts (Vatican & Sinai) altered the Words of *"the faith"* in at least 8,000 places. We must follow Paul in guarding the *"received Words"* of *"the faith"* in our day.

www.BibleForToday.org

BFT 3105 BK   ISBN #1-56848-060-1

www.ingramcontent.com/pod-product-compliance
Lightning Source LLC
Chambersburg PA
CBHW051043160426
43193CB00010B/1051